PLEASE ALLOW ME TO INTRODUCE MYSELF: ESSAYS ON DEBUT ALBUMS

PLEASE ALLOW ME TO INTRODUCE
MYSELF: ESSAYS ON DEBUT ALBUMS

for Julie, Anaïs, and Rivers
my First Glimmers
my Lasting Lights
Sparkle and Shine

Please Allow Me to Introduce Myself: Essays on Debut Albums

Edited by

GEORGE PLASKETES
Auburn University, Alabama, USA

Routledge
Taylor & Francis Group

LONDON AND NEW YORK

First Published 2013 by Ashgate Publisher

Published 2016 by Routledge
2 Park Square, Milton Park, Abingdon, Oxfordshire OX14 4RN
711 Third Avenue, New York, NY 10017, USA

First issued in paperback 2016

Routledge is an imprint of the Taylor & Francis Group, an informa business

British Library Cataloguing in Publication Data
Please allow me to introduce myself : essays on debut albums. – (Ashgate popular and folk music series)
  1. Popular music – History and criticism. 2. Popular music – Discography.
  I. Series II. Plasketes, George.
  782.4'21640266–dc23

The Library of Congress has cataloged the printed edition as follows:
Please allow me to introduce myself : essays on debut albums / edited by George Plasketes.
     pages cm.—(Ashgate popular and folk music series)
  Includes bibliographical references and index.
  ISBN 978-1-4094-4176-2 (hardcover)
1. Popular music—United States—History and
criticism. 2. Sound recording industry—United States. I. Plasketes, George, editor of compilation.

  ML3477.1.P54 2013
  781.640973—dc23

                                                                        2012044836

ISBN 13: 978-1-138-25698-9 (pbk)
ISBN 13: 978-1-4094-4176-2 (hbk)

Contents

List of Figures

Notes on Contributors

B. Lee Cooper is the author of 15 books on various aspects of popular music, including the three-volume series *Rock Music in American Popular Culture* (Routledge, 1995-1999) and more than 400 articles and book/record reviews.

Don Cusic is Music Row Professor of Music Industry at Belmont University in Nashville. As a premier country music historian, he is the author of hundreds of books and articles, among them a history of gospel music and biographies on Eddy Arnold and Gene Autry.

Andrew G. Davis is a PhD student in the Department of Communication Studies at the University of North Carolina-Chapel Hill. His research operates at the intersection of Cultural Studies and Media Studies, with emphases on Critical Political Economy and Rhetoric. He DJ's on the radio as host of *The Grown Folks' Show*, and in clubs as one-half of the Cosmic Liberation Front.

Marcello Giovanellli holds MA and PhD degrees from the University of Nottigham, UK, where he has taught English and stylistics. He has a long-standing interest in the "grunge" music scene of the 1980s and 1990s, particularly the relationship between the city of Seattle as a "cultural space" and the artist's sense of identity.

Joshua D. Hillyer is a Doctoral student and instructor in the College of Communication and Information Studies at the University of Kentucky. His research interests include instructional communication, computer-mediated communication and popular culture.

Kevin Holm-Hudson is Associate Professor of Music Theory at the University of Kentucky. He is the author of *Genesis and The Lamb Lies Down on Broadway* (Ashgate, 2008) and the editor of *Progressive Rock Reconsidered* (Routledge, 2002). He has published widely on popular music topics ranging from the Carpenters to Sigur Rós in *Music Theory Online*, *Popular Music and Society*, *American Music*, *Journal of Religion and Popular Culture*, and *Genre*. His other research interests include musical semiotics, aspects of musical symmetry and the music of John Cage and Karlheinz Stockhausen. He is currently preparing an undergraduate music theory text that blends popular, non-Western, and Western art-music repertoires.

PLEASE ALLOW ME TO INTRODUCE MYSELF

Ian Inglis is a Visiting Fellow in the School of Arts and Social Sciences at the University of Northumbria, Newcastle upon Tyne. His previous research interests have explored the music and career of the Beatles, the history of popular music, and forms of musical representation on stage, in live performance, and on television. His recent books include *The Words and Music of George Harrison* (Praeger, 2010), *Popular Music and Television in Britain* (Ashgate, 2010), and *The Beatles in Hamburg* (Reaktion, 2012).

David Janssen is a Professor of English and Honors Program Director at Gordon College in Barnseville, Georgia, and co-author of *Apocalypse Jukebox: The End of the World in Popular Music* (Soft Skull, 2009). Dr. J is a singer-songwriter on the weekends, and he hopes that he gets old before he dies.

Thomas M. Kitts, PhD, Professor of English and Chair of the Division of English/ Speech at St. John's University, New York, is the author/editor of *Finding Fogerty: Interdisciplinary Readings of John Fogerty and Creedence Clearwater Revival* (Lexington, 2013), *Literature and Work* (Longman, 2011), *Ray Davies: Not Like Everybody Else* (Routledge, 2008), *The Theatrical Life of George Henry Boker* (Peter Lang, 1994), and a play *Gypsies* (1994). His other publications include many articles, reviews, and several instruction manuals. He is the co-editor of *Popular Music and Society*, area chair of music for the national Popular and American Culture Associations' conference, and member of the board of directors of the Popular and American Culture Associations.

George H. Lewis is professor and chair of sociology at the University of the Pacific, Stockton California. He is past Music and Audio Reviews Editor for *Popular Music and Society* and has written extensively in the areas of contemporary culture and the sociology of music, including the books *Side-Saddle On The Golden Calf: Social Structure and Popular Culture in America* (Goodyear, 1972) and *All That Glitters: Country Music In America* (Popular Press, 1993). His article "Don' Go Down Waikiki: Social Protest and Popular Music in Hawaii" was a winner of the Marshall Fishwick Award for best article on popular culture in 1991. Lewis still clings to his original copy of *The "Chirping" Crickets,* the first LP he ever owned.

Nicole Marchesseau's award-winning creative work has been exhibited in Canada and overseas. Recent endeavors have included collaboration between her band Tuna Mind Melt and filmmaker/video artist Colt Jenders. In October 2010, she performed in Ottawa, Ontario with Jandek. She is currently researching Jandek's guitar-tuning systems as part of her doctoral studies at York University in Toronto.

George Plasketes is Professor of Radio-Television-Film & Popular Culture at Auburn University in Alabama. His writings include *B-Sides, Undercurrents* *and Overtones* (2009) the cover collection *Play It Again* (2010), both part of the Ashgate Popular and Folk Music Series, and *Images of Elvis Presley in American Culture, 1977-1997: The Mystery Terrain* (Haworth, 1997).

Rivers Plasketes is a Silas H. Rhodes Merit Scholar in Visual and Critical Studies at the School of Visual Arts in New York City, keeping one foot in the art world and the rest of his body in the real world.

Jerome Rodnitzky is Professor of history at the University of Texas at Arlington, where he specializes in recent American cultural history. His books include *Minstrels of the Dawn: The Folk Protest Singer as Cultural Hero* (Nelson-Hall, 1976), *Jazz-Age Boomtown* (Texaas A&M UP, 1997), *Feminist Phoenix; The Rise and Fall of a Feminist Counterculture* (Praeger, 1999), and *Lights, Camera, History: Portraying the Past in Film* (Texas A&M UP, 2007). He is a founding advisory editor of *Popular Music and Society* and *The Journal of Texas Music History*. He has a daughter named Joan Baez Rodnitzky.

Micah Rueber received his PhD in History from Mississippi State University. Following a two year Post-Doctoral Fellow at Auburn University, he joined the History faculty at Mississippi Valley State in the Delta. He is primarily interested in studying the intersections where technology and culture meet, such asthose factors that led to the pickup truck becoming the best-selling vehicle in the US.

William L. Schurk is the founder and Sound Recording Archivist at the Music Library at Bowling Green State University, Ohio. He has published extensively on record collecting.

Sarita M. Stewart currently serves as an instructor in the Entertainment Industry Studies program at Belmont University in Nashville, Tennessee. She has an MBA from Claremont Graduate University, and is completing a PhD in Mass Communication at the University of Alabama. Her primary research focus is music consumption, with accompanying interests in video games, social media and mood management. Stewart has extensive artists management experience in the entertainment industry, including Director of Marketing at Curb Records and US Marketing Manager at AKG Acoustics.

Deena Weinstein, Professor of Sociology at DePaul University in Chicago, specializes in rock music, popular culture, and social theory. She has published extensively on metal, including *Heavy Metal: The Music and its Culture* (DeCapo, 2000), and book chapters on the globalization of metal, and British Heavy Metal. She has also published many works on rock in general on the topics of cover songs, interaction in rock bands, protest songs, and rock criticism, among others. She has worked as a rock journalist, reviewing several hundred albums and concerts centering on extreme metal, and interviewing numerous metal musicians.

Edward Whitelock is a Professor of English and Chair of the Divison of Humanities at Gordon College in Barnesville, Georgia. He is co-author, with David Janssen, of *Apocalypse Jukebox: The End of the World in American Popular Music* (Soft Skull Press, 2009).

General Editor's Preface

The upheaval that occurred in musicology during the last two decades of the twentieth century has created a new urgency for the study of popular music alongside the development of new critical and theoretical models. A relativistic outlook has replaced the universal perspective of modernism (the international ambitions of the 12-note style); the grand narrative of the evolution and dissolution of tonality has been challenged, and emphasis has shifted to cultural context, reception and subject position. Together, these have conspired to eat away at the status of canonical composers and categories of high and low in music. A need has arisen, also, to recognize and address the emergence of crossovers, mixed and new genres, to engage in debates concerning the vexed problem of what constitutes authenticity in music and to offer a critique of musical practice as the product of free, individual expression.

Popular musicology is now a vital and exciting area of scholarship, and the *Ashgate Popular and Folk Music Series* presents some of the best research in the field. Authors are concerned with locating musical practices, values and meanings in cultural context, and may draw upon methodologies and theories developed in cultural studies, semiotics, poststructuralism, psychology and sociology. The series focuses on popular musics of the twentieth and twenty-first centuries. It is designed to embrace the world's popular musics from Acid Jazz to Zydeco, whether high tech or low tech, commercial or non-commercial, contemporary or traditional.

Derek B. Scott,
Professor of Critical Musicology,
University of Leeds, UK

Acknowledgments

Please Allow Me to Introduce Myself marks my third book in Ashgate's *Popular and Folk Music Series* (in case you missed the first two). In some literary circles, that might qualify as a Trilogy. No such pretensions here; I'm content with the less lofty "Trio." The alphabetical sequence of the Trio subjects—B-sides, Covers, Debuts—is an unintentional progression, a cosmic coincidence, perhaps subconsciously stirred by Sufjan Stevens's admirable, ambitious 50 state album concept that unfortunately stalled in the Midwest following *Illinois* and *Michigan*. Just as Sufjan Stevens is 48 shy of a Union, I currently don't have an epic master plan to develop music themed manuscripts with the remaining 23 letters of the alphabet.

Over the course of these three projects—all drafted on my dependable dinosaur Dell—I continue to accumulate an overwhelming debt of gratitude to everyone at Ashgate. My partnership with the press has been pure privilege, an experience that has been gratifying both personally and professionally. I cannot express how deeply grateful and honored I am to be a part of the Ashgate's impressive body of written works, and humbled I am to be in the company of its authors. My appreciation and respect to everyone for being so positive, professional, and pleasant: the series editor, Professor Derek Scott; Commissioning Editors for Music Studies—the ever excellent and encouraging Heidi Bishop, and Laura Macy, who initiated the project and steered the early stages; Senior Editor Sarah Charters, who valiantly directed the final phase; Nicole Norman, Sarah Noble and Luana Life in Marketing and the entire production staff. I admire your exhaustive efforts, open mindedness and standards of excellence. Endless thanks for believing in me, my ideas and my approach.

And then along comes Mary... Special thanks to Ashgate affiliate Mary Murphy for proofreading positive. Mary's masterful, meticulous caretaking and sharp editorial eye enhanced the manuscript appreciably. Hail, hail.

Here's to the contributing authors, the Debutantes—George H., Lee, Bill, Jerome, Don, Edward, Kevin, Ian, Tom, David, Nicole, Deena, Marcello, Sarita, Josh, Andrew, Micah, and favorite son Rivers. I was very encouraged by everyone's initial interest in the debut concept and subsequent willingness to come along for the writing ride. Thank you for delivering such a captivating assortment of perspectives, musical tastes, eras and experiences, expressed in each essay with sensitivity, intelligence, insight, fervor, and delight. While I was very fortunate to have a treasured father/son moment via our Go! Team(work) chapter, Josh and Marcello merit above and beyond recognition for writing their essays while in the midst of the bliss and sleepless state of new fatherhood, the ultimate "pleased to meet you" moment.

Sue Schrader at Blind/Blonde Ambition PR/Management promptly arranged my interviews with Steve Forbert. Steve was incredibly engaging, gracious and generous. Beyond my affection for what I consider to be the most fitting title for a debut album—*Alive on Arrival* (initially the title I intended to borrow for this book)—I appreciate Steve taking the time to talk with me, and the revealing conversations about his arrival; his tolerance of the requisite "next Dylan" line of questioning; and his courteous consent to quote his song lyrics and reproduce his debut album cover images in the book. Jandek and Corwood Industries, and Roger Miller and Mercury Records were similarly accommodating with permissions. Thanks also Lewton Cole/Alamy and LeAnn Rimes and Curb Records. It's always nice to have pictures.

My genuine appreciation to the all the artists featured in these chapters, for their first and lasting impressions, and the inspiration for *Please Allow Me to Introduce Myself*. And for Mick and Keith's sympathy for the book title.

There are places I remember... Enduring credit to several 1970's Oxford, Mississippi sources that surface in these pages: ear opening, eavesdropping sessions with George Stuart's record collection in Miller and Vaught Halls; Ronzo Shapiro compiling "Shap's Favorites" on cassette at the over the counter(culture) Hoka; and Meridian citizen John Lang force feeding Forbert's *Alive on Arrival,* that opening harmonica flutter forever fixed on my soundtrack.

I routinely benefit from the goodness and resourcefulness of a lot of folks at Auburn University. In the Department of Communication & Journalism, my chair Margaret Fitch Hauser; my kind colleagues, fellow faculty and staff; Shannon Solomon for her selfless, charitable allegiance; Whitney Hinson for research assistance; and at the Ralph Brown Draughon Library, archival sourceress Barb Bishop, and digital doyenne Eileen Hall for waving a magical wand to fine tune the manuscript's figures. I'm also grateful for the grant from the Bronczek Fund, which certainly came in handy.

Permanent thanks to the legendary Garys—Edgerton and Burns, the ubiquitous Greg Metcalf, faithful friend Bill Kolar, and to Jack Farrar for listening.

Of course, to my entire family, especially Dad and Mom for their presence in these pages; Rodger and Joan Williams, who define devotion; Matt Adams, Stanley the California Cat; sidekick Pancho; and loyal, lovable Lulu—"anything exceptional or remarkable"—our sweet and soulful shadow from room to room, companion down Jericho Road and back, in the yard and gardens, paths and porch, and in the solitude of The Woods.

Three Chords Good... The closing passage is always reserved for my true Trio—my wife Julie Grace, daughter Anaïs and son Rivers. Long ago, Cat Stevens (Yusuf Islam) asked simply in song: "How can I tell you...?" He had a point; as I wonder the same well beyond three minutes. A lifetime of words and expressions of love and gratitude are so insufficient. Julie's, Anaïs's and Rivers's arrivals in my life changed me forever. And they have continued to do so, shaping my entire being and outlook in countless and wondrous ways, making every moment meaningful, every day sacred and full of grace. In my setting due South, Anaïs is my West, Rivers my East, Julie my True North. Together, my Direction Home. A lean on a lyric from Arlo Guthrie's "Wedding Song" is fitting: "we spent the rest of our lives together, making our debut." Great Big Love, *yeah, yeah, yeah.*

Introduction

The First Cut is the Deepest

George Plasketes

> We shall not cease from exploration
> And the end of all our exploring
> Will be to arrive where we started
> And know the place for the first time.
>
> —T.S. Eliot, "Little Giddings" (1944)

> Following an incredible debut is impossible. You can't follow it. Because you can never debut again. It's not just the album that was great, it was the debut that was great. It was the arrival.
>
> —singer-songwriter Rickie Lee Jones (Zollo 1991: 136)

In the film, *Scott Pilgrim vs. the World* (dir. Edgar Wright, 2010), there is a party scene in which the hipster Comeau pontificates, "Their first album is better than their first album." The echo-speak conceit is a prologue analogous with superfluous layerings such as "first things first things first," "in the beginning of the beginning" or "once upon a once upon a time." Comeau's ricochet riff is simultaneously ridiculing and reverent; the stereotypical indie rock disdain and deification perhaps a pretentious paraphrase of the proverbial debut album proclamations "auspicious" and "eponymous." And a fitting pre(r)amble for this project.

Whether the first album or the first album, "firsts" carry considerable personal, social, historical and cultural importance and meaning. From relationships and romance—"love at first sight"—to experiences and events, artifacts and inventions, discoveries and achievements, "the first time" is a momentous marker in an individual or collective chronology. A place, a beginning, that we frequently, if not inevitably, circle back to as T.S. Eliot suggests in "Little Gidding" in *Four Quartets* (1944) (see epigraph above). "Firsts" are synonymous with fresh, original, new, and the never before. While something may be repeated, perhaps even evolving into a pattern or ritual, there is only one "first time." It is a singular moment or sensation. A celebration, because there is nothing quite like the first time.

Culturally, the newness inherent in a "first" is a norm that is not only expected, but appreciated and valued. Obvious examples span the performing arts to professional athletics, which annually recognize breakout performances with "Rookie of the Year" or "Best Newcomer" honors, while the Recording Industry awards a Grammy for the "Best New Artist." The common acknowledgement of newness is a cultural condition of continuous anticipation and anointing "the next best thing."

Every year, among the estimated 30,000 records produced and distributed throughout the music marketplace—a substantial number of those releases are first time recordings, artists making their debuts.[1] Whether a burst of glory that announces a new sound, a voice, songwriting style or presence; the arrival of an enduring, influential, impacting career, a cultural or genre touchstone, a signal of an epic masterpiece or movement, or an overlooked gem or a shooting star that fades, the debut album provides a "first impression."

As a meaningful, intriguing musical text, the debut album is more than a trend. Among other attributes, the debut embodies elements of genre and ritual. A first record is also universal and biographical. Every artist—past, present, future— has or will have a debut album, whether disc or digital. While there are many factors, there is no formula for the debut.[2] Arguably, each record by an artist can be singularly examined within its time, place, genre, and subsequently within the context of the artist's entire body of works. However, the debut album does contain its own exclusivity; its frame of reference confined to its initial entry into the listening sphere, music marketplace and a prospective discography. The beginning of a career arc. A promisingprelude.

In its purest sense, the debut album is an introduction, an announcement, an arrival. It is a beginning, a birth, a baptism, and sometimes, a breakthrough. Possibility and potential are its intrinsic qualities, though there are no guarantees of growth and artistic advancement. Indicators of promise may go unfilled or veer in another direction. Or the debut can be an ignition, a detonation expanding from a defining achievement into an enduring movement; its impact immediate or belated, minimal or momentous. The debut can preview a glimpse of greatness, or a revelation that becomes a revolution.

The debut album is a variation of an established music tradition. For classically trained musicians and vocalists, many of whom study at the most prestigious conservatories, the debut has customarily been an event and spectacle. Music debutantes participate in a season of performances staged at esteemed recital and symphony halls in major international cities, before sophisticated audiences, mentors, managers, agents, employers, sponsors, and critics.

In popular music, the debut album is a component of an artist's rite of passage. While the record may not necessarily be the very first step in a career path, it is nonetheless an integral stage, one that represents a sense of validation for the

---

[1]   Though seemingly a high count for an average number of annual record releases, 30,000 is the figure cited in Seabrook (2003).

[2]   John Leckie, producer of debuts by Stone Roses, XTC, Magazine, The Verve, Muse, and Kula Shaker, suggests Five Golden Rules for how to make that all-important first album: 1) have good songs, 2) running order and structure, especially an opener, are important, 3) know every song inside out, 4) be committed but enjoy it, and 5) get a good producer (Leckie "2006").

artist, an initial identity. The record deal or contract, and subsequent first record, is often a hard-earned reward following a dues-paying period that commonly includes cutting and shopping demos, touring as an opening act, or playing the small club circuit. Some have circumvented this time-honored toil through the glut of televised talent show shortcuts such as *American Idol.* Following the record's release, further substantiation, acceptance, or rejection await via critic and audience responses as well as sales and awards.

From a commercial perspective, the debut album is analogous with the introduction of a new product line or brand. Production of culture studies suggest that innovation in the music industry can be measured by the number of debut albums released in a year—in other words, by the number of new artists gaining access to a means of production and distribution (Christianen 1995). The "debut album" can be grouped among the music market's litany of generic product classifications for records. Among these tags are the breakthrough, follow-up, farewell, concept, concert, comeback, live, duet, unplugged, solo, reunion, greatest hits, and essentials.

One of the interesting attributes of the debut album is expectation, or perhaps more conspicuously, the absence of it. With the debut album in general, there is minimal anticipation compared to the level of expectancy and hype that accompanies a record release by an established artist. With the exception of record label promotion and touring, the primary source of expectation for the debut is, for the most part, generated by the designated single (or multiple songs as was common with the early rock era), that precedes and promotes the album's release. The mid-format Extended Play (EP)—longer than single but shorter than an album—serves a similar purpose. Thus, the debut album is a more formal and comprehensive introduction beyond the single(s), a showcase of 10-14 songs that are more or less representative of an artist's style and sound. During earlier eras, the primary exposure for the hopeful hit was limited to radio rotation airplay, with perhaps an occasional live performance on a television variety show. Over the years, the channels of dissemination for the single (and eventual album) have evolved into a multimedia marketplace of synergy beyond the exclusivity of the radio realm. The availability is vast—music videos; film and television soundtracks; placement in advertising and commercials; artist, record label, and fan music spaces and websites; Internet leaks or downloads; word of mouth or listen-up mentions in music blogs or magazine columns; and live performance and touring. As the song circulates, the listener's hope, no matter the era or mode of distribution, is that the remainder of the album's songs live up to the three-minute preview and promising precursor of the single.

Popular music's history is brimming with cases of "one hit wonders" who were unable to sustain beyond the one catchy tune chosen as the single. As is the case with a subsequent performance from a "Rookie of the Year" in sports or "Best New Artist" winner, the debut album, particularly if it is well received critically and/or commercially, establishes an identity. A precedent and an initial set of standards are established for the artist. Those creative and commercial criteria become credentials that are immediately attached to the next project. Inevitable expectation and comparison ensue. While an artist can certainly duplicate or advance beyond their initial recording, a follow-up to a successful debut can also be a set-up for a proverbial "sophomore slump" or "jinx," whether real or perceived. The task of producing a follow-up record that lives up to or exceeds the musical, critical, and or/ commercial impact of successful debut is a considerable challenge, if not impossible, as Rickie Lee Jones suggests (see epigraph above); a "follow-that problem" similar to that faced by Lewis Carroll with *Through the Looking Glass* after *Alice's Adventures in Wonderland* (Rushdie 2012),

Nominees and winners in the Grammy Awards "Best New Artist" category (see Appendix B) provide one strand of evidence that suggests it is not unusual for an artist's career arc to advance from launch to letdown over the course of their first two records. Starland Vocal Band (1977), Christopher Cross (1981), Milli Vanilli (1990), and Paula Cole (1998) are among cases which illustrate the swift descent from Best New Artist to "whatever happened to?" trivia. There are other peculiar post-debut fade-outs, such as Best New Artist (1999) Lauryn Hill, whose first record, *The Miseducation of Lauryn Hill* (1998), was awarded five Grammys, including Album of the Year. After an *Unplugged* follow up in 2002, the former Fugee's self-imposed absence from the music industry continued until late 2010, when she began touring again with hints of a new studio record.

Counter to the common perception, the Recording Academy's criteria and eligibility requirements for "new artist" do not specify a "debut." Though an album release is required in order to be nominated, a "breakthrough" and "advance toward prominence" have become nebulous voter variables that often override a debut. As a result, the nominees and eventual winner are capable of generating as much, if not more contentiousness, than other Grammy categories. The 53rd annual ceremony in 2011 was no exception as jazz bassist Esperanza Spalding's win was considered a surprise, if not an upset. Justin Bieber was widely deemed the favorite in a strong field that also included rapper Drake, Mumford and Sons, and Florence and the Machine. The "new artist" misnomer was at the forefront of the post-Grammy divisive dialogue, particularly among the teen idol's dismayed "true beliebers," who emphasized that Spalding had recorded three albums since 2006.

New Kid in Town

As a topic, the "debut album" contains music category conversation appeal, and is a rich resource of record store dialogue reminiscent of scenes from Nick Hornby's *High Fidelity*. Subjective "Best" and "Disappointing" lists can be found scattered across music journalism, from longtime music critic Dave Marsh's *New Book of Rock Lists* (1994) to Internet web sites such as dkpresents.wordpress.com (2008) and music blogs. Music magazines *Uncut* (2006), *New Musical Express* (2010) and *Rolling Stone* (2013) devoted special issues to "Best" and "Greatest" debut album lists. While engaging perusals, these lists are devoid of any critical context beyond a capsule summary of the album. (See Appendices C,D,E,F,G.)

Qualifying, ranking, or evaluating debut albums as "great" or "best" is not the aim of this collection (though there is a presumption of author appreciation of the album each writes about). Nor is the goal to establish a "debut album canon." Beyond my own attraction to the circumstance of debut albums, the overarching aim in conceptualizing this project was to generate some critical thought, appreciation, and discussion on this interesting, important, and neglected subject. The volume was designed to offer an opportunity for writers to sing the praises of, or make a case for, a debut album that marked their time line and musical experience in a meaningful way. The task was for contributors to choose a debut album and thoughtfully offer critical perspective on its time, place and significance, whether culturally, musically, historically, and/or personally. As the ensuing chapters will reveal, the submissions proved to be a satisfying and surprising sampling in many ways—content, quality, diversity and critical approaches.

Multi-author collections such as this can be uneven and inconsistent, even when there is a theme or topical thread of continuity. The value of a variety of viewpoints outweighed the merits of approaching this debut project as a solo venture. Like any music fan, collector, critic, or scholar, I carry an inventory of debuts in my music listography that strike a curious chord on some level and mark my timeline and tastes. Debuts were not only a more substantial introduction to artists beyond the singles on the AM radio airwaves, many of which became part of my cherished 45 collection, they were part of my initiation to the album experience, an ascension to enhanced 33⅓ status and the beginning of a lifelong collection. Before settling upon a series of 1970s-centric songwriters (Willis Alan Ramsey, Warren Zevon, Steve Forbert, Rickie Lee Jones), and a more current collaboration with our son Rivers (The Go! Team), an array of debuts and annotations crossed my mind while formulating chapters for this collection. Among them are the 1960s Chicago suburb locals the Cryan' Shames and Ides of March; the obvious *Mr. Tambourine Man*, with the Byrds' transcendent harmonies; Roger McGuinn's signature 12-string Rickenbacker, Dylan covers, and Gene Clark originals; my soft spot for *Along Comes the Association* and the Left Banke's elegant "Baroque and roll" with "Pretty Ballerina" and "Walk Away Renee"; the Buffalo Springfield, Beau Brummels and British Invaders, particularly the underappreciated Dave Clark Five, the Hollies, and the Kinks. A lot of my 1970s debut listening was California dreaming: Karla Bonoff's Ronstadt reservoir; Buckingham/Nicks' duo debut as an audition for Fleetwood Mac; Illinois migrant Dan Fogelberg's college café mellow on *Home Free* before the coffeehouse trend, the album cover's pencil on parchment self-portrait matted on green a curious cross between a beginning drawing project and crime suspect sketch. I vividly recall being convinced that a "Horse with No Name" was a new Neil Young song until America's debut;[3] and remain mildly wounded from my high school English teacher's refusal to

---

[3] The Young/America case of mistaken identity was apparently common. In his memoirs, *Waging Heavy Peace* (2012: 124), Neil Young writes: "People have tried to sound like me to the point where my dad thought 'A Horse With No Name' was mine!"

allow me to do my "song lyrics as poetry" project on Jackson Browne's precocious debut (mistakenly referred to as *Saturate Before Using*) because he was "not established enough" (or maybe that my tastes were more California-cool than the teacher's). There were post-Buffalo Springfield Americana precursors Poco and Pure Prairie League (described by Counting Crowe Adam Durwitz as "the Beatles on bourbon"); Steely Dan's covert cool jazzy yacht rock on *Can't Buy A Thrill*, and the Roche sisters whimsy (which my wife introduced me to in the early 1980s).

Cyndi Lauper's multiple hit *She's So Unusual* caricatured the early MTV era, the same decade that included Suzanne Vega's small blue brittle folk, Marshall Crenshaw's best Beatle- meets-Buddy Holly, Tracy Chapman's social consciousness highlighted by "Fast Car" and "Talkin' 'Bout a Revolution"; James McMurtry's nasal novella *Too Long in the Wasteland* that sounded like Lou Reed singing Woody Guthrie songs with John Mellencamp's band; Keith Richards's and Robbie Robertson's solos, the Bo Deans' roots rock produced by T-Bone Burnett; the Scottish Blue Nile's haunting atmospherics; Syd Straw's post-Golden Palomino *Surprise*; and Timbuk 3—Pat and Barbara K. MacDonald and boom box backing—bridging Sonny and Cher, Delaney and Bonnie, and Richard and Linda Thompson with contemporary couplets such as the Weepies, Submarines, Civil Wars, Kaiser Cartell, HoneyHoney, Gillian Welch/David Rawlings, Robert Plant/ Alison Krauss, Jenny and Johnny, and She and Him. My post-1980s stack includes Liz Phair's ambitious, loose interpretation of the Rolling Stones' *Exile on Main Street* on *Exit in Guyville*, Madeleine Peyroux's *sway*but *Dreamland*, Tift Merritt's *Bramble Rose*, and the Neil-nodding, Lucinda-like Kathleen Edwards's *Failer*.

Categories are easily compiled, along with patterns and themes. Cases of prolonged self-exilesuch as Greg Copeland's and Mary Margaret O'Hara's following their critically acclaimed debuts—*Revenge Will Come* (1982) and *Miss America* (1988), respectively—have always mystified me. (Chapter 9 presents what is perhaps the most mythical "one and done" debut case in Willis Alan Ramsey.) There are artists who stepped from the band background to the forefront rather than emerging out of nowhere: James Taylor background vocalist David Lasley's blue eyed soul *Missin' Twenty Grand* (1982); and sessionist, sideman extraordinaire David Lindley's solo venture *El Rayo-X* (1981); *Rumble Doll* (1993) by Bruce Springsteen's wife and fellow E Streeter, Patti Scialfa. The faux debuts by "Chris Gaines," Garth Brooks's alter ego, and the pseudo surf supergroup "Blue Stingrays," a Tom Petty project, contain conceptual and novelty appeal, as does his higher-profile all-star amalgam, the Traveling Wilburys, also with adopted surnames for Petty, Dylan, Harrison, Orbison, and Lynne.

The delayed debut of Rising Sons (featuring Taj Mahal and Ry Cooder) is an unusual case, its recordings released from the vault 25 years after their formation. The transcendent arc of Sixto Rodriguez's deferred debut, *Cold Fact* (1969), is similarly intriguing, though more enigmatic and mythical. Released in 1970, the album, featuring Dylanesque anti-establishment Blues, went unnoticed in the U.S.,then surfaced in the South African underground where it became a vital voice in anti-Apartheid movement. While Rodriguez's music became a word of mouth, bootleg and trade sensation, his life was shrouded in mystery and rumour. Rediscovered in his hometown Detroit in the late 1990s, his fascinating story was increasingly presented in media outlets, among them the iconic CBS news magazine show *60 Minutes*. The re-introduction culminated with the Academy Award-winning documentary *Searching for Sugar Man* (2012).

This random rundown provides a glimpse of what this collection might have read like had this been lone authorship. While the abbreviated survey likely forms a profile of an acoustic wimp fond of jangling guitars and harmonies, it more significantly magnifies one of the benefits of multiple author perspectives.

Whether a sampling be of 23 albums—as assembled in this collection—or of 223, omissions are inevitable. Some debut absences may be more conspicuous than others. For example, some of the UK's biggest selling first records—Norah Jones, Meat Loaf, Dido, Mike Oldfield—are certainly worthy subjects beyond their huge commercial successes. Among rock's most important, enduring artists, there is no denying the powerful opening statements of *Elvis Presley* and the Beatles' *Please Please Me*. Or the influence of *Bob Dylan*, despite *The Freewheelin'* follow-up being widely viewed as more important and superior artistically. Bruce Springsteen's relatively overlooked debut, *Greetings from Asbury Park*, did not anoint The Boss as "the future of rock and roll" the way *Born to Run* did, with *The Wild, the Innocent and the E-Street Shuffle* in between. Joni Mitchell's self-titled, David Crosby-produced debut in 1968—the same year her song "Both Sides Now" was a hit for Judy Collins—pales as a prologue to a remarkable run of canyon confessionals that followed between 1969 and 1972: *Clouds, Ladies of the Canyon, Blue, For the Roses.*[4]

Not having these successful albums and prominent artists included among the debut case studies does not diminish the depth, value, appeal, and most of all the originality of this collection. Critical documentation and analysis of the Elvis, Beatles, Dylan, Springsteen, Joni Mitchell et al. song books, which obviously includes their debuts, is as vast a critical body of works as their discographies themselves.

Pleased to Meet You

As a collection, *Please Allow Me to Introduce Myself* contains its own "eponymous debut" nature as the volume lies at the forefront of popular music literature on this subject, scratching the surface of critical discussion devoted to dimensions of the debut album. Greil Marcus's album anthology, *Stranded: Rock and Roll for a Desert Island* (1979) is a conceptual kindred spirit. And some resemblance may also be found in the Continuum Press's superb *33⅓* series, which features

---

[4] In *Uncut*'s "Debut Albums" issue (August 2006: 60), *Joni Mitchell* was listed #4 among "false starts." The list also included debuts by Primal Scream, David Bowie, Prince, Teenage Fanclub, The Beach Boys, Radiohead, Pulp, Cocteau Twins, and Nirvana.

concise critical and creative profiles of individual albums. But there are no written works—scholarly, popular or otherwise—beyond lists, devoted to the exploration of the debut as a genre.

The essays in this volume are all original works written exclusively for this collection. Thus, the inclusion of notable debuts such as Jeff Buckley's *Grace*, Patti Smith's poetic *Horses,* and R.E.M.'s punky *Murmur*, following their EP *Chronic Town,* would have been duplication that undermined the aims of originality since those records have been featured in the *33 1/3* catalog. The lack of literature on the debut album should not be interpreted as an indication that this subject does not merit critical inquiry. As these eclectic essays demonstrate, debuts are an abundantly meaningful, multifarious music text. The interdisciplinary group of contributing authors represents a generational variance of esteemed and emerging scholars who infuse the debut discussion with a diverse set of critical and creative perspectives, musical tastes, and experiences.

The chapters present close, comprehensive readings by the authors of their chosen debut, from the album concept, cover art design and images to lyrics, music, song sequence and genre to sociocultural, historical and biographical backgrounds. Career context is also significant, from launch to letdown or longevity and legend, with analysis that considers the album's impact and influence, and the artist's subsequent recordings and creative evolution following the debut album. Several of the essays are enhanced by the author participant observation accounts and personal interviews and performances with artists.

The case studies emphasize the creative and commercial circumstances within the organizational context of a variety of record companies and major and independent contrasts. The scope of the discussions also addresses the role of producers from discovery to debut, from signing a deal to studio recording sessions; and the impact of music critics and journalists. Settings are also relevant, with a broad geographical cross section of regions, locales, and cities as music venues central to the narratives.

Though the absence of rap, hip hop, jazz, and blues are lamentable genre holes in the collection, the broad music spectrum covers country, comedy, progressive country, alternative, grunge, metal, folk, British folk, rock, soul, DIY, outsider folk blues, R&B, indie rock, and sampling. Just as solo singer-songwriter studies outnumber bands here, the allocation of debut albums from era to era is also uneven, with the biggest concentration located across the 1970s. However, there is representation from each of the six decades. Though a wishful aim, the genre, artist and era planets aligning evenly for this project was not necessarily an editorial expectation or priority. Achieving proportionality is challenging with the inherent randomness and variables involved in soliciting and recruiting potential contributors. Despite some limitations, there is representation and balance on many levels.

As for degrees of successes, the critical and commercial responses are varying; some debuts shout popular, obvious and hit from the mainstream and charts while others, overlooked and obscure, whisper anonymously "won't you guess my name?" from the fringes to cult followings.

Perhaps the most obvious attribute that links these debuts is conspicuous youth. With the early teen exception of LeAnn Rimes at 13, artists almost exclusively "burst on the scene" with their first album in their early twenties, "trying to take advantage of that youthful energy," in the view of singer-songwriter Steve Forbert (see Chapter 13).

Beyond the common chord of age range, the narratives are a medley of unique facets. There are thematic debut variations—the one and done, solo, dual, major label and UK/US versions. For two artists, their debuts were the only albums they ever recorded. The assortment of artists includes an activist, piano-pounding pranksters, a solo Beatle and a next Dylan, an "Elvis" alias and a nom de guerre, a "clown prince" and a "cosmic cowboy"; a burn victim and runaway, a desperado, and duo dynamic. Among these debut records is the first single-artist triple album; one that underwent a title change after its release; and another whose title is derived from rolling papers. One album is comprised of cover songs and another contains incomplete songs; a few resemble greatest hits collections, and most pronounce a signature song such as "That'll Be the Day," "In the Midnight Hour," "Rockin' Pneumonia and the Boogie Woogie Flu," "Tutti Fruitti," "Alison," and "Chuck E.'s in Love."

In addition to each album's textual totality and musicultural importance, there is a consistent complementary undercurrent of personal meanings conveyed throughout the essays. The authors' admiration and affection for each record shimmer just beneath the surface of their critical analysis, weaving *Wonder Years* glimpses of their debut album experiences.

The Debutantes

The 23 debut albums in *Please Allow Me to Introduce Myself* are presented chronologically over 50-year span beginning with a Holly hiccup and the Crickets chirping in 1957, and extending to the global glee of the The Go! Team in 2004.

The lead chapter announces the arrival of the Buddy Holly-led band The Crickets, and their debut, *The "Chirping" Crickets* (Brunswick 1957), featuring a trio of singles, "That'll Be the Day," "Oh Boy," and "Not Fade Away." George Lewis weaves his own coming-of-age narrative of the first album he ever owned with a detailed production of culture chronicle of the Crickets' debut within the context of rock and roll's early days. The focal points of this historic, innovative album include the garage and studio sessions in Lubbock, Nashville, and New Mexico with producer Norman Petty, Holly's Fender Stratocaster, record companies (Decca, Coral, RCA, Brunswick), and connections to the Quarrymen cutting a demo of "That'll Be the Day" in 1958 before they became the Beatles. Lewis's ardent parallel narrative foreshadows the personal tones that shade many of the essays in the chapters that follow.

Record archivists B. Lee Cooper and Bill Schurk are also in tune with 1957, specifically clown anarchists Little Richard and Huey "Piano" Smith. The prankish pouncing and pounding of these two relentless rollers helped establish the piano as the central syncopation of the "birth of rock" era. Their dexterous debut albums were not only testament to rock's careening energy, eccentricity and excesses, but typical of many early debuts with attributes of "greatest hits" collections. Just as Jerry Lee Lewis's initial long play, also released in 1957, was preceded by "Whole Lotta Shakin'" and other radio and jukebox hits, eight of the 12 songs on *Here's Little Richard* (Specialty 1957) were issued as 45s, notably "Tutti Fruitti," which, 50 years later, topped *Mojo* magazine's list of "The 100 Records that Changed the World" (June 2007). Smith's *Having A Good Time* (Ace 1959) was released two years after his whimsical signature song, "Rockin' Pneumonia and the Boogie Woogie Flu," and three other tunes reached the *Billboard* charts. The collaborative case study identifies intersections between Little Richard's iconic crossover contributions during rock's triumphal emergence, and Smith's hijinks within New Orleans' rich, rhythmic piano heritage.

The debut discussion shifts briefly from the playful to the political with Jerome Rodnitzky's chapter on *Joan Baez* (Vanguard 1960). This album, a showcase for Baez's social consciousness and soaring soprano, was a bridge between decades. Following a noteworthy performance at the 1959 Newport Folk Festival, Baez chose to concentrate exclusively on interpretations of traditional Anglo-American folk songs from 1600 to 1900 for her first record. Rodnitzky presents the Baez debut as a centerpiece of the 1960s folk revival and catalyst for the student activism across college campuses.

Country music and comedy converge in Roger Miller's 1964 debut album, originally titled *Roger and Out* then renamed *Dang Me/Chug-A-Lug*. Don Cusics's Nashville narrative documents the unusual strategies employed by Smash Records as well as the influence of popular comedy records on Miller's first release. With its two title tunes becoming crossover country and pop hits, Miller's debut held its own with the top albums of 1964, which included three Beatles records, Barbara Streisand's *People, The Beach Boys Concert, The Singing Nun,* and two releases of *Hello Dolly,* an original cast version and Louis Armstrong's. The record laid the groundwork for Miller's follow-up album that contained "King of the Road," the biggest single in the career of "the clown prince of country music."

There are intermittent cases that challenge the prevalent notion that an artist can only debut once. A first recording might be conveniently dismissed as "illegitimate" or a "false start," and relegated to a forgotten frontal footnote in an artist's discography, if released on an unknown or independent label, if sales do not reach a certain level, or if the record is unnoticed critically, among other factors.[5] The debut misnomer pertains to Alanis Morissette's international hit *Jagged*

---

[5]   Similarly in professional sports, a player has to appear in a certain number of games to qualify as a "rookie." If short of that number, the following season can be considered the "official" rookie season.

Little Pill (Maverick 1995), as the Grammy-winning album was preceded by two Canadian releases that earned her several Juno Award nominations, including one for Most Promising Female Vocalist. The dual debuts of singer-songwriter Sam Phillips (not the Sam of Sun Records) are a more unusual case that involves a name alteration and genre change. Phillips's first album, *The Turning* (Myrrh 1987), a contemporary Christian record produced by then-husband T-Bone Burnett, was released under her given name "Leslie Phillips." The following year, she returned, a fine-tuned reinvention as "Sam Phillips," with the more recognizable neo-1960s pop debut *The Indescribable Wow* (Virgin 1988).

Such debut dismissals are musical minutiae buried in backstory for several artists in this collection. Warren Zevon's *Wanted Dead or Alive* (Pickwick/Imperial 1969) was eclipsed by his "major-label debut," the more polished *Warren Zevon* (1976), released on David Geffen's Asylum Records (see Chapter 11); while LeAnn Rimes, at age 11, recorded *All That* on a Dallas independent label (Nor Va Jak 1994) before *Blue* (Curb 1996) (see Chapter 18).

The "debut do over" is at the forefront of Lee Cooper's review of Wilson Pickett's earliest R&B recordings in Chapter 5. Pickett's very first album, *It's Too Late* (1963) on Lloyd Price's diminutive Double-L label, was weakly promoted and poorly received. The following year, Pickett joined Atlantic Records, where under the auspices of Jerry Wexler and Ahmet Ertegun, he delivered what is regarded as his formal debut, *In the Midnight Hour* (1965). The title song became Pickett's anthem, and helped usher in the "Soulsville, USA" moniker for Stax Studios in Memphis.

The artists featured in the next two chapters became posthumous discoveries, the fragile melancholy of their debut albums reflecting the misfortune in their biographies.

Edward Whitelock revives the overlooked Jackson C. Frank story in a carnival centered chronicle that is triumphant and tragic At age 11, Frank suffered severe burns over half his body in an elementary school fire in which 14 students died. A family friend bought Frank a guitar, hoping it would help him to both regain dexterity and pass the time. Eleven years later, his first and only album, *Jackson C. Frank* (Columbia 1965), was released in London. The debut, featuring one of the classic songs of the era, "Blues Run the Game," became a touchstone of the British folk revival of the late 1960s.Its influence lingered into the singer-songwriter movement of the 1970s, with Paul Simon, Sandy Denny, and Al Stewart among notable threads connected to Frank.

Frank also introduced a unique fingerpicking style in alternate tuning that would inspire the English folk revival's own tragic enigma, Nick Drake. Kevin Holm-Hudson's keen reading of Drake's *Five Leaves Left* (Island, 1969) accentuates the ravishing, romantic debut's restrained, timeless beauty, its melancholy lyrics, delicate instrumental arrangements and arabesques, and the haunting tone of a world-weary 21-year-old's voice. *Five Leaves Left* resonates with transcendent stillness and passage of time. Even the album's title—derived from a slip of paper found inside a package of rolling papers—is an eerie countdown: as if grimly foreshadowing Drake would be dead five years later, the victim of a prescription drug overdose.

The calm continues with George Harrison, the "quiet (and 'cool') Beatle,"[6] in Chapter 8. Harrison's *All Things Must Pass* (Apple 1970) exemplifies an important and prolific strand of the debut genre: the "solo debut"—a record release by an individual artist beyond or concurrent with his/her band affiliation. Whether the hiatus is temporary or permanent, such independent pursuits are inevitable. Among those who have splintered into the solo subgenre are all of the Beatles; Crosby, Stills, Nash, and Young; Stones Jagger, Richards, Wood, and Wyman; the Who's Daltrey and Townshend; Van Morrison after Them; Eagles Henley, Frey, Walsh, Schmidt, and Meisner; Tom Petty minus the Heartbreakers; Bob Mould of Hüsker Dü; Paul Westerberg following the disbanded Replacements; Strokes' lead Julian Casablancas; Ian Hunter post-Mott the Hoople; Jack White without Meg, the White Stripes and Raconteurs; and Debbie Harry, Natalie Merchant, Aimee Mann, and Juliana Hatfield following their respective fronts for Blondie, 10,000 Maniacs, 'Til Tuesday, and the Blake Babies.

Harrison emerged from what is undoubtedly the longest songwriting duo and band shadows ever cast, with a simmering accumulation of his own compositions shaped into a transcendent statement of Spectorian splendor and spirituality. Longtime Beatles chronicler Ian Inglis regards the eclectic epic as Harrison's greatest achievement, and a pivotal moment in popular music. Working within a broad Fab Four framework, Inglis' immersion includes the Abbey Road recording sessions and careful consideration of the Harrison debut within the Lennon-McCartney songwriting duopoly, the post-Beatle era and the continuous crisscrossing comparisons of their individual works. Beyond being Harrison's post-Beatle baptism, *All Things Must Pass* marked other "firsts" as rock's first single-artist triple album (preceded by the various artist *Woodstock* by six months) and as the first solo Beatles record to top the charts.

"What was wrong with the first one?" is Willis Alan Ramsey's response when asked why he never released another record following his revered debut in 1972 on Leon Russell's Shelter label. *Willis Alan Ramsey* is the epitome of the peculiar and rare debut condition—the one and done. The hello goodbye. The opening farewell. The disappearing act. The chapter identifies Ramsey as one of the handful of artists who have released a critically acclaimed debut only to withdraw from the music scene for an extended time, without recording a follow-up album for decades—or ever, as is the case with the idiosyncratic Ramsey. Ramsey's debut had its biggest impact on the "progressive country" genre and "cosmic cowboy" Southwest songwriter circuit largely based in Austin, Texas, with one of its songs transformed into a two-time Top 40 soft pop/rock hit by both America and the

---

[6] In his posthumous appreciation of Harrison, music critic Bill Flanagan suggests "cool Beatle" is just as fitting a characterization for Harrison as the overused "quiet Beatle" (Commentary, CBS *Sunday Morning*, November 2011).

Captain and Tenille. The essay addresses the mythic nature of Ramsey's debut while considering the context of his reluctance or refusal to record again.

The New York Dolls, one of rock and roll's most raw and reckless bands, were the embodiment of New York City during its most vulnerable period. Their raucous, Todd Rundgren-produced debut, *New York Dolls* (Mercury 1973), updated rock's roots, anticipated the Sex Pistols and Ramones, and confused critics. The album and band were named on both "best" and "worst" music lists of 1973. With New York City's daring and decay as a context, Tom Kitts's analysis of the Dolls' debut concentrates on the chaotic convergence of the band's knowledge of popular music, their use of camp conventions of theatre and showmanship, and their influence on the British and American punk movement.

On the opposite US coast, the ubiquitous country/folk/rock of Los Angeles and vicinity was *the* American sound for much of the 1970s. Within this thriving singer-songwriter paradise, Warren Zevon was an iconocLAast whose "comic noir" and sardonic sensibility in songs such as "I'll Sleep When I'm Dead" cast a shadow over the scene's prevailing peaceful easy feelings. *Warren Zevon* (Asylum 1976), produced by Jackson Browne, is one of the most delightfully dark and demystifying documents of Hollywood desperation, decadence, and despair during its mid-decade music apex. The desperado debut brims with outlaws and outcasts on the outskirts, from the late 1880s American West frontier to 1970s Hollywood hangouts. Frank and Jesse James riding to clear their names. A heroin addict contemplating suicide. The village idiot, face all a-glow, up all night listening to "Mohammed's Radio." The chapter's prismatic perspective focuses on Zevon's literary, cinematic songwriting, while identifying subtle and stark contrasts between his Asylum labelmates, among them Browne, Linda Ronstadt (who recorded four songs from *Warren Zevon*), and the Eagles, specifically their fast-lane excess epic *Hotel California*, also released in 1976.

Comparable literate lyricism, wicked wit, and noir tones are among the attractions in Elvis Costello's *My Aim Is True* (Stiff/Columbia 1977), released in Britain one month before the other Elvis's death. David Janssen contemplates Costello's initial aims in his rich reading of the landmark debut. In addition to tracing the genesis of Costello's image from Declan MacManus to a cleverly calculated stage name and bespectacled, knock-kneed geek persona leering on the album's cover, Janssen's chapter also addresses the accompanying misperceptions of punk and Presley linkages. Much of the analysis is centered within a"guilt and revenge" manifesto, which, in Janssen's view, makes Costello's compelling "Alison" seem out of place.

Approximately since Bob Dylan's breakthrough album, *The Freewheelin' Bob Dylan* (1963), critics and music industry marketers and have routinely, albeit unfairly, designated artists "the next" or "new" Dylan. Despite the common knowledge and universal truth expressed in T-Bone Burnett's Rolling Thunder Revue logbook entry in the mid-1970s—"The Next Bob Dylan will not come around for another millennium or two, making it highly unlikely it will happen at all"—the cliché continues to expand into endlessness, subgenre status and prophecy unfulfilled. From Greil Marcus's mid-1990s inventory (Marsh 1994: 334-35) to Josh Lieberman's music blog entry "The Members of 'The Next Dylan' Club" in 2012, the roster of Dylancarnates is well documented. The list is exhaustive, with Dylan himself, and fittingly, his son Jakob, included.

Figure I.1   Steve Forbert's quintessential debut album title.

Steve Forbert was anointed another "next Dylan" with *Alive On Arrival* (Nemperor 1978). The debut may evoke Huck Finn, Tom Sawyer, and *Midnight Cowboy* as much as it does Dylan. Forbert's songs chronicle his "follow that dream" transition from Meridian, Mississippi to Manhattan, singing on street corners, subways, doorways, alleys, and Grand Central Station before landing gigs in the clubs along the legendary Bleecker Street and in Greenwich Village. The chapter is constructed around a series of my personal interviews with Forbert specifically for this debut collection. Among the central points of our conversations were 1970s New York City and its music scene, critic John Rockwell's role in launching Forbert'sdebut, the "next Dylan" designation, and the legacy of *Alive on Arrival*, including its ideal debut album title, which Forbert had decided on one year before he even signed his initial record deal.[7]

Previous to my receiving debut album proposals from potential contributors, my only awareness of Jandek was the result of a serendipitous encounter while compiling Jeff Tweedy stray solo recordings. My discovery of the Wilco front's contribution, "Crack a Smile," on *Down in a Mirror: A Second Jandek Tribute* (2005), was bewildering buried treasure that elicited further curiosity. For example, who or what is Jandek? And how can there be two tributes to anonymity? Nicole Marchesseau, who has performed with Jandek, unveils some of that mystery. Her exploration of the ramshackle, folk blues hobble of Jandek's DIY debut, *Ready for the House* (Corwood 1978) details the self-referential lyrical, musical, and visual motifs, and an array of strange album attributes that includes sonic isolation, near musical stasis, incantations and incomplete songs. The essay is a postcard from the edges of taste and genre that provides a revealing portrait of a persistent outsider artist and insights into an intriguing subculture.

The lone trace of jazz notes in these pages floats in the cool of *Rickie Lee Jones* (Warner Brothers 1979), widely recognized as one of the most striking debuts during the disco-dominated late 1970s, and perhaps all time. Previewed by Lowell George's version of Jones's "Easy Money" on his post-Little Feat debut released months earlier, and pronounced by the unlikely hits "Chuck E.'s in Love" and "Young Blood," the Top Ten album earned Jones a Grammy for Best New Artist. The streetwise, sophisticated songs, backed by folk, jazz, and rock styles and marked by Jones's distinctive vocal delivery and hip presence, created a Boho vibe disparate from the prevalent 1970s sound and her fellow female artists, particularly the West Coast canyon clique.

The direction of the debut case studies shifts perceptibly from being singer-songwriter centric to emphasis on bands from the 1980s into the first decade of the 2000s, with a broad stylistic range that spans metal, grunge, indie rock, R&B, sampling, and global glee, with a country bridge in between for balance. Two consecutive chapters illustrate the impact of debut albums on music genres.

Metallica's jaw-dropping debut, *Kill 'Em All* (Megaforce 1983), ushered in more than just a new band. The album brought thrash/speed into its own as a metal subgenre and was responsible for the creation and development of indie metal record labels. Deena Weinstein examines Metallica's imposing sound and sources, while considering the band dynamics, the consequences of signing a major label deal, and a powerful management agency and how those factors shaped their first recording. As a metal aficionado, Weinstein regards Metallica's debut as the band's best album despite selling fewer copies than any of its subsequent releases.

---

[7] *Alive on Arrival* was initially my working title for this book before acquiescing to the Glimmer Twins. Forbert was simultaneously flattered and forgiving, and gracious without grudge.

Marcello Giovanelli addresses the intriguing paradoxical nature that lies within Pearl Jam's influential debut *Ten* (Epic 1992), which became the quintessential sound of the Grunge movement's explosion in the early 1990s. The album embodied the convergence of the 'Seattle sound' of Green River and Mother Love Bone, and a more classic blues-rock with the dark, Morrisonesque angst of its front man Eddie Vedder and his haunting autobiographical lyrics. Despite creating an archetypal era-defining grunge/alternative rock album, breathtaking in its musicianship and depth of emotional intensity, Pearl Jam spent the rest of their careers progressively seeking to distance themselves from the benchmark, blueprint debut.

A country music interlude with Patsy Cline presence follows with an insider account of the making of LeAnn Rimes's *Blue* (Curb 1996). As Director of Marketing at Curb Records in Nashville, Sarita Stewart was an integral part of the team that helped launch Rimes as the youngest country star since Tanya Tucker in the 1970s. Rimes proved to be "the right voice" for the album's title tune, which was written by disc jockey Bill Mack in 1958 with Cline in mind. Stewart's unique point of view profiles Rimes, her family, and label founder Mike Curb during the record's production stages.

The writing returns to rock with Third Eye Blind. Their self-titled, 14-song debut (Elektra 1997) featured five popular singles and sold over six million copies, an impressive accomplishment within the 1990s rap-happy music marketplace infatuated with boy bands and digital downloading. Josh Hillyer asserts that there is a depth and nuance in *Third Eye Blind* that is often overlooked, particularly the songwriting of Stephan Jenkins, valedictorian of Cal-Berkeley's Class of 1987. Hillyer highlights the debut's dark and subversive subject matter, its simplicity, wit, unique "three act" structure and lasting, albeit surprising, relevance in the punk and indie community.

Anachronistic authenticity is central to Andrew Davis's critical discussion of Sharon Jones's 2002 dap dippin' debut on the small Brooklyn label Daptone. Backed by the Dap Kings, who were major players for the late Amy Winehouse's *Back to Black* (2006) studio session and tour, Jones's record achieves genuine, honest-to-Stax R&B, funk, soul, groove, and blues without being retro or derivative. Davis contends that within the contemporary context of urban nu-soul hipsters, corporate music taste makers and their perception that R&B needed to be saved by hip-hop, rap, pop, and hollow marketing strategies, *Dap Dippin'* stands as a proud and defiant reminder of days when music was made by musicians and the house band was king.

Micah Rueber structures his postmodern, post-millennial perspective on the Libertines' neo-punk debut, *Up the Bracket* (EMI 2002), around a duo dynamic. Counter to their cool contemporaries—such as the Strokes, Hives, and the White Stripes—that feature a traditional front person, the Libertines' hip heroes, Pete Doherty and Carl Barat, share vocals, songwriting, and lead guitar. The dual duties of the Libertine leads continues a rich British tradition of rock groups that feature two dominant personalities. Rueber's reading of *Up the Bracket* reveals brazen borrowing that is confronting and compelling, with connections to British and American touchstones that include the Beatles, Clash, Velvet Underground and Ramones.

The postmodern pastiche persists into the collection's finale, a collaborative essay that evolved out of my curiosity and subsequent conversations with our (then) teenage son, Rivers, about a catchy collage of retro reverberations overheard in his music rotation. The Go! Team's *Thunder, Lightning, Strike* (Memphis Industries 2004) is a cinematic, sampledelic spectrum of pep squad soundscapes, music styles, genres, and eras. With their resourceful excavation of musical flotsam and jetsam, the Brighton-based multinational sextet is true to the spirit of its name—derived from the units that are dispatched to clean up the wreckage after a plane crash. The chapter portrays the high-energy hipsters as inventive archival audio rearrangers and abstract expressionists who have orchestrated an exclamation point debut that is chaotic yet cohesive, cluttered and comprehensive, and as playful and picturesque as it is sweet and smart. *Thunder, Lightning, Strike*'s exotic, found sound resonance and fragments of familiarity are a fresh, fleet alternative of convergent commotion that bridges the Generational Divide.

In addition to a Discography listing the albums discussed, the chapters are complemented with several appendices that provide debut reference sources and list subjective samples: Grammy Awards for Best New Artist, 1959 to present; "Greatest" and "Best" debut albums lists from music magazines *Uncut*, *New Musical Express*, and *Rolling Stone*, and the website dkpresents.wordpress.com; and music journalist Dave Marsh's "Best" and "Most Disappointing" Debut Albums.

Once Upon a Time ...

The rhythms, tones, and narratives within *Please Allow Me to Introduce Myself* resemble a collection of reflective short stories. The essays exude a "once upon a time," "in the beginning" aura. After all, a debut album is the beginning of a story, with captivating, creative characters, conflicts, lively settings, plot twists and turns, endings, and to-be-continueds. The debut is the story. A burst on the scene.An entrance. An arrival—for artist, audience, and album as an artifact of affection, from cover image and design through a fresh song cycle Alive on arrival. An introduction. A "pleased to meet you" moment. First impressions and lasting impressions. Love at first sound.

Chapter 1

Lubbock or Leave It:
Buddy Holly, Norman Petty, and
The "Chirping" Cricket[1]

George H. Lewis

Cold. It's freezing, cold and clear this early winter morning near the Maine coast. The empty field across the road has been coated in new snow, overnight. I hear the crunch of boots on frost, on the porch. A soft knock at the door. I grab my books, my winter cap. Step outside where Jim waits, ears red from the cold, fists bunched in his jacket pockets, meeting me for our walk to school. It is Tuesday, February 3, 1959.

In another snow strewn field, this early morning, nearly a half a continent away and four miles outside of Clear Lake, Iowa, the broken body of Buddy Holly has just been identified. Buddy has lain in this field since late the night before, thrown from his small chartered plane as it corkscrewed into the ground, one wing tearing a dark gash into the frozen midnight field before ripping off, after take-off into the whipping wind and snow.

"Buddy Holly's dead," Jim says, his breath like cold white steam in the frigid morning air. "It's on the radio. All over."

Fifteen months earlier, in November of 1957, Brunswick Records had released the debut album of Buddy's group, The Crickets. Titled *The "Chirping" Crickets*, it included their smash hit single, "That'll Be The Day." It was the first album of recorded music I ever owned.

Mid-June of 1956, Lubbock, Texas. Buddy Holly, Jerry Allison, and Sonny Curtis duck out of the dusty summer heat and into the cool darkness of downtown's Lindsey Theatre to catch an early showing of John Wayne's new blockbuster film, *The Searchers*. Although attracted by Wayne's already larger-than-life persona, they are also more than likely drawn to the film by 17-year-old Natalie Wood, fresh from her starring role with James Dean in *Rebel Without A Cause*. In *The*

---

[1]   In addition to the music by Buddy Holly and The Crickets, the following sources were invaluable to the author in crafting this essay: Carr and Munde (1995); Gerron and Cameron (2008); Goldrosen (1975); Goldrosen and Beecher (1996); Jensen (1998); Laing (2010); Leigh (2009); Sprech (2003). If the reader is interested in pursuing The Crickets' early work, these sources are highly recommended.

Searchers, Wood plays the part of Debbie Edwards, the older teen who was kidnapped by Comanches and whom Wayne ultimately tracks down in this now classic John Ford Western.

Natalie Wood has, by this time, also attracted the attention of Elvis Presley, who was very popular early in his career in this flat and dusty northwestern part of Texas and who had played Lubbock five times in 1955 (once on the back of a flat bed truck), where Buddy's then country band had opened for him. Presley had actually attended the Lindsey himself, one time that year, with Buddy and the other performers, laughing and nudging each other, as they caught a showing of *Gentlemen Prefer Blondes*, with Marilyn Monroe and Jane Russell. By this time, Elvis had also flown Natalie Wood to Memphis for a date, so Buddy and the gang were certainly interested in checking her out, this June afternoon, in the cool dusk of the Lindsey. Along with Wood's performance, they also come away with a catch phrase of Wayne's, uttered with self-confident bravado several times throughout the film—"That'll be the day!" It wasn't long before Allison and Holly had crafted a song around that phrase, and headed to Nashville, armed with a contract from Decca, to record it.

The July 1956 road trip to Nashville, in actuality, was their second of the year. Decca Records, eager to find a rockabilly singer to put up against RCA's recent Elvis Presley signing, had offered Buddy a contract in January. His sessions were overseen by Owen Bradley, the man responsible for recording Patsy Cline, Ernest Tubb, Kitty Wells, and other country legends. The problem was, as good as these cats were at creating country hits, Nashville pickers and producers had little clue as to how to play or record rock and roll. Buddy Holly's Fender Stratocaster, for example, was likely one of the first of these solid body guitars seen in Nashville. Originally produced in California in 1954, with its revolutionary cutaway design, it later became the focal instrument of early rockabilly and rock and roll. But Buddy was an innovator, and one of the first to use it. (In 1957 he holds it proudly on the cover photo of the group on their debut album, a revolutionary and defining image for rock and roll.)

That July session in Owen Bradley's famous Quonset Hut (804 16th Avenue South) was a ragtag mix of naive Texas boys trying to figure out how to play rock and roll with established country music session men. It wasn't pretty. "That'll Be The Day," begins with a too-short and nervous sounding Chuck Berry-style Strat intro from Buddy. Then Nashville takes over with a rigid and steady "country-pop" beat and rhythm, a higher pitched and strained "country" vocal from Buddy as he attempts to overcompensate for a lack of background voices, and an unsupported (although quite good) Strat guitar solo, all wrapped up in an overdone heavy echo effect that reached for, but could not duplicate, the sound that Sam Phillips had created for Elvis in Memphis at his tiny Sun Studio, before RCA had gobbled him up with the (thitherto) largest recording contract in history. In the end, Decca decided not to release "That'll Be The Day," or any other songs recorded at the July sessions.

On the rebound from Decca, Buddy Holly looked West, to New Mexico and a small independent studio for whom he had cut some demos in 1955 and early 1956. The studio was in Clovis and was run by Norman Petty and his wife, Vi. At the time of these recordings, Petty—who even then was impressed with Buddy's potential—advised him to go back to Lubbock, form a group and work up some original material, then to come back to Clovis and record seriously.

By late 1956, Petty had recorded Buddy Knox's "Party Doll" and Jimmy Bowen's "I'm Sticking with You," both of which he contracted out to larger New York-based labels and each of which sold over a million copies. Rock and roll was becoming commercial in a big way, and Petty was not locked into any pre-existing commercial musical genre that precluded him recognizing and hearing this. Like George Martin later with the Beatles, he encouraged innovation in his studio, even contributing to it himself. Major labels in New York were slowly realizing there was money to be made in rock and roll, and several had begun to look to Petty as one of the few independent producers who seemed to deliver bankable music of this emerging and, to them, unknowable style. When Buddy showed up in Clovis, with his band, ready to record, Petty was ecstatic. In their first 1957 session, they cut two songs Buddy Holly and Jerry Allison had brought with them—"I'm Looking for Someone to Love" and "That'll Be the Day."

Everyone involved was excited about the sound of these two recordings. On "That'll Be the Day," especially, Holly had developed a new, more original introductory guitar pattern that led far more smoothly into the song itself. He sang with excitement and intensity in his voice, now with the backing vocals he had wanted, but was denied in Nashville. Jerry Allison's muscular drumming and unique cymbal work both provided the strong foundation the song needed and propelled Buddy through the verses and his now classic Fender Strat guitar solo. The song, as reworked in Clovis, was musically tight, emotionally bright, packed with musical and vocal hooks, innovative, and melodically catchy. But there was a problem. Even though Decca had chosen not to release the recorded Nashville version, they still had Buddy under contract, and a legal right to his work, especially this song.

When Norman Petty tested the waters by shopping the master in New York, the individual most interested turned out to be Bob Thiele, head of Coral Records—which, of all things, was a subsidiary of Decca. After some delicate negotiations, during which it was pointed out that, if Buddy signed with Coral and Decca exercised its legal rights in court, it would actually be suing itself, Decca's Nashville division allowed Buddy to sign with Coral Records. Decca retained rights to their own unreleased version of "That'll Be The Day" and the other songs recorded in the Nashville sessions, and allowed Norman Petty's re-recorded "That'll Be The Day" to be released on a subsidiary label of Coral's that was used for African American pop and R&B artists, Brunswick Records. Perhaps they hoped this would bury the Clovis recording in an obscure and low-selling urban ethnic market where music created by a white group would have no chance. Little did they know of the emerging dynamics of rock and roll!

To be on the safe side, Norman and Buddy agreed to release the two songs on Brunswick as a single, but under a "group" name, rather than Holly's own. Buddy also used his first and middle names, "Charles Hardin," as songwriter when publishing the song, to avoid any possible legal issues on that front, as well. For his help in the studio and in obtaining the new contract, Norman Petty put his name on the song, along with "Charles Hardin" and Jerry Allison, as a co-writer (a questionable tactic, yet not uncommon for independent record producers in that era, and one that Petty continued to employ with Holly, The Crickets and other artists he recorded at his Clovis studio).

Holly and Allison now needed a formal name for their group to record under. Perhaps, knowing their recording would be released by an R&B label, they were influenced by African American R&B group names like The Spiders, The Termites, or The Fireflies, dance styles like the Jitterbug, or perhaps the release, in 1957, of "I'm A King Bee" by Slim Harpo, but in any event Holly and Allison decided to search for an insect name—then chose The Crickets, insects that do, indeed, "sing." So, by the summer of 1957, a new rock and roll group named The Crickets released their first single, "That'll Be the Day," on a New York-based black rhythm and blues label, Brunswick Records. The song entered *Billboard's* Top 100 in June and remained there for an amazing 23 weeks, reaching #1 in many regional markets, #3 nationally in the pop chart, and #2 in the R&B chart. By the fall of 1957, the Crickets had arrived.

It's late October 1957 and Jim's dad is out of prison. Slouching back on the family couch for hours on end, he drinks Pepsi, smokes Camels and listens to his old 45's on a battered player at his feet. "Whisperin' Bells." "Old Shep." "I Walk The Line." Says he'll drive us to Ellsworth, 40 miles down the coast, to buy a record, if we give him the gas money. Jim and I spend Saturday walking Salisbury Cove Road, snagging tossed empty bottles from under dusty fallen leaves in the ditches on both sides until we have enough to trade in for the needed cash. Then, together, he and I push his dad's rust-pocked 1953 black Studebaker backwards out of the drive—the tranny's lost reverse gear—and we head out over the Trenton flats towards Ellsworth. WMEX Boston plays through dry static over the car radio. Arnie Woo-Woo Ginsburg's show. "That'll Be the Day," by the Crickets comes on along with Arnie's trademark whistles and toots—"Still Boston's number one song, brought to you by Adventure Car Hop." We all three sing along. "Damn good song," Jim's dad says. I'm surprised, as his dad seldom says a thing, these days. "You're getting the Crickets, right?" he asks us. "Oh yeah," Jim says, then pauses—"well, them or 'Jailhouse Rock.'"

With a single out and moving into the charts, it is important to work the music on the road, and that is what the Crickets—Holly, Allison, Joe Mauldin, and Niki Sullivan—did, sometimes playing two or even three shows a day. In those early rock and roll and R&B shows, several artists would tour together as a "package," with some artists moving into and out of the package as the tour progressed across the country or region. Each act might play three to five songs as their part of the show, though some bands—The Crickets were one—also played behind other solo performers or acts as their band, to save the promoter money. This was exhausting work, but it also forged strong links among performers and expanded many artists' abilities to work in multiple musical genres, as backups to other artists. An evolved, supposedly communal version of this early model was likely behind Bob Dylan's concept of the "Rolling Thunder Review" which gained and shed artists as it moved across America in the mid-1970s, and both forms were likely ultimately based historically on the traveling minstrel show—at one time, America's most popular mode of song and entertainment.

For their part of this package show, The Crickets were not lacking for material. In addition to both sides of their current single, they had other original material, including their forthcoming second single, "Oh Boy," and a host of covers to draw from. Not only had Holly played country music in Lubbock bands for years, he was very familiar with R&B music. Lubbock had a relatively small African American population, but it was the only large town in the West Texas region, so many R&B groups and black dance bands played there, outside the official city limits where liquor was legal, in clubs like the Hi Hat and the Cotton Club. This is where Buddy went to hear performers like (especially) Little Richard (and to invite him home to dinner and, later, to tour with him). And then there was Elvis, who was very popular in Lubbock and who Buddy knew personally from his shared performances and visits.

The Crickets were not naive country boys from West Texas where music was concerned. They were well aware of rockabilly, R&B, blues and country, had played these musics and mixed them gleefully in their shared and emergent creations at the heart of American rock and roll. In so doing, Holly and his band created a distinctive vocal and musical style—intimate, breathy and confessional, yet at the same time filled with energy and outbreaks of exultation. One can hear traces of African American singers like Little Richard in Holly's sometimes frenetic bursts of vocal energy and his switching from low to high vocal registers, a bit of Elvis in his growl—though not nearly as sexually aggressive as Elvis managed to sound—and pure Buddy Holly with his melismatic hiccup that made his songs instantly recognizable as his own (and very difficult for other vocalists to cover, as well).

Coupled with Jerry Allison's innovative rhythmic ideas and his percussive shading and power, and the clean clear sound of Holly's electric Fender leads (which contain hints of Chuck Berry R&B solos, some Scotty Moore and (plugged in) traditional country acoustic and banjo pick and brush techniques), The Crickets were an exciting band to hear—breaking new musical ground with each recorded or live performance they undertook.

Among their many other performances, the 1957 tour behind "That'll Be the Day" booked The Crickets into three of the country's leading African American theatres, including a week-long residence at Harlem's famed Apollo in New York City. All the other performers on this bill were African American, as was the audience—most of whom expected The Crickets, from their name, their sound, their spot on the R&B chart, and their record label, to be African American as well. The silence that greeted them as they stepped on stage and sang "That'll Be the Day" dissolved, though, as Buddy sized up the situation and immediately jumped into a driving version of "Bo Diddley." The band was moving, all over the stage, sweating, dancing, and driving to the beat. The Crickets were, as Bo Diddley himself, one of the loudest live bands playing at the time, and they broke the Apollo up.

No accident, then, that the flip side of The Crickets' second single, "Not Fade Away," rode a bright and driving Bo Diddley beat and became a signature live song for them—as well as the initial breakthrough for the Rolling Stones, who covered it for their first hit single in 1964, and for the Grateful Dead, who played it live 530 times across their career, making it their seventh most often performed song. (And speaking of Cricket covers, "That'll Be The Day" was not only a huge hit for Linda Ronstadt in 1976 but also the first demo cut by the Quarrymen in 1958 (before they renamed themselves The Beatles—perhaps with The Crickets in mind not just for this particular song, but also as inspiration for their own new group name?)

By the fall of 1957, The Crickets were, in pop music terms, in the best situation they could have found themselves. Contracted to a major label with a national distribution network, they were recording with a bright, musically talented and inventive independent producer in his own studio, where they could make their own rules, rather than be dictated to by the corporate music industry. In Nashville, for instance, studio engineers had little experience in properly recording a solid body Fender Stratocaster with its three electric pickups. Further, studio time was strictly allocated in three-hour blocks, per agreement between the large recording companies and the American Federation of Musicians, and non-AFT musicians were not allowed to play on sessions. At Petty's Clovis studio, recording Holly's Stratocaster was an exciting challenge and there were no time limits or restrictions on musicians other than those set by Petty and whomever he was recording at the time. Recording sessions could (and sometimes did) last all night (with the only restriction being they could not begin until the gas station run by Petty's father next door had closed for the day, so traffic noise would not leak across and onto the recording). The studio itself was converted from a former grocery store run by Petty's aunt and was very small. There was one tiny "isolation" room in which Jerry Allison many times found himself, so his percussion would not leak into the other mics. The problem was that the room was too small to hold his complete drum kit so, for example, on "Not Fade Away" Allison drums the Bo Diddley beat on a cleverly miked cardboard box and for "Everyday" (a song that was recorded in this same time period but released under Holly's name rather than The Crickets'), Allison uses his own body as a percussion instrument, slapping his thighs, chest and knees to help obtain the unique percussive rhythm that is the signature of that song). When his full kit was needed, Allison moved out of the studio and into the hallway, then was miked back in.

A room over Petty's dad's garage next door was also turned into an ambient echo chamber, with sound from the studio fed in by cable through a speaker, miked in the room and sent back to the control room. This effect is used on Holly's lead vocals on "It's Too Late," and "Send Me Some Lovin'" among other songs. Finally, tape overdubbing was utilized to double track both guitar and voice on several songs, from "I'm Looking for Someone to Love," to "Words of Love" (another Holly solo song that was recorded with The Crickets at this same time). Although introduced by Les Paul and Mary Ford in the early 1950s, tape overdubbing had been used very little in pop music before Petty and Holly teamed up to create audio effects on both Crickets and Buddy Holly solo songs—effects that had not been heard before and which made these recordings even more innovative as artifacts of rock history—innovation similar in spirit and collaboration with what George Martin accomplished with the Beatles a decade or so later.

By mid-fall, 1957, Buddy Holly owned the pop airwaves. The Crickets' "That'll Be the Day" was in the top ten, as was Holly's solo single, "Peggy Sue." To muddy the waters further, Decca decided to finally release their Nashville version of "That'll Be the Day" to try and catch a piece of the action. Finally, not realizing the incredible staying power of "That'll Be the Day," Brunswick issued The Crickets' second single, "Oh Boy," backed with "Not Fade Away." That single began its climb to a #1 place on the charts by the year's end. In all, Buddy Holly and The Crickets had four (or if you count the flip side of "Oh Boy," five) recordings in the pop charts, issued by three different labels (Brunswick, Coral, and Decca), all at the same time. There had been nothing like it in pop music history, and wouldn't be again until the Beatles "invaded" America on Capitol Records in January of 1964.

An album was at this point a clear and obvious necessity, and The Crickets and Norman Petty went about compiling one. Titled "The 'Chirping' Crickets" (and quaintly identified on the back cover as "vocal group with orchestra") the album featured a full color photo of the group, neatly dressed in coats and ties and smiling under a bright blue sky. (This was Petty's doing. Buddy was usually as scruffy as the Beatles—or Elvis—before their managers cleaned their images up for broad public consumption.) The album photo, with Buddy holding his iconic Fender guitar, also served another purpose. Since Brunswick was known as an African American label, it showed the larger (white) teen buying public (and their parents) that The Crickets were white performers. It also showed radio DJs who would likely not play "race" music (especially, though not exclusively, in the South) the same thing. As with Elvis, whose handlers had initiated this whole "cover photo" concept for the same reasons, the clean and neat white image cleared the way for sales to the largest sector of the mass audience.

Released in November of 1957, the album contains the first three Crickets singles and flip sides, even though the third ("Maybe Baby/Tell Me How") had not yet been released. These six cuts are among the most innovative and influential in the history of rock and roll and they are all included on this amazing album. Of the remaining six, one, "Last Night," was written by Joe Mauldin, the Crickets bass player and is a solid contribution, as well. Two others are covers of African American artists Holly admired—Chuck Willis's "It's Too Late" and Little Richard's "Send Me Some Lovin'." Both emotional "soul" ballads, they would have been easily identified by African Americans who were browsing recordings on the Brunswick label and added some extra "cred" to Holly's place on the R&B charts and to his placement on Brunswick Records. By this point, white teens "in the know" would also recognize these names, as both artists were being played on early rock and roll radio programs such as Alan Freed's at WINS in New York or Arnie Ginsberg's at WMEX in Boston. These two covers by The Crickets are also great white soul interpretations, although the Jordanaire-type background vocals (sung by the Picks and dubbed in by Petty) tend to distract from the emotional intensity of Holly's treatments of each.

Two other songs ("You've Got Love" and "An Empty Cup") were written by Roy Orbison who, in 1957, was just beginning his recording career in rockabilly at Sun Records in Memphis. Orbison grew up in a small West Texas town about 60 miles from Lubbock and had initially recorded a few songs with Norman Petty in Clovis. These are good early attempts, and "An Empty Cup" suggests the sort of tragic story-ballad Orbison would later become known for. However, at this point in time, Orbison was just beginning to record rockabilly for iconic Sun Records— and he was also a local boy. Score large points for The Crickets on both counts, in including covers of these early songs on their album. (And in quite another vein, Orbison and Holly, both West Texas boys also made it cool for rock stars to wear dark thick-rimmed glasses. Where would Elton John and Elvis Costello have been later, without the trail these earlier two blazed, image-wise?)

The "Chirping" Crickets closes with a near novelty number, Shorty Long's "Rock Me My Baby." Later, Long would join Motown and would write "Devil in a Blue Dress", "Here Comes the Judge," and, in a strange twist of fate, would record "Chantilly Lace" the song that made The Big Bopper famous enough to put him on that same ill-fated tour, and plane, that killed Buddy Holly in Clear Lake, Iowa on January 3, 1959. Shorty Long was a name African Americans would recognize even as early as 1957—a name likely unknown outside their own musical community. "Rock Me My Baby" is a bouncy, happy song and gives Holly a chance to inject some killer Fender runs into a benign R&B novelty number, as well as to further establish his creds with the R&B crowd—while bringing this historic, innovative album to a pleasurable, though surprisingly unremarkable close.

Mid-December, 1957. The grey sky spits snow as I walk carefully down the icy sidewalk toward West Market Square in Bangor, Maine. Sam Viner's Music Company rises above me, three stories high. If anyone will have it, they will, I think, as I step inside. Pianos crouch round the main showroom, and I see racks of clarinets and horns, smell the tang of valve oil and brass polish. Somewhere, someone is quietly tuning an acoustic guitar. I ask at the main counter.

"Let's look." Viner moves to the racks of LPs that fill the rear of his store, flips through a few, pulls out an album and hands it to me. Through the translucent

plastic store sleeve, I can see The Crickets, dressed as neatly as Mr. Viner beside me. A group photo, everyone smiling, taken under an intense summer-blue sky. "Wanna hear it?" Viner asks.

"I guess ... sure," I stammer, having no idea that such was possible. Sam leads me to a listening booth, slides the album out of its protective sleeve, and shows me how to cue it up on the inside turntable. Then he leaves me to listen. "Oh Boy," the album's first cut, tumbles joyously from the speaker. Entranced, in another world, I stand there and listen to the album, all the way through.

Afterwards I hurry to meet my dad at the car, where we had agreed. Snow is still falling, and the wind has picked up. I'm late and my dad is worried about the weather. We have a long drive home and, at 4 in the afternoon, it is beginning to get dark. I tell him I was at Viner's, looking at band instruments. We have no pop music at home. No phonograph player. My dad wouldn't know Buddy Holly from Adam. Would probably care less.

He tells me he has one last errand to run, and asks me to sit in the car and wait for him. I dig my hands in my pockets to keep warm and try to play The "Chirping" Crickets *back, in my head, in my imagination. My dad returns, stuffs a package in the back, and we head for home.*

A week later, on Christmas morning, The "Chirping" Crickets *is waiting for me, propped carefully under the tree. Beside it is a new portable phonograph machine—from Sam Viner's. My mom and I dance to "Rock Me My Baby," stepping through Christmas wrappings that cover the living room floor. Tree lights shine. Tinsel glistens. This is the first album of recorded music I have ever owned.*

Chapter 2

Good Time Rollers: Little Richard and Huey "Piano" Smith

B. Lee Cooper and William L. Schurk

In the summer of 1957, I was a teenager mesmerized by the madcap lyrics and jump and holler piano rhythms of "Rockin' Pneumonia and the Boogie Woogie Flu." The melody was haunting, the lyrics catchy, mysterious and nonsensical. I would never have guessed that wily composer Huey Smith had co-opted phrases from Chuck Berry ("I got the rockin' pneumonia ...") and from Roy Brown ("Young man rhythm ...") and then created his own unique rhyme schemes to formulate the strange audio tale. The meandering keyboard introduction that kicked off "Rockin' Pneumonia" was undoubtedly grounded in Smith's years of piano apprenticeship in smoky saloons and dingy dance halls in his native New Orleans and extensive session work.

"Rockin' Pneumonia" expressed a similar vibrant, anarchistic spirit to that of Little Richard's "Tutti Fruitti," from a year and half earlier. Perhaps it was no coincidence. Huey Smith backed Little Richard during his Specialty sessions, the two taking turns on tunes, listening to each other play. Smith was regarded as a far more adept player, with Little Richard known for commonly banging out "wrong notes." Studio circumstances resulted in Little Richard taking over the piano on the raving "Tutti Fruitti." The song was an afterthought, and Little Richard's manager/producer Bumps Blackwell had only 15 minutes of studio time left to cut the song, not enough time to teach Smith the arrangement (Cocks 1979: 151). Songs from the Specialty sessions became hits and were subsequently consolidated into the debut album *Here's Little Richard* in 1957. Two years later, "Rockin Pneumonia" headlined Huey Smith and his Clowns' first album, *Having A Good Time* on Ace Records. Together, the Little Richard and Huey "Piano" Smith debut albums provide a composite of the energetic, eccentric, agile piano stylings that were central to the sound of the of the birth of rock era.

Here's Little Richard

It is impossible to elaborate the history of 20th-century popular music without focusing on Little Richard's distinctive, crossover contributions and energetic presence. Richard certainly ranks among rock's iconic pioneers such as Chuck Berry, Bo Diddley, Carl Perkins, and Elvis Presley, among others. His songs—

"Keep A Knockin'," "Heebie Jeebies," "Good Golly, Miss Molly," and "Tutti Frutti" are equally emblematic and arguably as essential to rock and roll's emergence as other touchstone tunes such as Willie Mae's "Big Mama," Thornton's "Hound Dog," "(We're Gonna) Rock Around the Clock" by Bill Haley and the Comets, Big Joe Turner's "Shake, Rattle and Roll," "Maybelline," "Blue Suede Shoes," and "Whole Lotta Shakin' Goin' On."

In early 1955, the American recording industry was tamer, pop singers were still safe and predictable, and radio melodies were rarely rocking. Admittedly, blues shouter Big Joe Turner and country music expatriate Bill Haley were shaking and rattling—and R&B piano man Fats Domino was gently rolling. Then came "Tutti Frutti"! For crooner Frank Sinatra and jazz critic Gene Lees it was considered lyrical nonsense sung by a wailing maniac. The frantic trills and gospel-tinged pitch of Little Richard gleefully announced that R&B had exploded into an entirely new sonic dimension (Coleman 1989: 18-27; Doggett 1990: 62-65).

The screaming tenor saxophone of Lee Allen and the honking baritone horn of Alvin "Red" Tyler reverberated with instrumental messages of chaos and ecstasy. The drum kit of Earl Palmer exploded with the signature rhythms of rock 'n' roll. And on piano, filling in for the more subtle Huey Smith, Little Richard crushed the keys into submission. Like nothing ever recorded before, Little Richard and his J&M Studio session-mates produced a feverish sound that was daring and danceable. The record that emerged from the Specialty Records studio September 14, 1955 announced Little Richard and magnified rock and roll (see Blackwell 2000: 100-101; Bowen 1989: 4-8; Watson 1990: 24-26).

Richard Wayne Penniman, born on December 5, 1935 in Macon, Georgia, was the third child of Bud and Leva Mae Penniman. The fundamentalist father and his devout wife would eventually produce a family of 13 youngsters. The traditional gospel renderings of the youthful Penniman Singers were countered by the attention-grabbing antics, cross-dressing, and bizarre sexual behavior of Richard Wayne. Eventually, his parents renounced him at age 13; two years later he was adopted by Ann and Johnny Johnson. Singing and cavorting were deeply ingrained in Richard Wayne's spirit. He began performing at the Tick Tock Club in Macon. Then he started touring the Southern states with Dr. Hudson's Medicine Show and Sugarfoot Sam's Minstrel Show. In 1951, performing as "Little Richard," he won an Atlanta talent contest sponsored by Fulton County radio personality Zenas Sears. This triumph led to a recording contract with RCA Victor Records. However, Little Richard's vocal efforts on "Taxi Blues" and "Every Hour" proved to be commercially inauspicious. Later single releases on Don Robey's Peacock label in Houston flopped as well. Tour dates as the lead singer for The Tempo Toppers yielded a reasonable weekly income, but Little Richard continued to harbor much bigger personal dreams. He longed to control the big stage like Cab Calloway and Roy Brown and echo the haunting singing styles of Marion Williams and Billy Wright; he hoped to play piano with the flair of Esquerita and desired the fan adulation and sexual liberties that he had witnessed at the Dew Drop Inn in New Orleans. (Kirby 2009: 63-121; Winner 1992: 52-59) In 1955, thanks in large part to Specialty Records A&R man and producer Robert "Bumps" Blackwell, Little Richard's frenetic energy and style would be captured, and released with the proclamation: "A wop bop a lu bop, a lop bam boom!"

As a debut record, *Here's Little Richard* was fresh but familiar, with attributes of a "greatest hits" compilation. Of the 12 songs on the album, "Tutti Frutti," "Long Tall Sally," "Slippin' and Slidin'," "Rip It Up," "Ready Teddy," "She's Got It," "Jenny, Jenny," and "Miss Ann" had previously been issued in 45 r.p.m. format. Each of these tunes had charted as *Billboard* R&B hits. Demonstrating Little Richard's exceptional commercial crossover prowess, seven of these recordings had also achieved *Billboard* Pop chart status. In 1958, another track from the album, "True, Fine Mama," would also reach both industry charts. The impact could be traced in the vocal styles and performing approaches of James Brown, Etta James, Big Al Downing, Otis Redding, Thurston Harris, Ronnie Molleen, Richard Berry, and Lowell Fulson. Attempting to co-opt the juggernaut jive featured in Little Richard's infectious recordings, notables Pat Boone, Bill Haley, and Elvis Presley released cover versions of several hit numbers. For years, the animated songs from *Here's Little Richard* continued to attract interpreters such as Paul McCartney, John Lennon, the Rolling Stones, John Fogerty, and Mitch Ryder.

Little Richard's dynamic debut record conceals as much as it reveals about its title character. The contemporary tributes—including the Rock and Roll Hall of Fame induction in 1986, a Grammy Lifetime Achievement Award in 1993, two songs placed in the Grammy Hall of Fame, and various *Rolling Stone* accolades—mask much of Little Richard's personal narrative. Like many of his fellow artists from the era, among them, Jerry Lee Lewis, his white counterpart in piano-playing mayhem, Little Richard was frequently torn between his religious devotion and the seductions of the lustfullifestyle of rock and roll. The internal spiritual conflict was one dimension of Little Richard's complex image marked by scars of Southern racism, parental rejection, the social stigma of an androgynous presence—mascara, makeup, and a six-inch high pompadour—and allegations of miscegenation stemming from mixed-race concert attendance. While Little Richard achieved considerable success as a groundbreaking crossover artist, the notoriety may have hindered a higher rise to prominence within an increasingly competitive, crowded recording industry and its predominantly white teenage record-buying audience (Simels 1985; Hirshey 1984).

Having a Good Time

Piano players like Huey Smith populated the 20th-century performing landscape and propelled wide diversity within American popular music. Among the endless variations are: Albert Ammons, Meade Lux Lewis, and Pete Johnson who demonstrated left-handed magic (see Silvester 1988). Mischievous Fats Waller with "Honeysuckle Rose" and "Ain't Misbehavin'," country artists Moon

Mullican and Merrill Moore, Johnny Maddox's tinkling honky-tonk, comedic keyboardist Victor Borge, and George Shearing, Art Tatum, and Oscar Peterson who accentuated and innovated the jazz idiom. Cecil Gant, Charles Brown, and Amos Milburn helped make the rhythm 'n' blues dance-scene roll while Liberace vamped and Nat King Cole methodically, smoothly synthesized jazz and pop. And Jerry Lee Lewis, Johnnie Johnson, and Ray Charles established piano vitality and vigor as a central element of rock 'n' roll that continued through Billy Joel and Elton John (Doerschuk 1982, 1985; Leavell 1990).

Huey Smith's hometown New Orleans is a piano-playing Mecca, a city with an unwavering cultural bias toward idiosyncratic keyboard artistry. Crescent City ethnomusicologist and music maven Jeff Hannusch (1985) is among those who have documented the ubiquitous presence of pianos in cafes, bars, dance halls, beauty shops, churches, fish fries, and motion picture parlors.[1] Of course, bold and bawdy jazz rhythms were born on keyboards nestled in barrelhouses and brothels throughout southern Louisiana. There are reportedly hundreds of "lost" piano performers—Sullivan Rock, Frank Duston, Drive 'Em Down, Kid Stormy Weather, Boogus, Robert Bertrand—who were never recorded. Other Louisiana keyboard giants whose keyboard mastery has been chronicled include Clarence Williams, Buddy Christian, Spencer Williams, Jelly Roll Morton, Champion Jack Dupree, Archibald, and, of course, Professor Longhair.

These performing legends and stylistic shadows stretch forward over more than six decades (Cooper 2008). During the 1950s and 1960s, a new generation of New Orleans piano prodigies emerged. Their nationwide influence was embodied in Fats Domino. Between 1950 and 1964, The Fat Man from the Ninth Ward placed 61 songs on *Billboard* R&B charts. Even more significantly, from 1955 to 1968 he charted a staggering 77 hits on *Billboard* Pop lists (Whitburn 2004, 2009), Other notable Louisiana keyboard specialists from this mid-century period included Tuts Washington, Allen Toussaint, Dave "Fat Man" Williams, James Booker, Little Brother Montgomery, Eddie Bo, Tommy Ridgley, Esquerita, and Mac "Dr. John" Rebennack. It is within the rich heritage of this piano-centered culture that Huey Smith was born on January 26, 1934.

Having a Good Time is an exciting, but atypical debut record. Issued in 1959 by Ace Records of Jackson, Mississippi, this 12-song album wasn't really an introduction to Huey "Piano" Smith and His Clowns. Record buyers and radio listeners in New Orleans and throughout the United States had initially encountered the madcap, Crescent City-based combo in 1957 when the two-sided single version of "Rockin' Pneumonia and the Boogie Woogie Flu" spent 13 weeks on the *Billboard* Pop charts. The following year, three more Smith compositions performed by the Clowns on the Ace label also secured *Billboard* rankings: "Don't You Just Know It," "High Blood Pressure," and "Don't You Know Yockomo."

---

[1]   There are a number of fine sources documenting New Orleans pianists, among them Berry (1986); Broven (1978); Callahan (1981); Lichtenstein and Dankner (1993); McNutt (2002); Shaw (1973); Winner (1980).

The four charting singles did not translate into album success when compiled into the long-play debut. *Having a Good Time* received neither popular acclaim nor positive critical commentary, nor did it attain a *Billboard* listing.

Despite this album's commercial disappointment, Huey "Piano" Smith persisted, his keyboard career similar to many other piano-playing Louisiana legends (Cocks 1979: 148-60). Smith was raised in the Garden District. At eight years of age, he formed the vocal duo of Slick and Dark, who serenaded their neighborhood mates with the self-constructed "Robertson Street Boogie." Piano playing by his uncle prompted the young Huey to listen intently to the recorded stylings of Dinah Washington, Ivory Joe Hunter, Bull Moose Jackson, and Charles Brown. The jukebox chatter and R&B rhythms of Louis Jordan were especially impressive to Smith. He possessed a keen ear for catchy phrases, jive talk, jump-rope cadences, and street slang that proved crucial to his future lyric structures. As Smith began performing professionally at 15, his touring experiences with Earl King, Roland Cook, and Eddie "Guitar Slim" Jones and his studio work with Smiley Lewis, Lloyd Price, and Little Richard helped move him from a session pianist to a more autonomous composer, arranger, and finally a band leader. Negative dealings with Ace Records owner Johnny Vincent concerning falsified artistic attributions and the theft of a song shaped Huey Smith's frustrations about the nature of the record business (Berry et al. 1986: 80-91; Hannusch 1985: 37-44; McNutt 2002).

Huey "Piano" Smith's lyrical wit and unquenchable zeal for producing dance numbers eventually prompted him to assemble his own crew of off-the-wall instrumentalists and singers. Lacking distinctive vocal talent himself, Smith recruited an ensemble of entertainers who, much like Jerry Leiber and Mike Stoller's Coasters, were unabashed audio comics. Smith christened his group "The Clowns." It is impossible to determine the precise personnel within Huey "Piano" Smith and His Clowns on any given day. Between their formation in 1957 and the release of their debut two years later, lead singing assignments alternated among James Black, Bobby Marchan, Gerri Hall, and Smith. Others members of the touring troupe included Willie Nettles, James Rivers, Raymond Lewis, Walter Kimble, Curley Moore, "Scarface" John Williams, Roosevelt Wright, Curley Smith, Robert Parker, and Jessie Hill. After "Rockin' Pneumonia" hit big in 1957, Smith ceased touring with The Clowns in order to devote more time to songwriting. Thereafter the outrageous and brilliant James Booker impersonated Smith as a touring piano-pounder. No matter the composition of the band's personnel, the good times rocked and rolled in New Orleans or elsewhere whenever The Clowns performed. The legacy of Huey "Piano" Smith is cemented in his magnificent array of Big Easy party songs—from "High Blood Pressure" to "Sea Cruise"—and in his ability to meld lyrical wackiness with rhythmic infection.

The original *Having A Good Time* debut album has been expanded and reissued in CD formats several times since its initial 1959 appearance. Four recent illustrations of this recycling are *Huey "Piano" Smith's Rock and Roll Revival* (Ace 1990), *Having A Good Time with Huey "Piano" Smith and His Clowns*

(Westside 1997), *High Blood Pressure* (Aim 2005), and *The Best of Huey "Piano" Smith and His Clowns* (Fuel 2000, 2009). "Rockin' Pneumonia and the Boogie Woogie Flu," has been anthologized as a regional rock anthem in several Big Easy music salutes, among them *The Hit Sounds of New Orleans* (Charly 1995), *Kings of New Orleans Rock 'n' Roll* (Music Club 1998), and *Glory Days of Rock 'n' Roll: New Orleans* (Time-Life Music 2000). Finally, throughout his concert performances and touring career, the legendary Dr. John has honored his Crescent City comrade by featuring medleys of Huey Smith compositions. Examples of these tributes are found on *Gumbo* (Atco 1972) featuring "High Blood Pressure/ Don't You Just Know It/Well I'll Be John Brown" and in *All By Hisself* (Skinji Brim 2003), containing "Rockin' Pneumonia/High Blood Pressure/Don't You Just Know It/Don't You Know Yockomo." Baton Rouge singer-songwriter Johnny Rivers is also among the Smith interpreters, recording a hit version of "Rockin' Pneumonia and the Boogie Woogie Flu" in 1972.

Rambling and Rolling On

The personal controversies in Little Richard's life may have been distractions, but ultimately did not fully devalue his pioneering crossover contributions and musical legacy. Though Huey "Piano" Smith may be overshadowed by fellow New Orleanian legends Professor Longhair, Fats Domino, and Allen Toussaint, the joker is nonetheless an undeniable premier Crescent City roller. Both artists embody rock's careening excesses. Their charisma, irrepressible energy and flamboyant presence as performers translated into uncompromising debut records characterized by banshee shrieks, lyrical nonsense, and rambling piano-pounding. The verve, power, manic exuberance, eccentricity, and electricity in the grooves of both *Here's Little Richard* and *Having a Good Time*, notably their signature songs "Tutti Frutti" and "Rocking Pneumonia and the Boogie Woogie Flu," make these debuts ideal samplers of American rock 'n' roll and its innate wild spirit that stretches from Macon to New Orleans and beyond, from the late 1950s to the present.

Chapter 3
Joan Baez:
The Classic 1960s Folk Heroine

Jerome Rodnitzky

Joan Baez was born in 1941 and continues to record and give concerts today. However, Baez is a child of the 1960s, when she had her central influence on America and its popular culture. Her rise was mostly timing— for Baez grew up with the decade. In 1960 she was a largely unknown 19-year-old singer, famous for popularizing folk music and centuries-old Anglo-American folk songs in particular. But she increasingly also became famous for activism and pacifism, because of the songs she sang, her concert appearances, and her participation in mass street protests.

Baez's debut album, simply titled *Joan Baez* (Vanguard 1960), is completely comprised of folksongs from 1600-1900. Most of the songs are Anglo-American songs, often telling sad stories, such as "Fare Thee Well" and "Rake and Rambling Boy." There are also two upbeat love songs—"Wildwood Flower" and "John Riley." Some ballads were 19th-century Appalachian folk songs, such as "All My Trials" and "Wildwood Flower." Another, "Donna Donna," came from the early 20th-century Yiddish musical theater, while "The House of the Rising Sun" is a Negro folk song and "El Preso Numero Nueve" (The Ninth Prisoner) was a 20th-century Mexican ballad.

Although Baez never identified herself as a feminist, several of the debut album ballads, and many of her later songs as well, centered on the plight of wronged women. On the debut album, "Silver Dagger" has a daughter complaining about the common philandering of men, including her father. It ends with the vow that she will sleep alone the rest of her life. Another debut song, "House of the Rising Sun," tells about a young girl trapped in the life of a New Orleans prostitute and yet another, "Mary Hamilton," relates the sad story of a woman killed because of English royal court politics. Also Baez, along with a few other women folksingers such as Peggy Seeger, was among the first women to sing songs meant to be sung by men. Good examples would be the song "Fare Thee Well" and "Rake and Rambling Boy." This made it easier much later for Janis Joplin to make a big hit of Kris Kristofferson's song "Me and Bobby McGee," which he wrote to be sung by a man.

Her follow-up second album, *Joan Baez, Vol. 2* (Vanguard 1961), was in most regards a duplicate of the first as far as content. The record had three Child Ballads, "The Cherry Tree Carol," "Barbara Allen," and "Silkie," and an old English ballad, "The Trees Do Grow High," but featured a larger number of American folk songs. The American ballads included "Waggoner's Lad," "The Lilly of the West," "Engine 143," "Pal of Mine," and "Old Blue," a song about a faithful dog.[1] Both Baez and Vanguard Records likely wanted to capitalize on the success of her debut album and not tamper too much with the folk content.

At first glance the first two albums seem rather unrelated to her increasing political activism. However, the albums were right in the middle of the folk revival that, almost unnoticed, had been sweeping the college campuses and influencing student activists during the late 1950s. Vanguard Records specialized in folk music and had already recorded groups such as The Weavers which featured Pete Seeger. These musicians sang Anglo-American folk songs mixed with labor union songs and Negro spirituals, and this music attracted college activists. Their work also attracted Bob Dylan as well as Baez.

Seeger had become particularly successful with a new folk quartet, The Weavers, which included Lee Hays, Fred Hellerman, and Ronnie Gilbert. Hellerman played guitar to back up Seeger's banjo and Hays contributed his deep bass voice. They all sang, but the singing star was Gilbert, who had a stunning high-pitched voice that often made their records musically artistic. Gilbert was perhaps the only folk singer with a voice anywhere near as striking as Baez's, but she was not quite in the same class as Baez. The Weavers had a few top-ten hits such as "Tzena, Tzena," an Israeli folk song and "Goodnight Irene," a Leadbelly folk song. Their albums, however, mixed Guthrie songs, protest songs, and traditional folk songs. The Weavers championed civil rights and pacifism in their concerts and the success of their records also encouraged many new non-political 1950s folk groups such as The Kingston Trio and The Brothers Four.

The Weavers' political protest songs could not be played on radio, but they were popular at college concerts. And even though the hit folk records of The Kingston Trio did not protest anything, folk music in general became associated with campus activism. By the late 1950s almost every college had a campus folk club where student activists often congregated. And since songs for the folk were identified as songs for the masses of Americans, that also tied folk music to activism. The campus folk craze was well summarized by a 1961 *Newsweek* comment: "Basically the schools and students that support causes support folk music. Find a campus that breeds Freedom Riders, anti-Birch demonstrators and anti-bomb societies and you'll find a folk group. The connection is not fortuitous" ("Hoots and Hollers on Campus" 1961).

In the 1950s, most rock music had become too juvenile for college students (consider lyrics such as "Shboom" and "Splish splash, I was taking a bath"). Meanwhile jazz had become too esoteric, complicated, and clearly not aimed at the masses, especially the young. Thus, folk music moved into the campus musical vacuum and this explains why a wide variety of folk music became popular in the late 1950s and early 1960s. Non-political groups like the The Kingston Trio

---

[1]   Joan Baez, *Joan Baez, Vol. 2* (Vanguard Records, VSD-79094, 1961).

and The Brothers Four were also popular with high school kids and their records were best sellers. But Baez was more influenced by the somewhat more political and satiric successful folk groups such as The Chad Mitchell Trio and Peter, Paul and Mary, and especially by the largely unknown folksingers in the folk clubs she attended in Boston. Having moved with her family to Boston in 1959, she dropped out of college after a semester at Boston University. Thus she was one among such early college dropouts as Bob Dylan and Microsoft's Bill Gates. Perhaps she dropped out of college because her father, Dr. Alberto Baez, was a university physicist who expected her to attend college. She later asserted college was just another way for parents to hang on to their children.

However, she continued to hang around the various Boston campus-based folk clubs and eventually started to perform there herself. By this time Baez's almost completely untrained, but very striking voice quickly made her a local star at Boston coffeehouses. And she rapidly picked up guitar and folk technique from folksingers such as Eric Von Schmidt. More importantly, in 1959, while she performed at the famed Gate of Horn folk club in Chicago, she met the premier national folksinger, Bob Gibson. That summer Gibson introduced Baez at the Newport Folk Festival and they performed a duet of a classic folk ballad, "Virgin Mary." Baez was a smash hit at Newport and was quickly offered a record contract by both Vanguard Records and the record industry giant, Columbia Records. She chose the smaller Vanguard group because they had already devoted themselves to folk music and appeared to be more interested in music and less completely wrapped up in commerce. Vanguard retained her loyalty for a dozen years, because they continued to turn out a vast array of folk albums by artists Baez admired.

Baez obviously chose to concentrate on folk music because the connection between campus activism and folk music was now clear. And she likely chose an album of older Anglo-American folk songs to show off her unique voice, which soared through the soprano register like almost no other. She had picked up a love and knowledge of some of these songs in the folk clubs of New York and Boston. Also most of the American folksingers sang very few older Anglo-American songs. Richard Dyer Bennett, an English-born folksinger did concentrate on these older songs and his renditions were well researched and authentic. However, he was 47 years old in 1960 and his voice was rather ordinary. Moreover, his 13 different LP records, put out by his own record company, did not sell very well.

Thus Baez's debut album stepped into somewhat of a folk vacuum. As a college undergraduate and folk music fan in 1960, I was completely blown away by Baez's voice and artistic delivery. Her debut album added a new dimension to American folk music. Other political folksingers such as Oscar Brand and Theo Bikel had been selling records, but their albums were largely unknown to college students. Baez, and later Bob Dylan and Judy Collins, took the campuses by storm and began performing on-campus concerts.

Baez's debut album cover was very strange. It has a large image of a woman playing a guitar, but it is piecemeal white-dot illustration of a woman's face against a pitch black background. It is so hazy one cannot easily see it as the young Baez. On the back cover there is a small 2x2 black-and-white photo of Baez that the cover is supposedly based on. The back also features very good complete explanations of the 13 songs and their origins; the Mexican song, "The Ninth Prisoner," has the words reproduced in both Spanish and English. Baez concerts would often feature a Spanish or Mexican song sung in Spanish. In part this was perhaps a tribute to her Mexican-born father. And since her mother was Scottish and English, her repertoire might be perceived as partly ancestral. Although Baez was a non-denominational believer, both her parents were Quakers and this likely contributed to her pacifism.

Her 1960 debut album was followed by a number of very successful college campus tours. Suddenly, at age 20, Baez was the premier American folksinger. In her semi-autobiographical book *Daybreak*, Baez wrote that "to sing is to love and affirm, to fly and soar, that nothing is a promise, but that beauty exists, and must be hunted for and for and found" (1966: 77). If her singing did give Baez wings, it was seldom apparent at her early live performances. These had a solemn quality which the audience quickly sensed—people did not sway to the singing and clapping your hands would seem stupid. Her fragile lyrics and looks encouraged the audience to respond with a hushed silence.

The earlier concerts were rather mystical. I first heard Baez at her November 1962 concert at the University of Illinois. She walked out on the stage of an auditorium filled with a capacity 1,500 student audience. Baez was dressed in a plain blouse and skirt. Without a word, she sat down on a stool—guitar in hand— and started playing. After 50 minutes of songs, broken only by some brief song introductions and the dedication of one song to Pete Seeger, she walked off the stage at intermission, without even saying she was coming back. In style and format, her second-half program was a repeat of the first. Her concert ended with one encore song and a simple "Goodnight, thank you."

Baez's concerts since 1970 have steadily become more modern and effervescent, with much more rapport and conversation with the audience. This was likely encouraged by her use of different types of songs. Her repertory moved from older ballads to protest songs, to Dylan ballads and, finally, to some songs that she wrote herself. She could undoubtedly have attracted a bigger audience by singing some simple popular rock songs, but she refused to sing songs that did not tell a serious story and make a point. Early in her career she became one of the first performers to introduce the young Bob Dylan, who was her age, at folk festivals and they sang some duets together. But his fame and success quickly surpassed Baez's and she became known as just a friend of Dylan. And Baez was very disappointed when Dylan turned from writing protest songs to more general ballads.

Ironically, in 1962 when Dylan was writing a number of protest songs, he chided Baez for singing older folksongs instead of protest songs. Dylan noted:

> It ain't nothin' just to walk around and sing ... Take Joanie man, she's still
> singing about Mary Hamilton. I mean where is that at? She's walked around on
> picket lines ... so why ain't she stepping out? (Farina 1967)

However, by 1965 Dylan had stopped writing protest songs and Baez was always waiting for him to start writing protest songs again so she could again cover his songs.

Balance has been a constant strength of Baez's albums. She never selected one type of song and thus even her hard-core protest songs were seldom tedious on albums. Nevertheless, Baez always had critics. In regard to her early albums, *Little Sandy Review* (*LSR*), headquarters for "folkier than thou" criticism, conceded that Baez was "perhaps the most thrilling young voice of our time." But they sadly concluded that "her vocal gifts were far too rich to carry the simplicity of the humble folk song." When a traditional folksinger, such as Woody Guthrie or Leadbelly, sang a folk song, the *LSR* reviewers argued, "it described the basic nature of his land and people"; Baez, however, could only describe herself, for in "molding a song to her own powerful personality" she destroyed it. Joan did not lack defenders. After reviewing Baez's first album, the *LSR* reviewers noted that her many fervent fans had requested that they "quit picking on Joan" and "go back to beating their grandmothers with old Library of Congress albums" (Nelson and Panake 1961).

All through the 1960s Baez's voice soared through the soprano register, far above the social and political struggles. She was clearly the most distinct and artful singer in the folk field. Her record albums always sold well, but were not best sellers. And her relative lack of commercial success helped buttress her political credibility. Baez had only one top-ten hit— Robbie Robertson's "The Night They Drove Old Dixie Down," in 1971. And although that song highlighted the tragedy and futility of America's Civil War, as seen through the actual experiences of a Robertson ancestor, most young fans just swayed to the music and missed the real message. From the 1970s on, Baez's concert tours and record sales did much better in Europe (where folk music remained more popular) than in America. But even while her career faded somewhat, Baez continued to shine on late night talk shows—from Dick Cavett to David Frost to Les Crane—where she both sang and was interviewed.

Baez continued to be seen as the premier woman folksinger, but her popularity was increasingly due to her personal activism. Her role in civil rights and anti-war protest got her arrested several times and often put her in harm's way. A number of popular singers sang and wrote protest songs, but Baez was unique because she put her body and her money where her mouth was. She contributed large cash amounts to pacifist and activist foundations. She also turned down opportunities to record more rock and roll and thus earn much more. Instead she concentrated on little-known artistic folk and message songs on albums and in concerts.

Baez was never a great songwriter, but she likely hit her peak with her 1975 A&M album *Diamonds and Rust*, which featured four songs she wrote. The highlight was "Diamonds and Rust," the title song, clearly about her stormy relationship with folk icon Bob Dylan. Perhaps her best retrospective showcase is the 1976 dual record album, *From Every Stage*, which showcases her concert performances. Her early records were on the Vanguard label which still specialized in folk music; in the 1970s, she switched to A&M Records, which allowed her more artistic leeway and supported her activism.

The 1985 Live Aid concert in Philadelphia perhaps made the clearest connection between Baez's music, protest, and activism. Her six minutes on stage opened with two verses of "Amazing Grace" for the older people, followed by several verses of "We Are the World," so the young kids could sing along with a chorus they knew. But before singing, Baez opened the US portion of the worldwide show with a call to arms: "Good morning children of the Eighties! This is your Woodstock and it's long overdue. And it's nice to know the money out of your pocket will feed the hungry." It was reminiscent of her 1968 appearance at Woodstock. There, a noticeably pregnant Baez sang to a sleepy young crowd at 2 a.m. and dedicated a song to her husband, David Harris, who was in prison for resisting the draft. In 1985 at Live Aid, Baez had suddenly taken us back to the 1960s and used songs to cement old and young in a proactive group. As a unique popular singer that has been her most notable achievement

Joan Baez's voice no longer soars through the soprano register, but she remains a charismatic singer and performer at concerts.[2] An artist with such a unique and powerful singing voice should perhaps be most remembered for her art and folksinger presence that was showcased on her debut, but it is more likely that Joan Baez will also be identified with her consistent, career-long activism.

---

[2]   The 90-minute American Masters documentary *How Sweet the Sound* (2009), which aired on PBS, is an excellent career chronicle on Joan Baez. Other important music biographical sources include Fuss (1996); Rodnitzky (1976); "Playboy Interview" (1970); and Wakefield (1967).

Chapter 4

From *Roger and Out* into *Dang Me/Chug A Lug*: Roger Miller's Debut[1]

Don Cusic

During the 1950s and 1960s—and even into the 1970s—country music was a singles business; the major buyers for country music were jukeboxes. In fact, it wasn't until 1964 that *Billboard*, the trade magazine for the music industry, instituted a country album chart. Prior to that time, only a relative handful of country acts had released an album on the pop chart; Chet Atkins had charted eight albums on RCA, but he was an instrumentalist whose appeal went beyond the country audience. Eddy Arnold had charted four albums, but, again, his appeal extended beyond the traditional country audience.

It seems surprising, then, that when Roger Miller signed with Smash Records, an imprint of Mercury, the label planned an album for his first release. The reason is that there had been a number of successful comedy albums during the previous years. Vaughn Meader's album *The First Family*, a spoof on the Kennedy family when John Kennedy was President, was the #1 album on the LP charts for 12 consecutive weeks in 1962 and stayed on the chart for 49 weeks; it won the Grammy for "Album of the Year" for 1962. *The First Family, Vol. 2*, reached the #4 position. The assassination of President Kennedy in November, 1963, ended Meader's career of releasing Kennedy spoofs.

Allan Sherman had a string of #1 albums—*My Son, the Folk Singer*, *My Son, The Celebrity*, and *My Son, The Nut*—between 1962 and 1964, and his single, "Hello Muddah, Hello Faddah," reached #2 on the *Billboard* Hot 100 chart in the summer and fall of 1963. *The Button Down Mind* and the *Button Down Mind Strikes Back* by Bob Newhart were both #1 albums (the first was #1 for 14 consecutive weeks in 1960-1961 and remained on the charts for 108 weeks). Newhart's next two albums, *Behind the Button-Down Mind of Bob Newhart* and *The Button-Down Mind on TV*, also did well on the charts.

---

[1]   I am indebted to Jerry Kennedy, Shelby Singleton, Charlie Fach, Don Williams, Lou Dennis, Harold Bradley, and Bob Moore for conversations and interviews concerning Roger Miller and his career. The Belmont Library's archive of *Billboard* and *Variety* magazines, and the Frist Library at the Country Music Hall of Fame and Museum's Miller files and *Music Reporter*, were also valuable sources. While researching at the British Library in London, back issues of *Melody Maker* and *New Music Express* were particularly useful for context.

Roger Miller moved to Nashville after his release from the Army in the spring of 1957. That year, he recorded four songs for the Mercury/Starday company, which released two singles. In 1959, Miller recorded four songs during two separate sessions for Decca. These were released as singles, but there was no chart success. Meanwhile, he wrote hits for other artists: Ernest Tubb recorded "Half a Mind"; Ray Price and Rex Allen had "Invitation to the Blues"; "Tall Tall Trees" and "Nothing Can Stop Me" were recorded by George Jones; "That's the Way I Feel" by Faron Young; and "Billy Bayou" and "Home" were both hits for Jim Reeves.

In late 1959 and again in 1960 Roger Miller recorded eight "sound-a-likes" for the Starday label. These were covers of country hits, done as close as possible to the originals and released on a series of albums called *Hillbilly Hit Parade*. Miller also recorded an original song, "Playboy," for Starday. The songs Miller had written for other artists—as well as those penned for himself—fell into the category of "typical" country songs—they told a story, sounded similar to the country records doing well in the market and attracted coins to the jukeboxes. His first real "Roger song" was "In the Summertime," aka "You Don't Want My Love." This led Chet Atkins to sign Miller to RCA; his first session was in August, 1960 and he recorded "In the Summertime" and another song. The record did reasonably well; it rose to #14 on the country chart and stayed on that chart for 16 weeks. The song was covered by Andy Williams, whose version reached #64 on the pop chart but the song was more popular than its chart number indicates because Williams sang it on his top-rated television show.

During 1962-1963, Roger Miller recorded 19 songs for RCA; several made respectable showings on the country singles chart but none was a major hit. Because Miller felt frustration at RCA, during the fall of 1963, he approached Jerry Kennedy, an A&R executive for Mercury Records, about joining that label. Kennedy agreed and contacted Charlie Fach, head of the Smash imprint in Chicago to sign Miller to a recording contract. Fach's reaction was "is that the crazy guy I see on the Tonight Show?" Yes, it was.

Miller had become popular on television because of his quick wit, appealing personality, and because he made it easy for hosts like Merv Griffin, Johnny Carson, and Jimmy Dean to be funny and entertaining. Miller's television appearances on national shows began in 1962; in January 1963, Jimmy Dean hosted *The Tonight Show* while Johnny Carson took a two-week break. Dean invited Miller to the show several times.

During the annual Country Music Disc Jockey Convention in Nashville in November 1963, Irving Green, president of Mercury Records, Shelby Singleton, head of A&R, and Charlie Fach, head of Smash, happened to be in the restaurant at the same time as Roger Miller and his publisher, Buddy Killen of Tree Publishing. Singleton insisted to Green and Fach that they sign Miller. Ironically, although Fach agreed with Jerry Kennedy's suggestion to sign Miller several weeks earlier, he had not drawn up any contracts.

Tired and frustrated with Nashville, Miller had decided to move to Los Angeles. While the response to his telvision work was encouraging, his music career appeared stalled. In addition, his wife and family had left him. He hoped for a fresh start in California. During the negotiations for the recording contract in November and December, Miller requested a $1,600 advance. Fach shrewdly countered that he would give Miller $100 for each song recorded; if he recorded 16 songs, then he'd receive $1,600. Miller agreed.

Miller met with Jerry Kennedy on Thursday, January 9, 1964 in Kennedy's office and they went over the songs Roger wanted to record. Kennedy felt he needed to have a single for country radio and the jukeboxes and decided that one of Miller's songs, "Less and Less," along with "Ain't That Fine," a song written by Dorsey Burnett that Kennedy received from a publisher, would make a good "A-" and "B-side" single. The next day, Miller recorded those two songs and another, "Why?"

On Saturday, January 10, Miller entered the Quonset Hut studio—the first studio built on what became known as "Music Row"—and sat down with musicians Harold Bradley, Ray Edenton, and Jerry Kennedy on guitars, Bob Moore on upright bass, Hargus "Pig" Robbins on piano, and Buddy Harmon on drums. Miller also played guitar and sang as he played; the group was in a sort of circle in the studio, although it was more like two groups of musicians facing each other in two semi-circles. It was time to do Miller's "crazy" songs, the songs he sang when gathered with friends or on a TV talk show. "Chug-A-Lug" was the first song on that Saturday session; it was based on a character from Roger's hometown of Erick, Oklahoma who could drink a beer in three seconds—he called it "chug-a-lugging"—and Roger used that term in addition to some experiences from back in his younger days to craft that song. This was followed by "I Ain't Coming Home Tonight," then "Lou's Got the Flu," "The Moon Is High (and So Am I)," "Got 2 Again," and "Feel of Me." Next came "That's Why I Love You," "Squares Make the World Go Round," and then "Dang Me," the ninth song that day and the twelfth song during those two days of sessions.

"Dang Me" begins with a unique and distinctive guitar run off the E chord. Miller played that intro for Harold Bradley and asked him to play it for the record; both Harold and producer Jerry Kennedy agreed that only Roger could play that unique run that he had created. The song is delivered in a humorous vein, but it is a serious song about a husband and father "sitting 'round drinkin'" instead of being home. "Private John Q," inspired by Miller's duty in the Army, followed "Dang Me," then "If You Want Me To" and "It Takes All Kinds (To Make a World)." That ended the session, which produced 15 songs, not 16. Jerry Kennedy added strings to "Less and Less" after the sessions and the label was notified to prepare it, backed by "Ain't That Fine," for a single release.

In the days before cassette and compact disc formats, Nashville executives listened to recordings on reel-to-reel tape. A copy of the session was put on a 7-inch reel and given to Kennedy, who took it back to his office where he only had a 5-inch reel, so he could not hear the entire session. One of the songs he did not hear was "Dang Me."

Kennedy then took the tape home, where he found a 7-inch take-up reel, and proceeded to listen to the entire sessions. When "Dang Me" played, Kennedy's three young sons "went wild," dancing around the room. They wanted him to play it again, and he did—and then again and again. Kennedy was convinced that "Less and Less" backed with "Ain't That Fine" should be shelved and "Dang Me" released as the single. The problem was that "Less and Less" was already pressed on 45 r.p.m. records made for disc jockeys and ready to be shipped out.

When Kennedy called Charlie Fach in Chicago and told him he wanted to release "Dang Me" instead of "Less and Less," Fach replied, "Mr. Green will kill me if I pull that record now." Kennedy agreed to speak with Irving Green and, at the end of that phone conversation, Green agreed that "Dang Me" would be the initial single release. This fit into the initial plan from Mercury to release a "comedy" album. The album was titled *Roger and Out* because Miller intended this to be his farewell to Nashville.

Miller moved to Los Angeles after those sessions and started acting lessons; he studied with James Best, later famous as Sheriff Roscoe on *Dukes of Hazzard*. "Dang Me" was released as a single in early May and reviewed in the May 16 issue of *Billboard*, the review stating: "Very clever song taken from Roger's newest LP. In the light-vein it revolves around a really bad guy; 'Daddy was a pistol, and 'I'm a son-of-a-gun.'" On the B-side was "Got 2 Again." Both songs were short: "Dang Me" was 1:47 and "Got 2 Again" was 2:17.

There was an immediate reaction from radio to the record; Charlie Fach remembers that a Dallas program director, Ken Dow, called and wanted to make sure that records were in stock because, if he played it and it wasn't available for purchase, people would get mad at the radio station. Apparently, the distributor had put "Dang Me" on some jukeboxes in Dallas and it was getting heavy play and sales. WLS, the 50,000 watt station in Chicago, put it on, then KAAY, the 50,000 watt station in Little Rock programmed it so the record was breaking in the Midwest. In California, Smash promotion man Lou Dennis took Roger Miller to San Francisco to appear on a local television show on KPIX hosted by Dick Stewart. Stewart wasn't there that day; instead, sitting in was Don Sherwood, the top morning disc jockey at KSFO. Sherwood loved Roger and loved "Dang Me" so much that he invited Roger back on the show the next day and played "Dang Me" on his radio station. Ironically, *The Tennessee Ernie Ford Show*, a nationally televised show, was taped at the same studio as the local show TV show. Billy Strange, who was music director for the Ford Show, knew Miller, so he arranged for Miller to appear on the Ford Show, which meant "Dang Me" had national exposure.

"Dang Me" debuted at #41 on the Country Singles Chart in *Billboard* on June 6; in that same issue, "Dang Me" is listed as a "Breakout Single" in the pop market with Seattle and Houston noted for their activity. Miller did a ten-day promotional tour of the Midwest in June, starting in Denver and stopping at radio and TV stations to plug his song, which gained further airplay. The record hit the *Billboard* Hot 100, the major pop chart, on June 13 when it debuted at #94; "Dang Me" jumped from #40 to #27 on the Country Singles chart the following week. On July 4, "Dang Me" was #6 on the *Billboard* country chart and on July 18, sat at #1 on the Country Singles chart in *Billboard*, but Miller's album, *Roger and Out*, was not on the album chart.

In the August 1 issue of *Billboard*, "Dang Me" peaked at #7 in the *Billboard* Hot 100 chart; on August 8, the *Roger and Out* album entered the Billboard country album chart at #15; "Dang Me" was still #1 on the Country Singles chart; it stayed in that position for 6 consecutive weeks and 25 weeks overall.

Roger Miller needed management and obtained it with Bernard and Williams, the Los Angeles firm of Alan Bernard, who managed Mary Tyler Moore, and Don Williams, brother of Andy. Being in LA, and with "Dang Me" on the pop chart, made Miller accessible and attractive to West Coast management groups, which opened up bookings in dinner clubs and on the Las Vegas-Reno-Tahoe circuit. These were not venues where country artists were normally booked. Living in Los Angeles also made Miller available for more television appearances. Although Bernard and Williams did not manage Andy Williams, their connections with those around him helped secure top bookings for Roger Miller.

On August 29, "Dang Me" dropped out of the #1 slot on the Country Singles chart; the *Roger and Out* album was at #6. In late August, Miller went to New York and taped appearances on *The Steve Allen Show* (broadcast September 2), and *The Jimmy Dean Show* (broadcast September 19). That same month, an "answer song" to "Dang Me" was released: "Dern Ya" by Ruby Wright, daughter of Johnny Wright and Kitty Wells, told the "Dang Me" story from a woman's point of view.

The second single from the album, "Chug-A-Lug," was released on September 19 after Charlie Fach decided to ignore the concerns of the country division of Mercury in Nashville. The song talked about drinking and referred to "wine," so the Nashville executives were concerned this might be offensive to the country audience. Jerry Kennedy went into the studio and edited the word "wine" out of the song for the single release but Fach was convinced "Chug-A-Lug" would appeal to the college audience and he was right; the country fans also enjoyed it.

During the 39th Annual Grand Ole Opry Birthday Celebration—commonly called "the DJ Convention"—held during the first week of November, 1964 in Nashville, Miller won the "Most Promising Male Artist" award and came in third in the "Favorite Country Songwriter" category at the "*Billboard* Country Music Awards," a forerunner to the Country Music Association Awards.

In the November 7 pop chart in *Billboard*, "Chug-A-Lug" was #9. By December 12, the song dipped to #22, and was at #23 on *Billboard*'s country chart. In order to capitalize on the hit singles, the record label shrewdly, if not shamelessly, changed Miller's album title from *Roger and Out* to *Dang Me/Chug-A-Lug* (Figure 4.1). The album charted at #12. Another song from the album, "Less and Less," recorded by Charlie Louvin, was at #41 on the country chart.

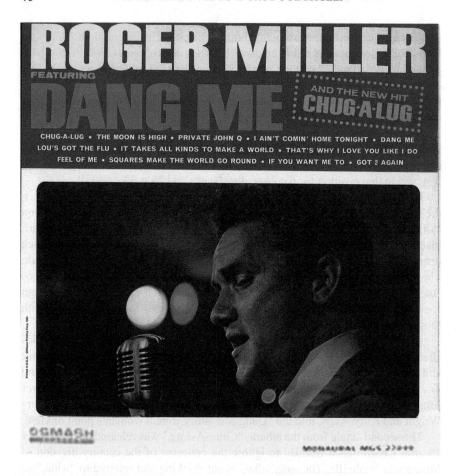

Figure 4.1   Smash Records' *Roger and Out* album title makeover.

The top two single records of 1964, based on *Billboard* chart activity, were "I Want To Hold Your Hand" and "She Loves You," both by the Beatles. These were followed by "Hello Dolly" by Louis Armstrong (#3), "Oh, Pretty Woman" by Roy Orbison (#4), "I Get Around" by The Beach Boys (#5), "Everybody Loves Somebody" by Dean Martin (#6), "My Guy" by Mary Wells (#7), "We'll Sing in the Sunshine" by Gale Garnett (#8), "Last Kiss" by J. Frank Wilson (#9) and "Where Did Our Love Go" by the Supremes (#10). The top albums of 1964 were *A Hard Day's Night, Meet the Beatles* and *The Beatles Second Album* by The Beatles; two releases of *Hello Dolly* (original cast version and Louis Armstrong's); *People* by Barbra Streisand, *The Singing Nun,* and *The Beach Boys Concert*. Roger Miller held his own in this impressive company; "Chug-A-Lug" and "Dang Me" were both among the top 100 records of 1964 and they received BMI Citations for the amount of radio airplay they received.

During the first week in January 1965, Miller debuted "King of the Road" on *The Jimmy Dean Show.* On February 6, the song jumped from #65 to #39 on the singles chart. His follow-up, *The Return of Roger Miller*, debuted on the LP chart at #135; while his re-titled debut album, *Dang Me/Chug-A-Lug*, sustained at #140.

The catchy "King of the Road," with sing-along appeal, was a massive pop hit in both the United States and England. It peaked at #4 on the *Billboard* Hot 100 chart at the end of March and in England it landed at #1 on the chart, ahead of "Ticket to Ride" by the Beatles, which was in the #2 slot. In fact, that week the British industry reported that "King of the Road" was the most played record on the BBC and had sold more sheet music than any other song. The other labels that Miller had recorded for cashed in on his success in 1964 and 1965: RCA released two albums and Starday released several singles and an album comprised of a number of the "sound-a-likes" that Miller recorded in 1959 and 1960.

"King of the Road" received heavy airplay on the radio during the time that the voting was conducted for the 1964 Grammy Awards. In April 1965, Miller swept all of the country awards, earning five Grammys: country song, single, album, male vocal and new artist.

Roger Miller's debut album, *Dang Me/Chug-A-Lug* (*Roger and Out*), was recorded in Nashville to satisfy the market for "comedy" records. Miller had established a career in country music—he was billed as "the clown prince of country music"—and had recorded several country singles that made respectable showings on the country charts. But Miller's debut album contained two songs, "Dang Me" and "Chug-A-Lug," that were pop as well as country hits. That album laid the groundwork for his follow-up album that contained "King of the Road," the biggest single in Miller's career and a "standard" in the American songbag. That led to Roger Miller becoming an international star and winning six Grammys for records released in 1965 ("King of the Road" beat out "Yesterday" for top pop song and Miller won top pop vocal over Paul McCartney). Those six Grammys held the record for most Grammys won by a single artist in a single year until Michael Jackson surpassed that figure in 1983.

Roger Miller's debut album eventually reached Gold status and paved the way for a career that included hosting a network TV show, being a top concert draw and, in 1985, winning a Tony Award for the songs he wrote for the Broadway musical *Big River*. Miller's records prior to "Dang Me," with the possible exception of "In the Summertime (You Don't Want My Love)," did not really reflect the witty, humorous side of Miller. His debut album, *Roger and Out* (turned *Dang Me/Chug A Lug*) captured Miller's wit and humor and allowed him to become a top star in both pop and country music. Arguably, no other debut album in the history of the music industry provided such a "course correction" for an artist. On the road between *Roger and Out* and *Dang Me/Chug A Lug*, Roger Miller became Roger Miller.

Chapter 5
Midnight in Memphis with the
Wicked Pickett

B. Lee Cooper

When is an initial album release not considered a debut record? The answer is multilayered, with significant commercial underpinnings. If an artist's first album disappoints commercially—by failing to establish popular name recognition, by failing to elicit either critical acclaim or even journalistic acknowledgement, by failing to attain any music trade paper chart visibility, and by failing to register in the public memory—it is historically inconsequential. Such debut dismissals are not uncommon in popular music. Among such false starts is *It's Too Late* (Double-L 2300) by Wilson Pickett. Released in 1963 by the diminutive Double-L label owned by Lloyd Price, this recording was weakly promoted and poorly received. Ironically, one of the songs featured on the unsuccessful album—"If You Need Me"—attracted the attention of Jerry Wexler, A&R head at Atlantic Records. Wexler purchased the rights to the song and, along with Bert Berns, helped produce Solomon Burke's popular cover version. The limited success of the Double-L release of "If You Need Me" prompted Pickett's decision to separate from his former R&B vocal mates, The Falcons. This action ultimately led to his 1964 agreement to join Wexler and Ahmet Ertegun on the prominent Atlantic label in New York.[1]

The search began immediately for material appropriate for a Wilson Pickett debut record. It would end with *In the Midnight Hour* (Atlantic 8114), a 12-song compilation that charted on October 30, 1965, spent a total of six weeks in the *Billboard* limelight, and yielded two single hits as well. "Don't Fight It" reached #4 on *Billboard* R&B charts and remained there for 13 weeks. The title track, however, became the signature song for Wilson Pickett. In addition, the song helped to usher in the "Soulsville, USA" moniker for Stax Studios in Memphis. "In The Midnight Hour" attained a #1 rank on *Billboard*'s R&B singles chart and remained commercially strong for 23 weeks. To Pickett's benefit, the song also crossed over onto the Pop charts for 12 weeks, peaking at #21. The cumulative

---

[1]   Among the most insightful biomusical sources on this stage of Pickett's career are Jerry Wexler's account in *Rhythm and Blues: A Life in American Music* (1993: 156-57); Leo Sacks's essay in Rhino Records compilation *A Man and A Half: The Best of Wilson Pickett,* (1992: 4-7); and White and Bronson's *The Billboard Book of Number One Rhythm and Blues Hits* (1993: 8-9).

effect translated into an announcement of Wilson Pickett's arrival (Wexler 1993: 175-80; Whitburn 2009: 759-60).

Pickett's biography and socioeconomic circumstances provide some context to his career evolution and major label debut. The rural South, specifically Prattville, located north of Montgomery in Central Alabama, was Wilson Pickett's coming-of-age region between 1941 through 1957. Biographical documentation suggests Pickett's disdain for cotton picking, corporal punishment as administered by his mother and his grandfather, the arrogance and disrespect of local whites toward all members of his family, and the attitudes of servitude exhibited within the black community. Music largely defined Pickett's dream of a better life beyond Alabama. His activities included singing in the church choir and with the Sons of Zion, listening to records by Louis Jordan and The Blind Boys of Alabama (Dahl 1993: 230-63; Hirshey 1984: 42-53). Because his mother considered the teenage Wilson too independent-minded, bold, and dangerous to survive in the pre-Civil Rights Era South, she sent him north to Detroit, where he joined his father who was an auto worker. In Michigan, Pickett remained focused on his singing and performing aspirations.

Mid-century Detroit was musically vibrant, even prior to the explosion of Berry Gordy's renowned Motown enterprise. Gospel harmonies echoed from the Bethel Baptist Church of civil rights activist Rev. C.L. Franklin. Pickett listened. Mahalia Jackson, Sam Cooke and The Soul Stirrers, Clara Ward, The Staple Singers, James Cleveland, and The Mighty Clouds of Joy were also part of the rich environment . As an aspiring vocalist and egotistical entertainer, Pickett was especially intrigued by the vocal arrangements of R.H. Harris and the lead singing techniques of Archie Brownlee, Clarence Fountain, and Julius Cheeks. During his Motor City years, Pickett performed with The Violinaires and The Spiritual Five. He honed his skills at recognizing harmonies, distinguishing song structures, developing stage dominance, adapting lyric idioms, and asserting vocal range and control. Of course, he also stretched his performance and vocal styling beyond sanctified songs toward "the Devil's music" (Marsh 1985: 286-90). Detroit's rhythm and blues scene was dynamic. Jukeboxes and radios blared the sensual messages of Little Willie John, Nolan Strong and The Diablos, Jackie Wilson, The Moonglows, Hank Ballard, and The Dominoes. In 1961, Pickett found his way from gospel to R&B by joining an established local troupe that included Eddie Floyd, Mack Rice, Joe Stubbs, and Willie Schofield. The Falcons, who had already scored a 1959 hit with "You're So Fine," were a far, far cry from The Sensational Nightingales. The members were gritty and tough. They were young talents who would eventually find their own separate routes to musical success. Writing the tune and singing lead in 1962, Wilson Pickett touched the *Billboard* charts briefly with The Falcons' "I Found a Love." Driven to greater personal attention and individual glory, Pickett departed to a new record label in 1963 (Shapiro 2006: 309-11).

Handsome, well-groomed, sharply-dressed, and cocky, Wilson Pickett was ready to set the music world on fire for Double-L Records. The first offering he co-authored and recorded for them was "If You Need Me". The fact that this audio gem was snatched away from him by a wily record business veteran and then performed by a more widely-promoted vocalist was a bitter lesson in Pickett's professional development. Such narratives of exploitation were commonplace in the early rock era. Later the same year, Pickett succeeded with "It's Too Late" and found himself connected with his former tormentor, Jerry Wexler, who believed Atlantic Records was better suited to Pickett's potential. Wexler was confident that he could steer the arrogant, demanding, brash singer from Alabama forward into music's mainstream. The only question was: Where was the proper material for Pickett's Atlantic debut album? The initial single releases were disastrous, demonstrating that symphonic soul sounds and Bert Berns's production style were not compatible with Pickett. Wexler chose to fly to Memphis with his young vocalist (Nooger 1987: 79-80).[2]

One of the key players in Pickett's development was guitarist Steve Cropper. The insightful guitar player, arranger, and songwriter at the 926 East McLemore studios of Stax Records knew nothing about Wilson Pickett. But upon learning that Wexler was bringing the singer to Memphis, Cropper managed to locate and review a few of Pickett's early gospel 45s, along with the single hit "It's Too Late." From this research, Cropper fashioned a distinctive rhythm pattern and even a few lyric lines that captured Pickett's imagination during their initial meeting. It seems unbelievable that Cropper and Pickett co-authored "In The Midnight Hour" in less than two hours together—or that they added "Don't Fight It" that same evening. Wexler was influential in suggesting and then humorously demonstrating the danceable jerk beat for the "Midnight" composition. The New York executive was impressed—if not overwhelmed—by the precision, camaraderie, and creativity that was manifested by the musicians in Stax studios. The Memphis sound behind the screaming Pickett vocals was produced by Joe Hall on piano, Cropper on guitar, Donald "Duck" Dunn on bass, Al Jackson, Jr. on drums, Wayne Jackson on trumpet, Charles "Packy" Axton and Andrew Love on tenor sax, and Floyd Newman on baritone sax. Booker T. Jones, the leader of the Memphis group, the MGs, was a notable absentee from the Pickett session (Doggett 1983:18-21; Shannon and Javna 1986: 122).[3]

Wilson Pickett's ascendancy as a soul-singing monarch was announced by the title track on *In the Midnight Hour*. Without Pickett's extensive gospel music experiences and minus his hardscrabble R&B touring with The Falcons, his vocal styling likely would never have evolved to the sound expressed in the

---

[2]   In addition to Wexler's personal account (1993: 175-80), the best chronicles of this era, record labels, and the R&B and soul genres are Peter Guralnick's *Sweet Soul Music* (1986, 1999) and Gerri Hirshey's *Nowhere to Run* (1984). The Shannon and Javna's Pickett biography (1986) is useful, though less analytical. The documentation in these three sources is consistent with Wexler's first-hand account of dealing with Pickett.

[3]   Booker T.'s notoriety may have created the expectation that he would be included in any Stax session. Accounts of the recording session make little of Jones's absence, other than to state he was simply "unavailable."

Atlantic debut. In Detroit, Pickett had also begun to manifest his audience-thrilling charisma and his son-construction talent. But prior to the May 1965 recording session in Memphis, the steamrolling rhythms and the self-aggrandizing lyrical patterns that would become his trademarks had eluded The Wicked One. Cropper and Pickett had excellent personal and professional rapport; they were "soul brothers" in a sense that defies both race and culture. The duo venerated the music they designed and performed together. This Stax studio chemistry continued for Pickett and Cropper from May through two more recording sessions in September and December. Unfortunately, personal frictions with the Stax management over Pickett's increasingly volatile behavior and Wexler's greed ended the striking Memphis soul experiment.

In the Midnight Hour is a longitudinal debut disc. That is, it features a dozen songs that were originally recorded between 1962 and 1965 in four different studios in Cincinnati, Detroit, New York, and Memphis. The album is undeniably an aesthetic assortment. At the same time, it is a culmination and an indelible introduction to Wilson Pickett as a performer. The fingerprints of other singers, instrumentalists, composers, and producers are obvious throughout the 12 songs on the debut album. Interestingly, the record accomplished precisely what the uncompromising tandem Pickett and Wexler each desired. As a debut, *In the Midnight Hour* personifies Pickett as an R&B artist and performer, and embodies the iconic Atlantic and Stax record labels, Memphis and the Soulsville sound. Pickett's major label debut paved the way for 11 more career-, era-, record label- and genre-defining Atlantic albums—beginning with highly successful *The Exciting Wilson Pickett* (1966) and ending with *Don't Knock My Love* (1972)— that all charted as R&B and Pop hits.

Chapter 6
Jackson C. Frank:
Play the Game of Carnival

Edward Whitelock

Witnesses spoke of the "soft, booming sound" the explosion inside the schoolhouse made—one called it a "thud like puff"—and of flames leaping 50 feet high from the line of windows where, after it was extinguished, the bodies of 10 of the 15 children claimed by the fire were found (Marek 2011). Eleven-year-old Jackson C. Frank was there that day, just before the lunchtime bell, with his fellow sixth graders in the music class at Cleveland Hill Elementary School in Cheektowaga, New York, a suburb of Buffalo. He survived the fire seemingly by the hand of chance. He was pushed through a broken window by a student teacher on her final day of assignment, his clothes aflame, and his classmates piled snow on him as he lay on the ground to extinguish the fire. Burns covered more than half of his body, necessitating a seven-month long hospital convalescence. He underwent weeks of immersion therapy in preparation for skin grafts to his face and chest, and when the time came, so much skin had to be taken from his legs that he would walk with a pronounced limp for the rest of his life. There was a concern that he'd never fully recover the use of his hands and fingers, so a family friend bought him a guitar, hoping it would help him to both regain dexterity and pass the time.

He'd been born on March 2, 1943, an only child who showed early a propensity for music, but it was the Cleveland Hill Elementary School fire that birthed the songwriter Jackson C. Frank, author of "Blues Run the Game," one of the best regarded and most widely covered songs of the 1960s folk revival. In the 15 years following the fire, Frank would become both a legend and a tragedy, an inspiration and a mystery. Those 15 years was all the fates dealt Jackson C. Frank, the folksinger, one of the first to wear the moniker singer-songwriter. The man's life would go on, but the musician's existence extended only from that first guitar though his single, self-titled album, his failure to produce a follow-up, and his descent into a long-gestating madness that, too, had been born on that morning of fire.

The most repeated story of Jackson C. Frank is that he wrote his most famous song, "Blues Run the Game," with its opening lines of "Catch a boat to England, baby, / Maybe to Spain" while he was indeed on a boat to England in 1964, armed with a guitar and the small fortune he had come into upon reaching his 21st birthday, an $80,000 insurance settlement from the fire. By all accounts of those who knew him, he had every intention of burning through the money via high-performance cars and a bon vivant lifestyle. His companion on that trip, his girlfriend at the time, Katherine Henry, noted his discomfort with the money and its source, saying "The money he came into was a door that he stepped through and he was a different person on one side than the other" (qtd. in Male 2009). One of the many lessons the fire taught Frank, apparently, was that nothing lasts, and it inspired in him a live-for-today mentality. Another guiding principle—quite logical considering what he'd been through—was that blind chance rules all, and this proved, for a time at least, a useful talisman.

It had been blind chance, after all, that Elvis was home at Graceland on the day Frank's mother took him to the newly built home and rang the bell at the gate; Elvis remembered having written Jackson a note during his convalescence and invited the star-struck 14-year-old and his mother in for lunch with his own parents. In London, it was blind chance that led him to Judith Piepe, a bohemian at heart, who ran a boarding house that welcomed fledgling musicians. She invited him to share a room with two other American boarders then trying their luck in the growing London folk scene, Paul Simon and Art Garfunkel. Simon in particular was instantly taken by Frank's songwriting skills and helped him to sign to Columbia's UK imprint, and offered to produce an album himself, funded by the first royalty check he'd received for "The Sound of Silence," which was just beginning its chart ascent in America. It was chance that led Frank to a Greek restaurant in the Soho district whose owners had allowed their son, Andy Matheou, to open a music club in the basement. That club, Les Cousins, became the hub for the key players in England's folk revival: Davey Graham, Burt Jansch, John Renbourn, Al Stewart, Roy Harper, John Martyn, and, at Frank's own urging since he was dating the shy novice singer at the time, Sandy Denny.

Frank's acceptance, indeed his adoration, within the London folk scene was practically instantaneous and must have been disconcerting to someone more attuned by circumstance to solitude, but, for a while, he thrived within the chaos of so much newness. The damage to his hands and fingers created limitations necessitating a unique guitar-picking style and encouraged Frank to explore alternate guitar tunings that, while a practical necessity for him, became stylistic guideposts for his peers. John Renbourn has said of Frank, "In the early days of the singer-songwriter, he was the best," while Burt Jansch compared him to another American songwriter beginning to make inroads on the British charts: "Dylan was surfacing around the same time, but to me [Frank's style] seemed like a different approach. It just blew me away" (qtd. in Allen 2009: 69-70). To someone who hasn't heard Frank's music, the artist whose playing and tuning style most resembles Frank is, surprisingly, the British folk revival's most famous tragic figure, Nick Drake. But Drake, too, was drawn into the Les Cousins scene— it's one of the few clubs where he actually performed on stage—and, after his own tragic passing, a collection of home recordings he had made in his bedroom became available, handed out freely by Drake's parents to fans of his music who made a pilgrimage to his family home at Tanworth-in-Arden. Contained on those tapes were Drake's versions of four of the ten songs on Jackson C. Frank's sole, eponymous album: "Blues Run the Game," "Here Come the Blues," "Kimbee," and "Milk and Honey."

That album, *Jackson C. Frank*, "influenced just about everyone who heard it." According to Jansch, "You could say that it changed the face of the contemporary songwriting world" (qtd. in Harper 2003). Released in 1965, the album became a common reference point for the in-the-know members of the scene and, witness the evidence of Drake's home tapes, an inspiration and guidepost for a new kind of playing. And yet, commercially, it was a failure, selling poorly in the UK and worse upon limited release in the US. It was, however, unlike anything anyone had heard up to that time, with even its creation shrouded in mystery and myth.

Al Stewart, who made his recording debut providing guitar accompaniment on "Yellow Walls," described the process as "probably the strangest recording session I've ever been to." He described Frank playing behind a screen because he claimed to be too shy to sing while being stared at and recalled long periods of silence from behind that screen while Frank pumped himself up to perform—"And then this beautiful guitar and voice would emerge" (qtd. in Means 1995). One can only speculate what was going through Frank's mind during those pauses, what mantra he may have whispered to himself for strength or what visions may have colored his mind as he sought inspiration, but one thing that must have been part of his private visionary process was certainly the Cleveland Hill School fire. The album that resulted is full of references direct and symbolic to that fire which almost killed him but set him instead on a path to a completely different life than had been a previous option. The central symbol of the album, though, is not fire itself; it is, instead, a reflection of the holistic experience of the fire, its happenstance, its confusion, its force, and the luck of survival. Whereas the central theme of the album is chance, its primary symbol is the carnival.

If one has ever been lost, even momentarily, within a carnival or fair, one knows what it is to become displaced amidst an overload of external stimuli and signs, where the normal and predictable have been abandoned by all that is visible, where sense and sensibility are compromised more deeply by each internalized image. The carnival is a place of overstimulation, of noise and brightness and swirling confusion, and it is a place where, at the center of everything lie the games of chance, which are, of course, fixed in such a way that "the house wins" more often than not. If one has ever been lost inside a carnival, one knows, as well, a little something of what it is like to be lost inside a disaster such as the Cleveland Hill School fire, where normal has been displaced, where a confusing overload of external stimuli cloud clarity, where brightness and darkness exchange their promised meanings, where chance rules survival and the house will take its cut. Mikhail Bakhtin introduced the term *carnivalesque* to literary study, explaining that it "brings together, unifies, weds, and combines the sacred with the profane, the lofty with the low, the great with the insignificant, the wise with the stupid" (1984: 123). While Frank would not have been familiar with Bakhtin's theories, his album serves as a precise demonstration of the carnivalesque, where extremes are interwoven, where perception is compromised, and where random chance is the only certainty. "Carnival," Michael E. Gardiner notes, "is steeped in the everyday" (2000: 65). Frank's everyday was steeped in echoes of his past tragedy, creating a carnivalesque personal vision and voice.

The first four songs on the album are each a completely different type of song from the others: "Blues Run the Game," the classic, is a revivalist blues piece; "Don't Look Back" is a (somewhat naive) protest song; "Kimbee" is an archival rearrangement of Bascomb Lamar Lunsford's "I Wish I Was a Mole in the Ground," gleaned from Harry Smith's *Anthology of American Folk Music*, which was quickly becoming the bible of the folk revival; and "Yellow Walls," most importantly, is a deeply personal, symbolic piece of confessional songwriting. Here is a framework for the singer-songwriter era that was to follow, the four dominant song types that would define the genre: revival, archival, protest, and personal. That Frank opens the record with these four diverse songs creates a type of tutorial for those who follow while simultaneously frustrating any sense of unity or flow, creating instead a sense of displacement or dis-ease. Welcome to the carnival.

While "Blues Run the Game" is best known among the four opening songs, "Yellow Walls" is the most revelatory and, within its time, groundbreaking in its hyper-personalized symbolism. Katherine Henry describes it as "a hallucinatory experience of his being in hospital, probably in tremendous pain" (qtd. in Male 2009) and, if one has any awareness of the treatment and healing process that severe burn victims undergo, it becomes readily apparent that the room in which the singer describes being trapped is actually his own body. When Frank sings of "Dark green windows" that "Stare never closed / From yellow walls that shine like silver" he is describing what it is like to watch his own burned skin glisten as it slowly heals, through eyes that he can't close, since his eyelids have been burned off. This is more than a simple song of isolation, though isolation is another of the themes that run through the album; it is a song of prolonged torture. Yet, in the upside-down world of carnival, torture brings healing. Frank presents himself as a shadow self here, "Running naked and unmentioned / Through the death of a saltless sea." Life continues to go on outside the hospital walls, while inside Frank was subject to daily immersions in fluids which softened the bandages congealed to his wounds and prepared his damaged body to accept the skin grafts. Each immersion would be a shock, an all-encompassing surge of pain for reawakened nerve endings, torture in the service of healing. Chance had placed him here, cocooned and pupa-like, awaiting a sort of rebirth, while it had taken others completely and left still more others unscarred. Life continues to flow blindly on like the season cycle Franks sings of in "Milk and Honey" later on the album.

The album's centerpiece is "My Name is Carnival." Perhaps the masterpiece of the album, it's a curiosity that the song hasn't received more attention, something Frank himself commented on in a late interview with T.J. McGrath (1995): "I'm surprised that it wasn't picked up as cover material because it's got a great tune and the lyrics are interesting." A possible explanation for the song's failure to elicit a wide range of cover versions (though Burt Jansch did finally record a version late in his own career and the contemporary UK band Erland and The Carnival both cover and take their name from the song) is its hyper-personalized symbolic language. Unlike "Blues Run the Game," which presents a fairly open hint of a narrative into which any singer can easily insert himself (its multiple "babes" and "honeys" have dissuaded most female folksingers from covering it), "My Name is Carnival" presents a disjointed narrative and a private symbolic language into which one cannot step comfortably. It is a nightmare vision that captures the sinister notes of carnival in a way that few other songs of the era can. One wonders if Jim Morrison may have stumbled across a copy of Frank's album and found inspiration in this song for his own calliope-inflected apocalypse "The End." But even if he did, the evidence of that song is that he didn't quite get it, his own nightmare vision trapped within a stunted, Freud-lite version of adolescent sexuality.

Jackson C. Frank's apocalyptic carnival vision is horrific because he locates his nightmare within a childhood experience of displacement and disassociation, and, as in so many other places on the album, the childhood memories of the Cleveland Hill School fire bleed through. Frank in this song creates a precise enactment of Bakhtin's concept of heteroglossia where, "the processes of centralization and decentralization, of unification and disunification, intersect" and where "centrifugal as well as centripetal forces are brought to bear" (Bakhtin 2000: 271). Frank's every utterance, and the singer is speaking in the first-person as the personification of Carnival, is double-edged—both general and specific, literal and figurative, exuberant and traumatized. The joyful associations of carnival are here, but are instantly obscured by dark memories. The "Rise and fall / Spin and call" of sound becomes both joyful music and the echoes of sirens. Voices that "appear and disappear in the forest" are one moment laughing, the next screaming, at once immediate, then obscured by smoke and unreachable. Frank recalls "Strings of yellow tears" that "Drip from black wire fears in the meadow" which at one moment evoke the strings of lights along a carnival midway and frenzied anticipation but as quickly give way to an image of children's faces, burned black with soot, and the yellow traces tears would make. The most important lesson, Frank reveals is, simply, "Here there is no law / But the arcade's penny claw hanging empty." It bears repeating: at the center of every carnival lie the games of chance and they are fixed to appear easy but prove impossible. Losing is built into the game; winning is the odd happenstance, utterly random and hardly a reward. Rather, and even more sinister, winning ultimately serves the house: the few winners draw even more players into the trap, convincing them they have a shot. The claw is the one repeated symbol of the song as Frank sings "Clawed dreams all / In the name of carnival" into a fade. Ultimately, life is a game and the fulfillment of our dreams the prize. More often than not, though, we feed countless quarters into the machine only to be perpetually teased as the claw skirts, pushes, and flips the prize before rising empty, clasping air.

The final three songs on the album ricochet through an extreme mood swing, from "Dialogue," with its repeated refrain of "I want to be alone," to "Just Like

Anything," which meanders with such a sing-song naivety that one can almost picture Kermit the Frog strumming it on his banjo, then to "You Never Wanted Me, Babe," a fine folk break-up song that bookends the theme of chance that begins with "Blues Run the Game." It's a song that was probably written about Sandy Denny, and she actually covered it on her own debut album. For her follow-up, she wrote a song for Frank, titled "Next Time Around," where she asks, "Whatever came of his talented son / Who wrote me a Dialog set to a tune?" She recalls that he told her "of being alone, except for the stories about God and you." And asks if he still lives "there in Buffalo?" (Denny 1971). The answer to Denny's question is that the hand of chance dealt a new set of cards, and Frank's path shifted again. He left England when his insurance money ran out and he proved unable to bring his label a follow-up to his debut.

Frank first settled in Woodstock with his new wife, Elaine Sedgewick, a model and cousin of Andy Warhol's protégé Edie Sedgewick, to try his hand at journalism, which he had studied at college before catching that boat to England. He attempted a return to London and the Les Cousins scene in 1968 but, in the words of Al Stewart, "He proceeded to fall apart before our eyes" (qtd. in Means 1995). He hadn't written any new songs, and in the interim had suffered the loss of his infant son to cystic fibrosis. The scene had changed significantly since he left it and his new performances did nothing to re-establish an audience, Stewart describing them as "completely impenetrable ... psychological angst played at full volume" (qtd. in Harper 2003). Frank returned to the US permanently in 1969 and, though Sedgewick gave birth to a healthy daughter shortly thereafter, his increasingly fragile mental state led her to end the marriage and take the baby to her family home in England, where she would remain estranged from her father.

Stories of Frank's behavior became wilder and more bizarre as assorted friends reached out to him only to find themselves brushed aside. Shortly after dissolving his professional union with Paul Simon, Art Garfunkel sought out Frank for a collaborative project, but when he arrived at their arranged meeting place, Frank greeted him in disheveled street clothes with a group of his new homeless friends and hurled taunts at him until Garfunkel just drove away. John Renbourn visited Woodstock and was rebuffed with a cryptic phone call. Al Stewart managed to see him but "by then he'd become very strange. He was hiding behind pieces of furniture" (qtd. in Allen 2009: 72). There were stories of a naked man in a cape running around Woodstock and of a derelict that spent afternoons staring at traffic lights. Both descriptions matched Frank (Allen 2009: 72). He finally moved back in with his mother in Buffalo, but vanished while she was in the hospital for heart surgery. He said he was going to New York to catch up with Paul Simon, but ended up homeless, in and out of mental clinics, being treated and mistreated for a sequence of mental illnesses, none of them having to do with the fire that scarred him so thoroughly.

He lost touch so thoroughly that his family in Buffalo presumed him to be dead, but chance dealt Frank one more good hand, and he was rescued from the cycle of homelessness and institutionalization in the mid-1990s. Jim Abbott, a student and fan of the folk movement happened upon a copy of Al Stewart's *Year of the Cat* album in a used record bin. It had been inscribed to Frank by Stewart: "Regards to Jackson. The Blues Run the Game, Al" (qtd. in Means 1995) and the inscription inspired Abbott to find out who this "Jackson" was. Years later, one of Abbott's college professors turned out to be a childhood friend of Frank's to whom Frank had recently reached out to for help. Abbott became Frank's friend and advocate and, by 1997, had arranged for proper care and lodging for the ailing singer, now seriously overweight due to a glandular condition caused by his injuries from the fire, who had recently been blinded in one eye after having been shot with a pellet gun by bored kids hunting homeless people (Allen 2009: 74). Abbott even found him a guitar, and Frank began playing again. Thanks to Abbott, Frank's final years were as close to peaceful as his haunted soul could allow. Jackson C. Frank succumbed to a heart attack on March 3, 1999, at the age of 56. His beautiful and tragic game had been run.

Chapter 7
What Time Has Told Me about Nick Drake's *Five Leaves Left*

Kevin Holm-Hudson

When Island Records released Nick Drake's debut album *Five Leaves Left* in September 1969, its impact then was negligible; its impact on me when I sought out the album and heard it for the first time in 1978 (at the age of 16) considerable. Reading a profile of the then-obscure singer by Arthur Lubow in the magazine *New Times,* I was intrigued enough to seek out—and zealously cherish—expensive import copies of his albums: *Five Leaves Left, Bryter Layter,* and *Pink Moon.* None of my friends knew of Drake's work back then—several have thanked me, years later, for introducing his music to them. *Five Leaves Left* was the first Nick Drake album I heard, and I remember being very surprised by it. There is a restrained, timeless beauty to the album: melancholy lyrics, delicate instrumental arrangements, Drake's strong, bass-string-driven guitar arabesques, and Drake's haunting, smoky-velvet voice.

The sessions for *Five Leaves Left* began in July 1968, but—unusual for a debut album of the time—it took the better part of a year to make (Humphries 1998: 91). Perhaps because of the painstaking songwriting and recording process, *Five Leaves Left* is imbued with an unusual awareness of time's passing, from the opening "Time Has Told Me" to the foreboding of "Three Hours," the somber "Day is Done," and the elegiac "Saturday Sun" which, finally, "wept for a day gone by." Drake's meditations on the passing of time may be contrasted with the child's blissful unawareness of time expressed at about the same time by the Moody Blues in "Another Morning" from *Days of Future Passed*: "Time seems to stand quite still / in a child's world, it always will." Barely 21, Drake already sounds old and world-weary. Even the album's title, from a slip of paper found inside a package of Rizla rolling papers (Petrusich 2007: 32), is a warning of running out; coincidentally, Drake would be dead five years later from a prescription drug overdose. His life seemingly followed the grand Romantic narrative: young sensitive artist releases a work of ravishing beauty to a cold and indifferent world; artist grows despondent; artist takes own life; world posthumously discovers and celebrates the work of beauty left behind. Such a paradigm, however, ignores the fact that *Five Leaves Left,* like the Beach Boys' *Pet Sounds* before it, captures the feelings of a young man's shift from Blakeian innocence to experience, in a musical setting that transcends the time in which it was made and resonates forever in its stillness.

Five Leaves Left was recorded at Sound Techniques, an eight-track studio constructed in a converted cowshed in Chelsea (Petrusich 2007: 32-33); the album was produced by Joe Boyd, and the engineer was the studio's co-owner John Wood. One inspiration for the album's sound was Leonard Cohen's first album (Boyd 2006: 192); another inspiration was the debut album by Randy Newman (Humphries 1998: 90). Initial arranging efforts were made with Richard Hewson, who had done arrangements for James Taylor and would go on to work on the Beatles' *Let It Be*. The arrangements were judged to be "competent, mediocre and slightly fey, distracting from the songs rather than adding to them' (Boyd 2006: 193).[1] Drake suggested the services of a college friend, Robert Kirby, who was classically trained and knew Drake's music well. Boyd was skeptical, as was Wood, but they agreed to bring Kirby in. The decision was auspicious—Kirby approached his orchestrations with the restraint of a classical composer, not a pop arranger, and the album consequently avoids the pitfalls of embracing any of the faddish filigree often found in late-1960s productions.

Perhaps because the album was so "out of its time," it had trouble finding a niche. Released with little promotion, *Five Leaves Left* ultimately sold fewer than 3,000 copies during the singer's lifetime (Petrusich 2007: 35-36). Moreover, Petrusich hints that there may have been indifference from the record label, as "the record's sleeve contained no clues about the artist or the music within, 'Three Hours' was listed as 'Sundown,' and an unrecorded verse was included with the lyrics to 'River Man'" (Petrusich 2007: 35). Boyd expected that the album would sell around 100,000 copies, as Cohen's debut had, but the lack of "free-form" radio formats comparable to those in America at the time hurt sales. "John Peel played Nick's album, but he was one of the few; Radio One was all about 'pop' in its myriad British guises, none of which bore much resemblance to Nick" (Boyd 2006: 197-98).

Where the album attracted any press attention at all, it was with a similar lack of enthusiasm: A *New Musical Express* reviewer, identified only as "GC" wrote that Drake "obviously has a not inconsiderable amount of talent, but there is not nearly enough variety on this LP to make it entertaining" (Petrusich 2007: 35). *Melody Maker* dismissed the release as "an awkward mixture of folk and cocktail jazz" (Boyd 2006: 198).

It can be said that the lead-off track on an album—the "Side 1, Track 1," in vinyl terms—sets the tone for what is to follow; if that be so, the opening track on *Five Leaves Left*, "Time Has Told Me," presents the listener with a rather unusual sound space for a late-1960s production. Drake's voice and guitar are front and center, nimbly supported by Danny Thompson (best known at the time for his work with the British folk-jazz-rock outfit Pentangle) on double bass; there are no drums. Panned hard left in the stereo spectrum is the piano of Paul Harris, a

---

[1]   Evidence supporting this judgment can be heard on an early song, "I Was Made to Love Magic," which appears on the posthumous collection of outtakes and unreleased songs *Time of No Reply* (1986).

New York musician who had previously worked on John and Beverley Martyn's *Stormbringer* album, another Boyd production. Boyd (2006: 196) remembers that Harris worked with Nick for hours and was somewhat puzzled by Drake's reticent personality and his music, as was Fairport guitarist Richard Thompson, whose twangy electric guitar fills can be heard panned hard right in a dialogue of sorts with Harris's piano. Harris's playing does come across as hesitant at first, as if still feeling his way into the style of the song for its first two and a half minutes, especially when compared with Thompson's comfortable playing. One is also struck by the easy, almost sunny tone of the music—in C major—coupled with the somewhat brooding lyrics that reveal "a troubled mind."

If "Time Has Told Me" is simple and intimate, "River Man," the last song recorded in the *Five Leaves Left* sessions, presents a lush and expansive soundscape. Boyd recalls that Kirby felt he was not up to the challenge of orchestrating the song in a way that would do it justice and that would meet Drake's wishes. John Wood immediately suggested veteran arranger Harry Robinson: "Harry was a master mimic. You want Sibelius? He could give you Sibelius. Since Nick wanted 'River Man' to sound like Delius, Harry, said John, was our man" (Boyd 2006: 197). The session was recorded live, with Nick surrounded by the orchestra as Robinson conducted, "just like Nelson Riddle and Frank Sinatra" (Boyd 2006: 197). "River Man" is also in C, though—befitting its subject—the modality is more fluid, shifting between major and minor, moments of darkness interspersed with the light.

The dreamy and languid sound of "River Man" is soon undone by "Three Hours," the title of which, Boyd has reflected, may refer to the travel time from London to Drake's college home in Cambridge (Humphries 1998; 92). This song has a stark, urgent quality, the congas of Ghanaian percussionist Rocky Dzidzornu propelling the mix of double bass and Drake's kinetic guitar. The song opens with the image of a figure named Jeremy fleeing for shelter in a cave at "three hours before sundown," with the implied threat of some unnamed danger once darkness takes hold. "Three Hours" is in strophic form, like a folk ballad, in a folk mode—D Dorian mode, or a minor scale with a raised sixth scale degree (the same mode as "Scarborough Fair," which Drake's melody superficially resembles). Each verse introduces different characters and their reactions to being presented with their time running out. Drake's melody is cast in an unusual ABBA form, the B phrases of which have a C—B—A descending line.

The third verse of "Three Hours" is, unusually, in a much slower tempo and different meter; it concludes with the line "three hours to fall," at which point Drake's voices drops off to near inaudibility, as if the consequences awaiting the song's protagonists are too horrific to contemplate. This is followed by an extended instrumental passage, from 3:57 to 4:39, characterized by a descending chromatic line at (C—B—Bb—A) that can be regarded as an elaborated version of the Dorian descent (C—B—A) in the verses. This line is also similar to the descending chromatic bass line found in Baroque music that was intended to connote lamenting or grief; Baroque theorists even had a name for this gesture, calling it the *passus duriusculus* (translating roughly as "slightly harder steps"). There is an inexorable quality to the chromatic descent, driving the music toward its rest.[2] During a guitar solo in the song, Drake plays a guitar figure at 2:49-3:02 that anticipates "Free Ride" on his final album *Pink Moon*.

"Way to Blue" was the first song recorded for the album with Robert Kirby's arrangements. This song was recorded with a string sextet; perhaps in a nod to the Beatles' "Yesterday" and "Eleanor Rigby" (which, like "Way to Blue," is in E minor), Drake did not play guitar on the song. "As John [Wood] isolated the sound of each instrument, adjusting the mic position or the equalization, I could barely contain my impatience to hear the full sextet. The individual lines were tantalizing, unusual and strong. When at last John opened all the channels and we heard Robert's full arrangement... I almost wept with joy and relief" (Boyd, 194). Indeed, compared with Hewson's rather dated arrangements, Kirby's studied dissonances on this song bear a strong resemblance to those found in Baroque music, particularly Handel (Lubow, 58). The Baroque qualities of the song allow for a stylistic affinity with the middle section of "Three Hours" and with the song that follows "Way to Blue," "Day is Done."

"Day is Done" closes side 1 with a depiction of the close of a day, harkening back to the D minor tonality of "Three Hours" with a heavy sense of futility that recalls the preacher's lament in Ecclesiastes:

> "Vanity of vanities," says the Preacher; "Vanity of vanities, all is vanity."
> What does man gain from all his labor in which he labors under the sun?
> One generation goes, and another generation comes; but the earth remains forever.
> The sun also rises, and the sun goes down, and hurries to its place where it rises.
> The wind goes toward the south, and turns around to the north. It turns around continually as it goes, and the wind returns again to its courses.
> All the rivers run into the sea, yet the sea is not full. To the place where the rivers flow, there they flow again.
> All things are full of weariness beyond uttering. The eye is not satisfied with seeing, nor the ear filled with hearing.
> That which has been is that which shall be; and that which has been done is that which shall be done: and there is no new thing under the sun. (Ecclesiastes 1:2-9, KJV)

Ecclesiastes resonates with the theme of "vanity" or meaninglessness. The day's labors seem to be for naught, each day is like the next, and "all things are full of weariness beyond uttering" (v. 8). Drake's song develops a similar theme: the sun sets "along with everything that was lost and won," each day begins with a new

---

[2]   The well-known "Dido's Lament" from Henry Purcell's 1689 opera *Dido and Aeneas* is an excellent example of the affective use of the *passus duriusculus* in Baroque music, as is the "Crucifixus" from Bach's *Mass in B Minor*. In both pieces the descending line connotes a descent into death, which might be tied with the "sundown" imagery in "Three Hours."

race to run (only to "have to go back where you begun"), and there are images of discarded newspapers and the aftermath of a party where, Drake sings, "[you] didn't do the things you meant to do."

The cyclic futility of "Day is Done" is underscored by the musical structure, which unfolds as a *chaconne*—a Baroque form characterized by a repeating harmonic progression with an open ending, allowing for repetition and developing variation. The song's chord progression also features the return of the descending chromatic *passus duriusculus,* more explicitly this time than it was in its appearance in an inner voice of the guitar in the "Three Hours" interlude. The strings are also muted, giving the impression of a Baroque consort of viols and enhancing the overall melancholy of the song.

Side 2 opens with "Cello Song," a showcase for Drake's peerless fingerpicking technique and named for the cello line contributed by Clare Lowther. The song breaks the spell of the minor-key songs that concluded side 1, though its key—B-flat major—can still be considered a "dark" major key. "Cello Song" is a distant, more hopeful, cousin to "Three Hours," sharing its strophic form and the congas of Rocky Dzidzornu. While there are images of descent and decay, as seen earlier on "Day is Done" ("the earth sinks to its grave"), these are balanced this time by being carried by something inexorable, almost ecstatic ("you sail to the sky on the crest of a wave"). Toward the end we are indeed borne aloft "to your place in the clouds" on the wings of the cello line, ascending into a cloud of reverb.

"The Thoughts of Mary Jane" is next, a lovely, if perhaps slight and precious, relief from the album's overall melancholy mood, an elegaic portrayal of a girl (or is it a drug?). The song is pleasant enough but, in its released version, rather inconsequential, ending with an incongruously faster coda that seems to skitter away. An alternate version, released on the posthumous compilation *Time of No Reply*, is better, Drake's web-like guitar framing a closely recorded—almost whispered—vocal, with electric guitar fills added by Richard Thompson.

"Man in a Shed" reveals a jazzier side to Drake's playing, informed perhaps by contemporary guitarists Bert Jansch and Davey Graham and certainly pointing toward the more overtly jazz-inflected direction that Drake was to take on his "urban" album, *Bryter Layter.* Although Humphries calls the song a "juvenile narrative" and "a facile remake of the Beatles' 'Fixing a Hole'" (1998: 95), there is an added psychological dimension to Drake's song. The Beatles' song uses repairing a leak as a metaphor for avoiding needless distractions from "silly people," whereas "Man in a Shed" is actually the reverse: in the second verse, the man approaches a girl who rebuffs him with the remark, "I'm sorry, you'll just have to find a friend." By the third verse, the world is "raining through my head." As with "Time Has Told Me," these desperate lyrics are grafted to almost jaunty music, as if the musical setting depicted a world utterly indifferent to the man's loneliness and isolation.

"Fruit Tree" is one of the most beloved songs in the Drake canon, mainly because it seems to uncannily anticipate the indifference with which Drake's subsequent work would be met during his lifetime and his posthumous rediscovery and commercial canonization. As we listen we are reminded that we have not heard Robert Kirby's gorgeous arrangements since "Day is Done" at the end of side 1, and here Kirby does not disappoint, with a duet of oboe and English horn in the second verse especially beautiful. Again there are muted strings, as on "Day is Done," and beginning at 3:25 the *passus duriusculus* returns, again—as in "Three Hours"—during an instrumental interlude.

"Fruit Tree" seems to bring the album to a close with finality—the song is about death, the tree having been cut down ("they'll all stand and stare when you're gone"), and musically the song ties together preceding elements that have run like a thread through the album. After it, "Saturday Sun" seems like a coda of sorts, with a return to the jazz style introduced by "Man in a Shed" (perhaps because of its placement at the end of the album, Humphries again dismisses it as an "unsuccessful jazz meandering") (1998: 95). The vibraphone makes a new appearance of instrumental color, and the key of the song, C major—closely related to "Fruit Tree"—marks a cyclic return to the key of "Time Has Told Me." After Saturday is wistfully recalled, nevertheless the Saturday sun "won't come see me today" because it has "turned to Sunday's rain." (The final song on *Bryter Layter*, the brooding instrumental "Sunday," can also be seen as a sequel to this song.)

The final verse of "Saturday Sun," brooding on time, once again employs cyclic imagery that recalls the futility of "Day is Done": "stories with reason and rhyme" are "circling through your brain," and "people in their season and time" return "again and again and again and again." People return, seasons return, time returns—and just as side 1 closed with the ending of a day in a mood of futility, so does side 2. Another, seemingly perfect, day came and went, and—as in "Day is Done"—"no one knew what to do." And after this perfect day has gone, Sunday "wept for a day gone by."

Perhaps it is the thematic thread of time's passage and the return of certain musical elements (such as the *passus duriusculus*) that enables *Five Leaves Left*, in spite of its different styles, to sustain the mood that it does. *Bryter Layter* is more consistent in its musical direction but, conversely, seems like more of a "collection of songs" than a coherent album narrative. Drake's final release, *Pink Moon*, takes the idea of the thematic/musical thread explored in *Five Leaves Left* and hones it to a single-minded, harrowing intensity. All of these albums, beyond posthumous mythology, reverence, and exploitation, are exceptional, and all of them remain part of my regular listening. But it is still *Five Leaves Left* that I return to when I want to remember what it was like to be age 16, on the cusp of independence and adult responsibilities, still holding on to childhood's securities and dreams, awkwardly reaching out from my shed to girls who lived in mansions.

Chapter 8
The Voice of "the Quiet One": George Harrison's *All Things Must Pass*

Ian Inglis

Even from a distance of several decades, it is difficult not to be overwhelmed by the immensity of the Beatles' achievements in the 1960s. Prior to the group's global breakthrough in 1963 and 1964, the majority of pop stars had refrained from extra-musical comment and activities, allowed other people to control their affairs, recorded songs that were given to them by professional songwriters, and generally conformed to the performative expectations of a complacent and paternalistic industry. By the end of the decade much of that had changed, as increasing numbers of musicians followed the Beatles in making assertions of creative and financial independence. For many, the songs they recorded, the occasions on which they chose to perform them, the musicians and producers with whom they preferred to work, and the freedom to balance personal desires and professional obligations became crucial components of their working routines.

Thus, Paul McCartney's announcement (via the promotional material for his solo album *McCartney*) in April 1970 that he had left the Beatles not only brought to an end the career of popular music's most innovative and influential performers, but also demonstrated again the group's ability to defiantly steer its own course—however unpredictable or ill-advised it might seem—through the commercial and cultural landscape it had helped to construct. Of course, McCartney's decision was not unexpected. In the previous 18 months, John Lennon, George Harrison, and Ringo Starr had all temporarily resigned from the group, or signalled their intention to do so in the future. Furthermore, all had been actively engaged in individual recording projects. With Yoko Ono and/or the Plastic Ono Band, Lennon had released a stream of albums and singles: *Two Virgins* (November 1968), *Life with the Lions* (May 1969), *Wedding Album* (October 1969), *Live Peace in Toronto* (December 1969), "Give Peace A Chance" (July 1969), "Cold Turkey" (October 1969), and "Instant Karma" (February 1970). Starr's album *Sentimental Journey* was released in March 1970. Harrison had composed and produced the soundtrack album *Wonderwall Music* (November 1968), and demonstrated the properties of his newly acquired Moog synthesizer on *Electronic Sound* (May 1969). *McCartney* was therefore merely one in a long line of solo projects, rather than the definitive moment in the disintegration of the Beatles.

Nevertheless, it did mark a formal acknowledgement of the group's demise, and in 1970 each Beatle offered his own observations on its causes and consequences.

McCartney's published explanation (sleeve notes 1970) claimed that the split had come about because of "personal differences, business differences, musical differences, but most of all because I have a better time with my family." Lennon went out of his way to cynically dismiss the group and its accomplishments: "I don't believe in the Beatles. I don't believe in them, whatever they were supposed to be … it was a dream. I don't believe in the dream anymore" (Wenner 1971: 159-60). Starr's continuing optimism suggested that the group might yet re-form: "There's nothing wrong with the Beatles. When we've got something to do, we'll do it. We're all in touch" (Smith 1970). In contrast with the accusations, recriminations, and denials of the others, George Harrison was alone in immediately recognizing the musical opportunities that now lay before him. Just two weeks after McCartney's press release, he announced:

> I am going to be recording. I'm gonna start an album of my own [like] Ringo and Paul. This is gonna be the George album, and I start that in three to four weeks time, and I hope to do it with Phil Spector. I've had songs for a long time, and lots of new songs. I've got enough songs for about three or four albums, actually … It was the way the Beatles took off with Paul and John's songs, and it made it very difficult for me to get in, and also, I suppose at that time I didn't have as much confidence when it came down to pushing my own material … But now the output of songs is too much to be able to just sit around, you know, waiting to put two songs on an album. I've got to get them out, you know. (WABC-TV radio interview 1970)

Harrison's disappointment over his traditional allocation of two songs per album, and the secondary status it implied, was a perennial frustration to him. His popular characterization as "the quiet one" of the group and George Martin's description of him as "the third man" only added to his unease (Martin 1994: 123). Although he had been a regular vocalist during the group's formative years in Liverpool and Hamburg, and had (like Lennon) performed four of the fifteen songs recorded by the Beatles at their Decca audition in January 1962, his contributions had diminished as the Lennon-McCartney songwriting team developed. A pattern was established on the group's first album, *Please Please Me* (March 1963), when "Do You Want to Know A Secret" (written for him by Lennon-McCartney) and "Chains" (a cover version of the Cookies' single, composed by the Brill Building's Gerry Goffin and Carole King) were his only tracks as lead vocalist; the inclusion of "Don't Bother Me" on *With The Beatles* (November 1963) was the first occasion on which one of his own songs was recorded and released by the group. The persistence of this policy (with occasional minor variations) throughout the Beatles' career was a source of considerable irritation to Harrison, particularly as it took no account of the obvious quality of songs such as "While My Guitar Gently Weeps", "Here Comes the Sun" and "Something"—memorably described by Frank Sinatra as "the greatest love song of the last fifty years" (Schaffner 1977: 125). And despite the selection of "The Inner Light" as the B-side of "Lady Madonna" (March 1968) and "Old Brown Shoe" as the B-side of "The Ballad of John And Yoko" (May 1969), it was not until "Something" and "Come Together" were released as joint A-sides in October 1969 that he saw one of his songs become a legitimate hit single for the Beatles.

Of all the Beatles, Harrison was the member whose discontent with the chaotic conditions of live performance had definitively helped to propel the group away from the stage and into the studio, as he readily explained in 1968:

> We got in a rut, going round the world. It was a different audience each day, but
> we were doing the same things. There was no satisfaction in it. Nobody could
> hear. It was just a bloody big row. We got worse as musicians, playing the same
> old junk every day. There was no satisfaction at all. (Davies 1968: 232)

In fact, his painstaking emphasis on musical precision had been noted years earlier by Brian Epstein, who had described him as "very musicianly ... George takes enormous care ... he has a very fine ear for sound and for a delicate half-note, and the others respect him for it" (Epstein 1984: 92). It was, therefore, hardly surprising that the preparation for his first solo album involved detailed discussions with co-producer Spector and orchestral arranger John Barham, and a careful selection of those musicians he would invite to accompany him; and, as a Beatle, he knew that very few of his peers would refuse such an invitation.

Those who eventually participated in the recording sessions at Abbey Road included friends and colleagues from all stages of his career. The presence of Ringo Starr, Klaus Voormann, Billy Preston, and Tony Ashton recalled the Beatles' early years in Liverpool and Hamburg. Eric Clapton, Dave Mason, Gary Brooker, Ginger Baker, and Gary Wright represented contemporary British rock. Renowned US session musicians Jim Gordon, Bobby Keys, and Jim Price were joined by Carl Radle and Bobby Whitlock (who Harrison had met while guesting on the Delaney and Bonnie and Friends tour of the UK in December 1969, and who had subsequently been recruited by Clapton to form Derek and the Dominoes). Additional musicians included drummer Alan White, Nashville pedal steel guitarist Pete Drake, and Badfinger (signed by the Beatles to Apple in 1968). On later albums, such as *Somewhere in England* (1981) and *Cloud Nine* (1987), Harrison would surround himself with a small core of musicians but in view of his natural anxiety over his solo debut—and the knowledge that it would be rigorously compared with planned albums by Lennon, McCartney, and Starr—he opted for a flexible roster of participants with diverse talents and approaches.[1] The decision also reflected his evident realization, even at this early stage, that the planned number of tracks far exceeded normal expectations — although this was

---

[1]   In addition to the already-released *Sentimental Journey* and *McCartney*, the next few months would see the release of Starr's *Beaucoups of Blues* (September 1970), John Lennon's *John Lennon/Plastic Ono Band* (December 1970), and Paul McCartney's *Ram* (May 1971).

clearly a reflection of his musical ambitions, rather than a deliberate attempt to upstage the other Beatles:

> Though the sophistication and even the sheer size of the resources are not an unqualified asset, they cannot merely be dismissed as a product of pique — of a desire to "show us", and particularly to show Lennon and McCartney, what their once reticent colleague is capable of ... The resources are genuinely relevant to the nature of the music. (Mellers 1973: 147)

But while the desire to exceed the other Beatles in the aftermath of their separation may not have been the primary motivation for the planned album, it was certainly a relevant factor in its form and content. After all, several of the tracks that were subsequently recorded over the summer of 1970 had been previously offered by Harrison to the Beatles only to be rejected; others had been written during and about the group's internal conflicts over the previous two years; and some were composed with or for external collaborators whose importance in Harrison's life reflected his growing dissociation from Lennon, McCartney, and Starr.[2]

Thus, early versions of "All Things Must Pass" and "Hear Me Lord" had been initially recorded in February 1969, during the Beatles' *Let It Be* sessions. "Wah-Wah" was written at the same time (during his two-week departure from the group) and "Run Of The Mill" was his commentary on the increasing problems that plagued Apple. "I'd Have You Anytime" was composed with Bob Dylan while Harrison was staying at the singer's Woodstock home in November 1968; "Behind That Locked Door" was written about Dylan during his appearance at the Isle of Wight Festival in August 1969; and "If Not For You" was a cover of the song that would appear on Dylan's *New Morning* in October 1970. "Beware of Darkness," "Awaiting on You All" and "Art of Dying" testified to the depth of Harrison's immersion in the humanitarian spirituality he had first encountered in India in the mid-1960s.

All Things Must Pass was released in late November 1970. Despite Harrison's initial fears that a single release might damage album sales, "My Sweet Lord" (with "Isn't It a Pity" as the B-side) was released in the same week. Together, both enjoyed an extraordinary commercial and critical reception: in January 1971, Harrison held the #1 position in the singles and album charts of the UK and the US; indeed, he was the first of the solo Beatles to have a chart-topping single. "My Sweet Lord" rapidly sold around five million copies worldwide; and by the time of its re-release in 2001, the estimated total sales of *All Things Must Pass* were more than six million. In *Rolling Stone*, Ben Gerson described the album as "an intensely personal statement and a grandiose gesture ... the *War and Peace* of rock'n'roll" (qtd. in Schaffner 1977: 142, while *Melody Maker*'s Richard Williams concluded that its impact was "the rock equivalent of the shock felt by pre-war moviegoers when Garbo first opened her mouth in a talkie" (qtd. in Greene 2006:

---

[2]   Recording sessions began on 27 May 1970, and continued until late August.

221). Even George Martin, who had described Harrison's pre-*Revolver* songs with the Beatles as "awfully poor [and] dead boring," was moved to supply a much more positive reassessment of his abilities in the wake of the album's success:

> I have great admiration for George. He's done tremendously because it's a sort of devotion of duty as far as he's concerned ... He could never collaborate with anyone in his writing, and therefore, when the split came, he had more strength because he was forced to be alone. He learned an awful lot about producing, studio techniques, and so on ... To go along and actually produce good sounds and good music and good lyrics with it, is tremendous. I'm full of admiration for that. I think the other two have suffered by comparison. (Williams 1971)

Only Lennon was grudging in his praise. Interviewed shortly after the release of *All Things Must Pass*, he conceded:

> I think it's alright, you know. Personally, at home, I wouldn't play that kind of music, but I don't want to hurt George's feelings. I don't know how to say about it. I think it's better than Paul's. I thought Paul's was rubbish. (Wenner 1971: 42)

For many, the range and scale of the music itself was the album's most powerful characteristic. In its employment of multi-instrumental backing, prominent percussion, overdubbed backing vocals (provided by Harrison under the guise of the George O'Hara-Smith Singers), and insistent melodic narratives, the album exuded a forcefulness that, in part, reflected the "Wall of Sound" techniques created by co-producer Spector in the early 1960s. But Harrison's eclectic and sympathetic manipulation of influences drawn from gospel, country, soul, pop, and rock gave the songs a distinctive personal signature that confirmed his status as a mature and thoughtful musician in his own right, rather than merely a former Beatle—and which gave him the confidence to organize the Concert for Bangla Desh at New York's Madison Square Garden, in August 1971.[3]

However, the objective presentation of the album itself was of no less interest. In 1970, double albums were still comparatively rare: Dylan's *Blonde on Blonde* (1966) was rock's first example, and had been followed by others such as the Mothers of Invention's *Freak Out!* (1966), Jimi Hendrix's *Electric Ladyland* (1968), *The Beatles*, aka *The White Album* (1968), and The Who's *Tommy* (1969). Triple albums were virtually unknown.[4] Harrison's decision to release *All Things Must Pass* as rock's first triple album by a solo performer was therefore not only

---

[3]   The charity concert—to raise funds for refugees in the troubled region of Bangla Desh—was the first of its kind, and included performances by Harrison, Bob Dylan, Ringo Starr, Eric Clapton, Ravi Shankar, Leon Russell, and Billy Preston. With additional profits from the subsequent triple album and documentary film, the project eventually donated $15 million to the United Nations Relief Fund.

[4]   *Woodstock* (August 1970) was rock's first triple album.

an act of commercial bravado (its price in the UK of £4 19s 6d, or £4.99, was more than double that of a single LP) but also a strategic move that effectively overshadowed competing albums from the other Beatles before a single note had been heard.[5] The first two LPs contained eighteen songs (including two versions of "Isn't It a Pity") and the third ("Apple Jam") featured five tracks taken from informal jam sessions between various combinations of the participating musicians. Also included was a large colour poster of Harrison in the hallway of his home, Friar Park in Henley-on-Thames (which was itself the subject of "Ballad of Frankie Crisp"). The entire contents were packaged as a boxed set whose cover portrait depicted a dishevelled and unsmiling Harrison in the grounds of his home, surrounded by four reclining stone gnomes.

In the three decades between *All Things Must Pass* and Harrison's death in November 2001, he remained active as a songwriter, performer, and musician. He recorded a further nine solo studio albums, from *Living In The Material World* (1973) to *Brainwashed* (2002). He made numerous live appearances, including lengthy tours of North America in 1974 and Japan in 1991. In 1978, he co-founded Handmade Films, which went on to produce many of Britain's most successful movies of the next decade, such as *Monty Python's Life of Brian* (Terry Jones, 1979), *Time Bandits* (Terry Gilliam, 1981), *Mona Lisa* (Neil Jordan, 1986), and *Withnail and I* (Bruce Robinson, 1987). He had further #1 hit singles in the US with "Give Me Love" (June 1973) and "Got My Mind Set on You" (January 1988). In 1988, he formed the Traveling Wilburys, with Bob Dylan, Roy Orbison, Jeff Lynne, and Tom Petty, as a way of cementing his personal and professional friendships. He participated, with Paul McCartney and Ringo Starr, in the "Beatles reunion" of 1995 that produced "Free As A Bird" and "Real Love." And he continued to contribute to the studio recordings of many of his friends and peers, including John Lennon, Carl Perkins, Eric Clapton, Bob Dylan, Ravi Shankar, Alvin Lee, Ronnie Wood, and Nicky Hopkins.

However, it is his debut album of 1970 that remains his greatest achievement. Much of this may be to do with the status of "My Sweet Lord" which has become (along with "Blowin' in the Wind" and "Give Peace a Chance") one of popular music's most enduring and evocative anthems. Harrison's simple lyrics were not directed at a specific manifestation of a single faith's deity, but rather to the concept of one god whose essential nature is untouched by particular interpretations; it was this quality that kept it free from allegations of religious bigotry or proselytizing. The court case for alleged plagiarism brought against Harrison by the publisher and writer of the Chiffons' "He's So Fine" did little to undermine the song's reputation or popularity, and when it was re-released as a single in January 2002, it topped the UK charts once again.[6]

---

[5]   In the US, *All Things Must Pass* was priced at less than $10, at Harrison's request.

[6]   In 1976, Harrison was ordered to pay $500,000 in compensation to composer Ronnie Mack and publisher Bright Tunes.

Like any text (musical or otherwise), *All Things Must Pass* cannot be divorced from the time (or the place) in which it was created. In this respect, 1970 was a pivotal moment in the history of popular music. The 1960s had been a decade in which the major musical innovations had come from such varied sources as folk and "protest" music, Motown, British beat groups, West Coast harmony, bubblegum, soul, psychedelia, and the Beatles themselves. In the 1970s, the principal trends would include heavy metal, progressive rock, punk, reggae, country-rock, funk, disco, and glam rock. Moreover, 1970 itself was a year in which the unhurried introspection of contemporary singer-songwriters (Neil Young's *After the Goldrush*, James Taylor's *Sweet Baby James*, Joni Mitchell's *Blue*, Simon and Garfunkel's *Bridge Over Troubled Water*, Cat Stevens's *Tea for the Tillerman*) competed against the energy and excitement of contemporary rock (Pink Floyd's *Atom Heart Mother*, Deep Purple's *Deep Purple in Rock*, The Who's *Live at Leeds*, Led Zeppelin's *Led Zeppelin 3*, Free's *Fire and Water*). Through his astute choice of supporting musicians, his varied repertoire of songs, and the combination of his and Spector's production skills, Harrison was able to fashion an album that successfully bridged the gap between the two emergent genres, allowed him to draw on his spiritual beliefs in a way that had not been possible in the Beatles, and enabled him to escape the constant and claustrophobic comparisons with Lennon and McCartney.

When a remastered CD version of the album was released in 2001, Harrison reflected on the significance of *All Things Must Pass*:

> It's been thirty years since *All Things Must Pass* was recorded. I still like the songs on the album ... It was an important album for me and a timely vehicle for all the songs I'd been writing during the last period with the Beatles. I began recording just months after we had all finally decided to go our separate ways and I was looking forward to making the first solo album of songs ... I still see a number of the musicians and friends who helped me with the album [and] after thirty years of life's lessons, I'm grateful to have had three decades of friendship with them. (Harrison 2001)

His overt reference to the friendships acquired through the recording of the album is significant. Several of the musicians regularly appeared on his subsequent albums and many descriptions of Harrison have stressed the importance he attached to his friends. Tom Petty observed that "George really treasured his friends" (Love 2002: 223). Ravi Shankar described him as "so loving and magnanimous, going out of his way to help those whom he cares for" (Shankar 1992: 230). Paul Theroux referred to "his passion for music and his diverse and close friendships" (Harrison 2011: 13).

Perhaps this is the key to understanding the significance of *All Things Must Pass* in Harrison's career. Such was the acclaim that greeted the album that it was (and is) often forgotten that its preparation, recording, and release took place during a period of profound personal turmoil. Recently, and acrimoniously, separated from the friends with whom he had lived and worked for more than a decade, saddened by the death of his mother Louise in July (which brought a temporary halt to the recording sessions), and confused by the evident deterioration in his marriage to Pattie Boyd (who would eventually leave him for Eric Clapton in 1974), the album supplied him with the opportunity to find a refuge in music from the emotional pressures and lingering disappointments of his private life, and to draw strength and support from others. *All Things Must Pass* was, unequivocally, Harrison's album. But it was also an album on which the themes of love (spiritual and personal), affection and friendship were repeatedly explored and exposed—not just in the lyrics of its songs, but in the circumstances of its creation.

Chapter 9

"That's It": *Willis Alan Ramsey,* the Ballad of a Cosmic Cowboy

George Plasketes

> What was wrong with the first one?
>
> —Willis Alan Ramsey

There is an unusual false climax on "Northeast Texas Women," the concluding song on Willis Alan Ramsey's self-titled debut album from 1972. "The Birklettes," as they are credited, lead the sing-along chorus, accompanied by an odd array of found sound sources—bottle, south wall, coke crate, knees, cowbell, carpets, hallways—that blend with the more traditional fiddle, guitar, bass, and drums. The song fades into its apparent finish. However, after 15 seconds of silence, the music re-emerges, continuing as coda. When the instrumentation recedes again, Ramsey (presumably) affirms the finale, pronouncing with mildly upbeat inflection, "That's it." His simple declaration is both punctuation and prophecy, with reverberation beyond the recording session in the Beautiful Sound Studios in Memphis in 1971.

When *Willis Alan Ramsey* was released the following year, the album, despite meager sales, received widespread praise from Ramsey's music peers and critics. The venerated debut links Texas outlaw and troubadour masters, Willie Nelson, Guy Clark, and Townes van Zandt, among others, with the arrival of *Austin City Limits* in 1975 to contemporaries such as eclecticist Lyle Lovett and onto the ever expanding Americana/alternative country catalog. Forty years later, fans, artists and critics still await a Second Coming, an elusive follow-up record from the enigmatic Ramsey.[1]

Willis Alan Ramsey represents an intriguing strand of the debut genre. Call it "the one and done," for lack of a better or less rhyming phrase. A kindred to the single song sensation of the "one hit wonder" that is endemic in popular music, the less common "one and done" is album-oriented and largely artist-driven. The decision is in large part a personal and/or professional choice, rather than entirely being dictated by a record company, the music market, and its commercial imperatives. Such perplexing acts of self-banishment are relatively rare, with cases

---

[1]   I did not experience *Willis Alan Ramsey* first hand in 1972, rather as a latecomer. The album was not prominent in the FM station rotations or suburban record collections in my hometown Chicago during the 1970s. Despite America's popular "Muskrat Love" cover, Ramsey remained anonymous to me until around 1980 when I increasingly heard the record in Mississippi.

so minimal they may not qualify as a trend or even a pattern. Ramsey's disconnect in the early 1970s was an antecedent to a handful of artists—Greg Copeland, Mary Margaret O' Hara, and multiple Grammy winner Lauryn Hill, among the few— who also released critically acclaimed debuts and then withdrew from the music scene for an extended period of time, without recording a follow-up studio album for decades; and in some cases such as Ramsey, for ever.[2]

Ramsey's debut record coincided with the advent of "Progressive Country," a music format pioneered by KOKE-FM in Austin, Texas. The unconventional programming approach, initially limited to weekends, was endorsed by journalist Chet Flippo, who covered the Austin music scene for *Rolling Stone.* The small station's classification of country music was expansive, with an "anything remotely country sounding" rotation that ranged from Johnny Cash and Hank Williams, Jr. to the Allman Brothers and Flying Burrito Brothers to the Rolling Stones' "Dead Flowers" (see Reid 2004: 78-79; 268-69).

The Jagger/Richards hillbilly junkie tune was emblematic of the 1960s twilight that settled securely into the Southwest and progressive country genre. Austin's "alternative Nashville" music boom in the early years of the new decade tapped into a tributary of maverick country and western that swung back to Bob Willis and the Texas Playboys and evolved to Asleep at the Wheel and Willie Nelson. At the same time, there was clearly a counterculture undercurrent emerging, with "echoes and refrains of Ken Kesey's Merry Pranksters and *The Whole Earth Catalog*" (Reid 2004: 270). The post-hippie inferences conveniently connected KOKE's call letters with the rising popularity of cocaine in the area.

The broader cultural hostilities conveyed in Merle Haggard's sneering "We don't smoke marijuana in Muskogee," or in the closing scene of the film *Easy Rider* (1969), with rednecks blowing away long-haired bikers on Southern back roads, were not part of the burgeoning music community. At Armadillo World Headquarters in Austin, the home, hangout, and hub of the regional music movement, "rednecks with back pocket moonshine got blitzed with long haired pot smoking hippies" (Tramontana 2000). Jan Reid, author of the insightful Southwest region music chronicle, *The Improbable Rise of Redneck Rock* (2004), insists that

---

[2]   Copeland's brilliant *Revenge Will Come* (1982, out of print/never reissued), produced by Jackson Browne, made *Time*'s "Best of" year-end list alongside Bruce Springsteen's *Nebraska* and Richard and Linda Thompson's *Shoot Out the Lights.* He followed up the debut 26 years later with the gem *Diana and James* (2008). He also wrote the Nitty Gritty Dirt Band's first hit "Buy for Me the Rain." Toronto native and cult icon O'Hara, sister of comic actress Catherine O'Hara, was a striking vocalist whose odd syncopations and patterns of diction straddled Al Green and Patsy Cline. Following *Miss America* (1988) and struggles with stage fright, her reappearances have been sparse: the soundtrack *Apartment Hunting* (2001), stray vocals (Morrissey's "November Spawned a Monster"), compilation contributions, and a Christmas EP (see Roberts 2006). Hill, the former Fugee front and Best New Artist in 1999, followed *The Miseducation of Lauryn Hill* (1998) with *MTV Unplugged No. 2.0* (2002), but then took an extended hiatus due to music industry dissatisfaction. She resurfaced in 2010, with performances and plans for a new studio record.

Eddie Wilson's Armadillo World Headquarters "had more in common with Bill Graham's Fillmore than with the Grand Old Opry" (2004: 270).[3]

The musical convergence of counterculture and country, with common themes of individuality and freedom in their narratives, became patent among the "cosmic cowboys." A songwriting moniker and movement, the beards, boots and booze brand was adapted from Michael Murphey's popular sing-along song "Cosmic Cowboy, Pt. 1," featuring the catchy chorus—"riding the range and acting strange / that's where I want to be." Murphey, whose best known songs include "Geronimo's Cadillac," "Wildfire," and "Carolina in the Pines," is regarded as an intellect within the progressive country setting. He never intended for "Cosmic Cowboy" to be taken seriously, and purportedly wrote the song tongue-in-cheek. Much to Murphey's chagrin, the song became an anthem and convenient catchphrase for the hippie-redneck confluence that populated the vibrant music scene. The "supernatural country rockin' galoot" in the song personified the proliferation, ascendance and airs of this strand of 1970s songwriters (Reid 2004: 271).[4]

Willis Alan Ramsey was considered one of the "Cosmic Cowboys." Born in Birmingham, Alabama, Ramsey moved to Dallas with his family when he was a boy. In the late 1970s, at age 19, Ramsey began shopping his songwriting skills to various producers, but received little encouragement or interest. Ramsey eventually connected with the Allman Brothers and Leon Russell, who were in Austin for a performance and happened to be staying at the same hotel, the Villa Capri. They were impressed enough to invite Ramsey to record some demos. He went to Macon, Georgia with Gregg Allman, then to Los Angeles to audition for Russell at his home studio in Hollywood Hills. Russell, along with Denny Cordell, had just formed Shelter Records, an artist-owned, artist-friendly label that was designed to be an American version of the Beatles' Apple Records. Ramsey was soon signed to the Shelter roster that included Tom Petty, Phoebe Snow, The Grease Band, and Texas blues artist Freddie King.

The experience was overwhelming for Ramsey, who admittedly "had no idea how to record, much less make a record" (Tramontana 2000). Russell booked studio time for Ramsey with some impressive backing bands. Among the players were ubiquitous sessionists from the Southern California circuit, Leland Sklar, Russ Kunkel, Tim Drummond, Kenneth Buttrey, and Jim Keltner, whose extensive recording credits included James Taylor and Neil Young. Russell also played piano on two songs, and Shelter label mate J.J. Cale was also a drop-in. Recording

---

[3]   The Armadillo had four intangible "C's" which appealed to performers: a carpet, Coke machine, lack of cops, and the fervent crowd. Most stages were hardwood and "unfamiliar;" the carpet provided "cohesiveness and the feel of home for the band." The Coke machine was stocked with ten-cent long necked bottles of Texas beer. (See Reid 2004: 60-69.)

[4]   Murphey (later Michael Martin Murphey) considered the song, its lyrics, and impact regrettable. He fled the Austin scene, fearing that the cosmic cowboy fad of his own inadvertent making might jeopardize his career.

sessions took place in five different studios in Nashville, Memphis, Tyler, Texas, and two in Hollywood.

The multiple sessions generated a 40-minute album of 11 songs. There is a natural simplicity that pervades the acoustic country folk song cycle, with an overall tone that is more restrained than raucous. While traditional country sounds are present—harmonica, fiddle, and pedal steel—other instruments, such as a cello on "Angel Eyes" and Leon Russell's vibes on "Muskrat Candlelight," provide calming accents. The cosmic cowboy cosmetic is established on the album's lead cut, "Ballad of Spider John." An accordion wash, saxophone, and a string arrangement accompany the modern-day outlaw tale, with its familiar narrative conventions, among them a hobo robber man "on my way to nowhere / running from my past," and an object of sweet affection named "Diamond Lilly."

The melodic instrumentation throughout complements the charm in Ramsey's drawling tenor and vocal delivery that resembles Russell. Reid aptly characterizes Ramsey's singing style with lyrical detail: "bluesy in a Southern white kind of way ... whimsical, as if it belonged to a boy shuffling barefoot down sandy backwoods road. It was out of the Austin ordinary ..." (2004: 141). Ramsey's youthful, self-assured songwriting displays a flair that is varyingly vivid, romantic, mischievous, wry, witty, wistful and melancholy.

The rock and roll fantasy "Satin Sheets" is a meandering, tapping, "praise the Lord and pass the mescaline" precursor to Joe Walsh's chronicle of excess, "Life's Been Good." Ramsey pledges to "give all the pretty women the third degree and satin sheets / keep 'em off the streets." Similarly low-key, but with a more reverent tone and a pedal steel providing a graceful, wailing thread, "Boy from Oklahoma" is an ode to Woody Guthrie, his rambling, wandering, drifting "on an endless one night stand." The song sustains as one of the best Guthrie homages, a harbinger to the Billy Bragg and Wilco *Mermaid Sessions* and 100 Year commemorations such as *New Multitudes* (2012), featuring Jay Farrar, Will Johnson, Anders Parker, and Yim Yames

Ramsey readily wears his country heart on his sleeve, in pining, aching beats, with a trace of Hank Williams's lonesome disposition. "Goodbye Old Missoula" waltzes farewell to a heartbreak barmaid. The mid-tempo, fiddle-driven "Painted Lady" conveys a honky-tonk trucker's days-gone-by dreams of the Old West and his longing for a lovely, lonesome cowgirl by his side.

Ramsey balances the yearning with lightheartedness and intimate allusions from the nature trail. The album's most rambunctious song, the sing-along "Northeast Texas Women," praises "kisses sweeter than cactus" and "cotton-candy hair." "Geraldine and the Honeybee" is a playful compost pile and pollen ditty, with a smitten vow of "never going back to the honeysuckle vine." Desire translates into appetite under the shade of the big magnolia tree in the slide guitar, tapping, blues affectation in "Watermelon Man." "Muskrat Candlelight," the album's most recognizable tune, is a rodent romance between Suzy and skinny Sam, as they whirl, twirl, and tangle in a mating dance, "floating like the heavens above." Described by Ramsey as "just a little novelty song I wrote in fifteen minutes"

(Tramonta 2000), "Muskrat Candleight" was promptly transformed into a two-time Top 40 hit reminiscent of Bread's 1970 soft pop-rock hit "Make It With You." Retitled "Muskrat Love," Ramsey's song was first popularized by America, who had just won a Grammy for Best New Artist the same year Ramsey's debut was released. The harmonic folk-rock rendition was the lead song and single on *Hat Trick* (1973), the group's third album. In 1976, the Captain and Tenille's version ascended to #4 on the *Billboard* Hot 100.

Ramsey's precocious songwriting was infectious. In between the muskrat adaptations, Jimmy Buffet recorded "Ballad of Spider John" on the pre-Parrothead *Living and Dying in 3/4 Time* (1974), calling it "one of them songs I wish I had written." Eventually, more than one-third of the songs on *Willis Alan Ramsey* were recorded by other artists, among them "Ballad of Spider John" (Buffet, Sam Bush), "Goodbye Old Missoula" (Jimmie Dale Gilmore), "Satin Sheets" (Waylon Jennings, Shawn Colvin), and "Northeast Texas Women" (Buffet, Jerry Jeff Walker). The numerous cover versions and music chart success reinforced the critical merit of Ramsey's debut album, as well as his songwriting knack and the post-hippie appeal of progressive country. However, sales of the record itself were minimal, particularly beyond the Texas border. Ramsey joked, "I think I've met every single person that purchased it" (Tramontana 2000).

The reverence for the album among Ramsey's songwriter peers overshadowed the commercial disappointment. The palpable influence within the 1970s Austin scene and across the Southwest circuit extended to late 1980s progressives such as Shawn Colvin and Lyle Lovett. "I'd never heard the album before I moved to Austin in 1976, but just about everybody in Austin had it. It was very important to me. I really studied it," said Colvin (Tramontana 2000; Colvin 1994).

Lovett became one of *Willis Alan Ramsey*'s most avid advocates, gushing that it is "one of the greatest records of all time." "I learned every song off his record," said Lovett. "I went to see him every time he played, got tennis shoes like his. I wanted to be Willis Alan Ramsey" (willisalanramsey.com). When Lovett began performing during the late 1970s while earning degrees in journalism and German at Texas A&M, Ramsey's songs, along with many by Steve Fromholz and Michael Murphey, were central to Lovett's repertoire. "As much as I liked Willie Nelson, we didn't cover his songs. I wanted songs that were new to an audience, and Willie was on the radio all the time," said Lovett. "I sang 'Spider John' more times than I could count" (Reid 2004: 325).

Lovett was drawn to Ramsey's distinct style:

> Listening to Willis's record showed me that you don't have to play straight-ahead blues to have blues be a part of your music. He's so soulful…just with his vocal style. He's not playing the shuffle kind of stuff you hear at a bar on Sixth Street in Austin. He does it with narrative that's not restricted to the sixteen-bar blues form. (Reid 2004: 325-26)

Lovett's appreciation for Ramsey was clearly genuine and enduring. Ramsey performed "Angel Eyes" at the wedding ceremony of Lovett and actress Julia Roberts in 1993. The following year, he contributed background vocals on Lovett's *I Love Everybody* (1994), then co-wrote "That's Right (You're Not from Texas)" for *Road to Ensenada* (1996). Lovett's respect for Ramsey is further demonstrated in his double-disc Texas songwriter tribute, *Step Inside This House* (1998), which features the post-debut Ramsey composition "Sleepwalking."

Lone Star State of Mind

Though undeniably peculiar, Ramsey's vanishing act following his esteemed debut is more mythical than mysterious. The narrative is a familiar thread that features a stereotypical artist demeanor—youthful idealism, stubbornness, perfectionism—combined with record label conflict, and generic music industry frustration. Ramsey was not comfortable with the "big-time," professing not to "know how those people operate out in LA." His musical mindset was more regional than national, and he preferred his own studio to Shelter's setting. "It took me a year to make my record. I went through a whole lot of shit that I'd prefer not to go through again," he said. Ramsey had a five-year contract with Shelter that called for one album per year. Though an annual album was a fairly common expectation during the era, the deal was also generous and sanguine, considering Ramsey's unproven nature within the thriving 1970s singer-songwriter market. His contract was suspended by Shelter in the second year until Ramsey delivered a second album (Reid 2004: 146).

Ramsey appeared to be a self-saboteur, with little regard for fundamental music industry protocol, the binding nature of contractual agreements, and the role of booking agents and managers. He resisted promotion from Shelter and was defiant about touring to support his record's release:

> I asked them not to promote it ... I just don't like advertisement. I don't like somebody to feel like they've got to shove something down my throat before I'll find out about it. Because I know that people who listen to records as much as I do will gradually hear one if it's any good. Let it stand the test of time. Just float it out there and see what happens. If the record company can afford it, I can. (Reid 2004: 148)

Ramsey cancelled out of his first major tour on which he was scheduled to perform behind Delaney Bramlett at venues that included the renowned Troubadour in Los Angeles. To him, such "prestige" and "pressure" engagements were "not gigs that I covet." Music colleagues attributed Ramsey's indifference to his being young and immature. Armadillo owner Eddie Wilson said that, despite "writing some damn nice songs," Ramsey had "a terminal case of the kid. He's always running around worried about his attitude" (see Reid 2004: 145, 148). Ramsey cited creative constraints:

> I guess I'm one of those sensitive artist types that ends up being broke and at odds with everybody in the music industry. It seems like I'm fast working myself there. But I don't give a shit. If I've got something to say I want to be able to say it from start to finish and not have somebody come in and edit it and have somebody decide for me how to present it. (Reid 2004: 150)

A significant shift in the music scene also contributed to Ramsey's disillusion and detachment. By the end of the 1970s, the urban cowboy movement supplanted the cosmic cowboys. The songwriter-friendly venues became rowdy to the rafters, with mechanical bulls replacing laid-back hippies. "Everything just got kind of stressful for me," said Ramsey, in simplified summary (Schulian 2000).

During the decades of disconnect following his debut, Ramsey relocated to London, then to Scotland where he lived in an old signal tower outside Edinburgh. He returned in the 1990s, married, settled in Nashville, and eventually moved back to Texas where he continued to write songs and play gigs, living off songwriting royalties. Reflecting its creator, *Willis Alan Ramsey* remained out of print for many years until Koch reissued the record in 1999. Performance videos on You Tube document some of his appearances, among them Threadgills and Austin City Limits in 2001, where Ramsey introduced some new songs. In 2003, a 30th anniversary tour further showcased the latest material: "Boystown," "Mr. Lemon," "Mockingbird Blues," "Positively," and "Desireé." The new songs fortified the persistent rumors of a follow-up record, which incessantly torment the Ramsey cult. There is even an alleged working title for the record—*Gentilly.*

As an artist, Ramsey has redefined, if not ridiculed and eradicated, the notion of "work in progress." More abstractly, Ramsey and the circumstance of his debut record personify the motto "lone star state." The case illuminates nuances of the symbiotic or complementary relationship between a debut and second record. Arguably, the rare "one and done" is ultimately a safe route for an artist to chose, particularly if the work is critically acclaimed or approaches masterpiece status, as the Ramsey debut does. Caught up in the fable, few, if any, have suggested that Ramsey's reluctance to record again may reflect other "sensitive artist" traits such as fear, doubt, and insecurity as much as it does his stubbornness, perfectionism, and frustration. A new Ramsey record would naturally demystify the debut to some degree. It would provide closure and continuity; Ramsey's disconnect ends as does the record's singularity. A discography begins to build. And, as is the case with any second record, the follow-up, no matter how many years apart from the first, provides a frame of reference to revisit the debut and critically assess artistic advancement.

Beyond contractual obligation and the less binding expectations of the music marketplace, there is no statute of limitations or requirement that stipulates that an artist must follow up a debut, or any work. Continuity and its pace are largely a personal choice shaped by many factors. Ramsey is clearly no exception. During the 1960s and the 1970s, the standard for artists was to write and record enough songs for an album release on a yearly basis. That production cycle began to shift in the early 1980s, in large part due to MTV's arrival, and the synergy strategy of cross-media promotion between music, radio, music video, television, film, and commercials. In addition, artists no longer limited themselves to music, but explored multiple business and creative opportunities. As a result, the annual expectation diminished and the span between records widened. For decades, it has been uncommon for an artist to release a record in consecutive years. Two to four years tends to be the standard time frame, though there are always exceptions and extremes. Gillian Welch's eight years between *Soul Journey* (2003) and *The Harrow and the Harvest* (2011), and Bonnie Raitt's and Fiona Apple's seven-year break between albums (2005-2012 in both cases) are among the unusually long recording gaps of recent note.

Ramsey's recording hiatus is unprecedented by any era's standards. Forty years is an epic exile, one of Biblical proportion. As the years have accumulated into decades without a follow-up record, Ramsey's debut has ascended to a level of myth analogous with a career-ending death or band break-up. Absence makes the art grow fonder. And, there is a sense of bewilderment, betrayal, and increased expectation in the loss or absence. There *has* to be more: a second coming.

Such a mythology is arguably more easily cultivated from the masterful than the mediocre. Though the impressive music and songwriting of *Willis Alan Ramsey* sustain on their own, the "lone album saga" often overshadows the album's artistic virtues. The ongoing oddity has become fable and folklore. A small scale sequel to Elvis sightings with a hint of Celine Dion's pseudo-retirement. A running gag and skeptical "hell freezes over" colloquialism: "It'll happen when the second Willis Alan Ramsey album is released."

The Ramsey narrative is not a tabloid tale nor does it fit the VH-1 *Behind the Scenes* formula. Music journalism, in part, facilitates the cult fascination, from catchy article titles in the *New York Times*—"One Album to His Name, but It's the Stuff of Legend," (Schulian, 2000)—to being the featured "album from oblivion" in the UK music magazine *Mojo*'s "Buried Treasure" column (November 2000).

Among fans and followers, Internet threads with reviews, fond recollections, and rumors abound. There are stories of salvaging copies of the record at Goodwill and thrift stores, and passing the cherished vinyl artifact down the generations as family music heirlooms. Musician testimonies are plentiful beyond Lyle Lovett: Kevin Russell of the Gourds recalling how his uncle used to play him Ramsey's record and long for the good old days at the Armadillo (Reid 2004:352). Country star Clint Black listing *Willis Alan Ramsey* as one of his five "Desert Island" albums. Shawn Colvin buying copies of the reissued Ramsey CD to give out as gifts, and, in the liner notes of her album *Cover* Girl (1994), encouraging people to go buy the record.

Ramsey has always appeared more amused than annoyed by the debut phenomenon. "It just won't go away," he says (Tramontana 2000). He himself has perpetuated the myth and speculation by remaining ambiguous about his detachment and status as a singer-songwriter. Over the years, Ramsey has responded to the persistent inquiry about a second record with the clever comeback—"What was wrong with the first one?" This frequently cited quote has become part of his debut album's charming lore. The line would be a suitable caption for the photo on *Willis Alan Ramsey*'s iconic green cover: a shot of a 20-year-old Ramsey at ease with a Trickster smirk, bearing a slight resemblance to actor Woody Harrelson in cowboy costume. Like the album's concluding utterance in "Northeast Texas Women"—"That's it!"—Ramsey's remark about his debut is a shrug that conveys indifference more than it does defiance. The comment casually deflects, and at the same time it reflects the "sensitive artist" persona and its complex range of traits. The counter question raised by Ramsey has been answered repeatedly in the 40 years since the release of *Willis Alan Ramsey* in 1972. The consensus about his debut record has been that there is very little, if anything, "wrong with the first one"—other than that there has not been a second one. The Ramsey debut discourse is a Texas Two Step, a circle that remains unbroken. Without a sequel, *Willis Alan Ramsey*'s singularity persists, a cosmic cowboy ballad awaiting its next verse. The sound of one hand clapping.

Chapter 10

New York Dolls: "Ridin' right on the subway train"

Thomas M. Kitts

As a high school student in the very early 1970s in Staten Island, New York, I had been reading in the *Village Voice* about a reckless glam band called the New York Dolls. In late August 1973, approximately a month after the release of the Dolls' first album, a friend and I decided to venture into Max's Kansas City to give the band a hearing. We walked past the steak-and-potatoes diners downstairs and headed up to the small, dingy club. We took our seats, not more than 25 feet from the stage, and waited. Finally, after an opening act or two, the lights dimmed and a guitar roared the hypnotic chords of "(I'm Your) Hoochie Coochie Man." The lights came up on a frightening group of musicians. An elfin guitarist slammed the chords; a lead guitarist, all hair and heels, glared, seemingly right at us, as his lead lines seared over the top; the bulky bass player, larger than life in platforms and tights, suggested Frankenstein in drag; the drummer, barely visible under his hair, hammered hard; and the lead singer—heavily made-up, gangly in his heels with an open shirt and tights—shouted in a deep voice with effeminate enunciations: "The gypsy woman told my mother ..." His voice snarled and whined as lead riffs competed for space. Willie Dixon's staccatoed blues riffs could barely stave off the band's explosiveness—and, with the following number and for the rest of the night, the band did explode.

The next day, with my ears still ringing, I borrowed my parents' station wagon and drove to E.J. Korvette's to buy *New York Dolls*. The album didn't disappoint. I have been listening to the Dolls ever since.

New York Dolls was an album that almost didn't get done. The band's manager, Marty Thau, had a hard time finding a producer: "And do you think it's so easy to just get a good producer? Especially with a group like that, that some people maintained couldn't play for shit? It wasn't easy" (qtd. in Stegall 2005:86). Finally, they settled on or got lucky with Todd Rundgren, an art rocker formerly with Nazz and then riding the pop charts with his hit double album *Something/Anything?* and the hit singles "I Saw the Light" and "Hello It's Me." Rundgren explained why he took on the task of producing these crude and rudimentary rockers: "I was amused by them ... these guys walking around in hot pants, wearing girls' clothes all the time (qtd. in Needs and Porter 2006: 78). He explained further:

> The main reason that I did the Dolls album was because it was a New York
> City record. There was no reason to get David Bowie or some other weirdo to
> produce it; the only person who can logically produce a New York City record is
> someone who lives in New York. I live here, and I recognize all the things about
> New York that the Dolls recognize in their music. (qtd. in Edmonds 2007: 101)

But Rundgren had no idea what was in store for him. Recording began in
mid-April 1973 at the Record Plant, Studio B, on West 44th Street, in the heart of
the Broadway theatre district. Mercury Records wanted it done fast. They wanted
the band on the road selling this sure-fire gold record. In the adjoining studio
was folkie Livingston Taylor, James's brother, who was reportedly terrified of
the Dolls. Rundgren, for whom the studio could be a sacred place, and the Dolls
clashed immediately. The Dolls found Rundgren overly serious, cold, indifferent,
and anything but fun. The Dolls had never been in a studio and, to put it moderately,
they had a poor work ethic. Rundgren, however, had a tight, precise, technically
controlled recording process and solid work ethic. "The atmosphere in the studio
was carnival-like, I guess, because they did have such a large entourage," recalled
Rundgren. "I found it sort of annoying, but the band were only loosely held
together anyway" (qtd. in Needs 79). The Dolls partied mightily in the studio
with their hangers-on and their drugs of choice: alcohol, hash, and cocaine. At
one point, Rundgren walked away from the chaos with a curt dictate to one of his
assistants: "If they get any ideas call me" (qtd. in Needs 79).

Lead singer David Johansen said that "Todd needed a bullwhip and a chair.
He wasn't intimidated by us; just exasperated … We didn't know that you were
supposed to go to a studio and knuckle down. For us it was just another part of
this non-stop party we were living" (qtd. in Needs and Porter 2006: 79). Besides
partying, the Dolls had massive egos and none as large as the lead singer's and
the lead guitarist's. Ignoring Rundgren's technical savvy and precision, Johnny
Thunders played as loudly as he possibly could, as did his best friend in the band,
drummer Jerry Nolan, while David Jo insisted his vocals be clear. They would all
be angry with Todd for years. Whenever Thunders did a guest DJ gig on the radio,
he would dedicate a song to Todd: "Your Mama Don't Dance and Your Daddy
Don't Rock and Roll." But, as rhythm guitarist Sylvain Sylvain commented,
"Jesus Christ couldn't have done a better job, dealing with five guys all going,
'Hey, listen to me, put him down and put me up and fuck them'" (qtd. in Antonia
1998: 80). Shortly after the release, Rundgren commented on the music: "The
only thing that it testifies to is that they're punks"—not a compliment at the time
(qtd. in Edmonds 2007: 101).

Released on July 27, 1973, *New York Dolls* marks the debut of one of rock and
roll's most explosive and self-destructive bands. The album is a raucous rock-and-
roll record made by naive and defiant young men with loud guitars and plenty of
ego and bravado who look back at the roots of rock—updating Bo Diddley, for
instance—and forward to the future of rock, anticipating the Ramones and the
Sex Pistols. But at its release, *Dolls* did not have the commercial impact Mercury

anticipated, selling an underwhelming 110,000 copies and peaking at #116 on the *Billboard* charts. (Mercury expected a gold record, 500,000 sales.) The album and the band confused critics and rock listeners. In a year-end readers' poll for *Creem*, the Dolls achieved top ranking in two categories: the Best New Group of 1973 and the Worst New Group of 1973. Yet with time and with the Dolls' influence on the American and British punk movement in the 1970s and 1980s came respect. In 2003, *Rolling Stone* ranked *New York Dolls* at #213 on its list of "the 500 greatest albums of all time."

Sales were hurt by the album's cover which was, to put it mildly, controversial. As the band's soundman Nitebob says, "They got a big push then [from Mercury], they really did. But then, there was the album cover, which was a big error. The picture was way extreme. So many people were turned off by that" (qtd. in Stegall 2005: 86, 88). Paul Nelson, who as the head of Mercury's A&R department signed the Dolls and was later fired for so doing, tells of trying to promote the album to top FM stations whose DJs would refuse even to give it a listen because of the cover: "It created something that remained at the forefront of a lot of people's opinions, and they never got beyond that cover" (qtd. in Antonia 1998: 84).

The cover captures the Dolls in all their glory. Squeezed on an antique white sofa (shot in a downtown Third Avenue antique store) and doing Oscar Wilde proud, the band gives their best jaded, decadent, defiant, and drag-queen pose. From the left sits bassist Arthur Kane who, with fake pearls, a cigarette, and a cocktail, glares ahead with a tight pullover top sloped from one shoulder across his breasts; Sylvain, with heavily rouged face, wears roller skates and hangs one hand on Kane's bare shoulder while the other touches a silk handkerchief; Johansen, heavily made up, checks himself out in a compact mirror as he sits sideways in a tight open sweater and short, tight satin slacks that reveal hairy legs; Thunders, in black with huge white heels, stares into the camera and consumes more than his share of the sofa's space; and Jerry Nolan in his huge knee-high boots, tights, and scarf, clasps the bottom of his ornately lapelled smoking jacket as he straightens his backbone. Above the band, their name written in lipstick; beneath them, the debris of a trash-glam night on the town: a cigarette lighter, a pack of Lucky Strikes, a purse, and a Schlitz beer can with a straw. "We like to look bored to the bottom of our bowels," Johansen said (qtd. in Needs and Porter 2006: 40).

On the back cover, the Dolls pose in front of Gem Spa, a cigarette-newsstand on the corner of St. Marks Place and 2nd Avenue that still looks the same almost 40 years later. Johansen again in the center of the posse, resembling the drag-queen prostitutes who, at the time, solicited a few blocks away on 11th Street (between 2nd and 3rd Avenue) or, most especially, along the West Side Highway. With the album jacket, the Dolls proclaim to America, "This is our world and our music. Enter at your own risk."

The album kicks off with "Personality Crisis," the Dolls' signature song, with Nolan's slamming the cymbals and Sylvain's grinding out of the dominant chord progression for barely six beats before Rundgren sneaks in a piano trickle just ahead of the rest of the band and Johansen's full-blown scream, "Whoaaaaaa—

ooh, yeah yeah yeah, no no no no no no no." The Dolls are off at a blistering pace in this humorous tongue-in-cheek tale of celebrity culture, schizophrenia ("Your mirror's getting jammed up with all your friends"), and bitchiness. Johansen delivers all whistles, howls, and lyrics with a New York swagger and exaggerated diction ("You was butterflyin'") while Thunders crams lead lines in every available and unavailable space. These are the Dolls: loud, bold, riff-driven, funny, and in perpetual crisis of personality.

In "Looking for a Kiss," a small character portrait, the desperate singer has been "houndin' the street" and "haulin' booty all night long" in his quest for love. It is early Sunday morning and the singer encounters addicts shooting up (beautiful in their decadence and ennui, but "so obsessed with gloom") and "old ladies on their way to church." A mid-tempo rocker fueled by the rhythm section's steady beat, the Johansen composition borrows heavily from Chuck Berry via T. Rex's "Get It On" while taking its intro from the Shangri-Las' "Give Him a Great Big Kiss": "When I say I'm in love, you best believe I'm in love — L.U.V." The theatrical Johansen does one of his best drag queen imitations here.

"Subway Train," or the Dolls' "Orange Blossom Special"—inverted, of course—captures the New York City subway ride like nothing before or since. In "Orange Blossom Special," the rhythms are graceful and smooth, conjuring images of rolling hills and verdant valleys as the singer anticipates the return of his love and the loss of his New York City blues. In "Subway Train," however, Sylvain creates the rattling, careening, stop-and-go rhythm of a NYC subway, while Thunders's lead lines mimic the piercing screams of the rail. Johansen, as the neglected singer, whines with glam-queen affectation to his unresponsive lover: "I've been trying every night to hold you near me." His life, he gripes, is "cursed, poisoned, condemned." Still worse, even in the enclosed space of a subway car, he cannot usurp his lover's attention from friends and "Suzy Says," the gossip column in the *Daily News*. The subway and apparently the relationship grind on with no resolution.

There are several other classic Dolls tracks on the album, including "Trash," a tumbling love song that jolts along like an early morning garbage truck as the confused singer/lover seems on the verge of a murder-suicide—the Dolls gave "Trash" a haunting reggae treatment on 2009's *'Cause I Sez So*. Other standout performances include "Vietnamese Baby," in which Johansen promises to show us more mustard gas than we have ever seen; the raging rocker "Bad Girl"; the complaining singer of the gentle ballad "Lonely Planet Boy"; the rocking-and-rolling "Jet Boy," and the unruly cover of Bo Diddley's "Pills." Perhaps Thunders was not being facetious but prescient when he wanted the album to be called *The New York Dolls' Greatest Hits*.

The Dolls, band and album, derive their power from a chaotic convergence of several sources, but especially the following three:

1. Pop music. The Dolls had a deep and instinctive passion for and understanding of popular music and believed, above all, that rock and roll

had to be fun and uplifting. (Johansen and Thunders especially had an encyclopedic knowledge of popular music.) This passion—along with their explosiveness, reckless bravado, and volume—more than compensated for sloppy playing.

2. Theater, especially camp. The Dolls understood showmanship and were inspired by the emerging gay scene, which saw the first gay pride parade in 1970, and the downtown arts scene which included Charles Ludlum's flamboyant Ridiculous Theatrical Company, where Johansen had landed a small role as a spear carrier just before the Dolls. However, the Dolls always had a rock-and-roll undergirding, even when theatrical, whether imitating girl groups like the Shangra-las, or the Rolling Stones—Johansen and Thunders assumed Jagger/Richards posturing at about the same time as Steven Tyler and Joe Perry of Aerosmith. The Dolls loved to pose: whether it be as hardened drag queens or jaded fin-de-siècle throwbacks. As Mick Jones of the Clash once said in praise, "They were incredible and they blew my mind. The way that they looked, their whole kind of attitude ... They were a group that was all about style" (*Clash*).

3. New York City. A band's name might never have been so fitting. After over 20 years of unparalleled growth and development post World War II, New York City began a steep decline from about 1968 to the early 1980s, reaching its nadir in 1977 with the infamous blackout and widespread looting, the Son of Sam killings, a contentious and mean-spirited mayoral race, open air drug supermarkets in public parks, and the real threat of bankruptcy. Consider Frank Sinatra's comment on New York at the time: "It's sure changed, this town ... this was the greatest city in the whole goddamned world. It was like a big, beautiful lady. It's like a busted-down hooker now" (qtd. in Hamil 1980: 31). Formed in late 1971, the Dolls emerged out of the refuse of a city in decay, embodying Sinatra's "busted down" hookers, but full of energy, daring, revelry, fuzzy rebelliousness, over-the-edge fashion, and capriciousness.

Importantly, the Dolls may have been formed in the downtown arts scene, but they were all born, except for Sylvain and original drummer Billy Murcia, in one of the outer boroughs, and all, including Sylvain and Murcia (who died of a drug overdose before the recording of the first album) were raised in an outer borough: Johansen (Staten Island), Thunders, Sylvain, and Murcia (Queens), Kane (the Bronx), and Nolan (Brooklyn). Individually, they possessed that hard outer-borough edge and defiance, one developed from a sense of inferiority at not being artsy Manhattanites. They knew that they would have to scream to be heard— the band's operative term became *excess*. Camp provided the mask for them to be excessive and to allow their egos full play. They were not, after all, prissy, prep school Manhattan kids and they wanted all to know it. A few years later, the same attitude would infuse the Ramones, from Queens, but, later, lead to lingering questions about the rock authenticity of the prep school Strokes, from Manhattan.

But as much as these energies synergized in the Dolls, they also led to the band's hasty demise. Their campy glam limited the Dolls' appeal. Glam has always had a narrow market in America. With Ziggy Stardust, David Bowie's glam was more mythical or sci-fi, and Alice Cooper's greatest success came with rock theater, and despite his feminine name he was very masculine on stage, in voice, and with his boa constrictors.[1] Johansen's boas were of a feathery kind. Camp, long aligned with the gay community, could be threatening to suburban males (a large part of the rock record-buying demographic) and explains in part the limited success of Marc Bolan and T. Rex as well as the Dolls. Many missed Johansen's camp posturing in interviews to promote the album. In the *Record Mirror*, he bragged, "I wrote those songs, and my unbiased opinion is that they're great ... We've got pop prowess." Then, with absurd confidence, he said of record-buyers, "Don't worry they'll take anything we put out" (qtd. in Needs and Porter 2006: 81).

But, above all, what especially made the Dolls so exciting, so wildly explosive, and so successful (however commercially limited) was what destroyed them: their excesses, especially their egos (particularly Johansen's and Thunders's) and their booze and drug consumption, which has been called "heroic" (Needs and Porter 2006: 54). (Thunders became addicted to heroin after Iggy Pop introduced him to the drug in Los Angeles within weeks of *Dolls* release.) Their "reckless outrageousness," as John Rockwell termed it, made the Dolls a fragile entity at best and gave the *New York Times* critic "the impression ... that they were just unstable enough to tip over the edge at any minute." Of course, such excesses did little to develop a work ethic, and, thus, the Dolls failed to develop—their set list varied little from 1972 through 1975. Unlike the Ramones (guided at least in part by the military precision of guitarist Johnny Ramone), the Dolls lacked the persistence and endurance for long tours, which might have opened up American and global markets. In 1974, after the poor showing of their second album *Too Much Too Soon*, Mercury, who could be considered supportive even though they didn't really know how to market the band, dropped the Dolls. For all intent and purposes, the Dolls ended in early 1975 when Thunders and Nolan left the band during a tour of Florida. Kane, soaked in alcoholism, followed shortly afterwards while Johansen and Sylvain limped on with replacements for a bit.

In 2004, the three surviving Dolls (Johansen, Sylvain, and Kane) reunited for a concert in England, encouraged by former Doll UK fan club president Morrissey (yes, of the Smiths), who said, "Some bands grab you and they never let you go and, no matter what they do, they can never let you down ... The Dolls were that for me" (*New York Dolls* 2005). Drugs claimed the life of Thunders in 1991, and Nolan died from a stroke brought on by bacterial meningitis in 1992. Shortly after the reunion, Kane died from leukemia.

Sylvain and Johansen have continued as the Dolls after the initial reunion, releasing to date three fine studio albums: *One Day It Will Please Us to Remember*

---

[1]   Bowie once told the Dolls that they "had the energy of six English bands" (see Edmonds 2007: 101).

Even This (2006), *'Cause I Sez So* (2009), produced by Todd Rundgren, and *Dancing Backward in High Heels* (2011). The Dolls still perform, and, while they are far more skilled and disciplined and less reckless and flamboyant, they have, thankfully, not aged completely gracefully. But in their prime, which lasted for perhaps two years surrounding their debut album, the Dolls careened liked a New York City subway car: loud, rattling, sometimes at breakneck speed and sometimes paused, vulnerable to immediate breakdown, overcrowded with posturings and egos, but always on an adventurous and dangerous journey.

Chapter 11
Warren Zevon: Asylum IconocLAst

George Plasketes

It was as if a Laurel Canyon version of Elvis Costello had suddenly surfaced amidst Asylum's [Records] pervasive complacency.

—Barney Hoskyns, *Hotel California* (2006: 246)

With a cold eye, a boozer's humor, and a reprobate's sense of fate, this California rounder put Los Angeles back on the rock and roll map and nearly blew the Malibu singer-songwriter crowd right off it.

—culture/music critic Greil Marcus (qtd. in Hoskyns 2003: 281)

During the four-decade span of his career, Warren Zevon attracted an unusual number of inventive literary, film, music and art analogies from critics and contemporaries attempting to characterize his singular songwriting and presence. Among the associations are: "a Laurel Canyon version of Elvis Costello," "the 'Sam Peckinpah' and 'John Huston' of rock," "Jackson Browne's bad conscience," "the 'Ernest Hemingway' and 'Charles Bronson' of the 12-string guitar,"[1] "the Dorothy Parker of rock and roll," a "Dada-ist Bruce Springsteen," "Warren Warhol," and "F. Scott Fitzevon." While Springsteen read Nathanael West in Zevon, singer Bonnie Raitt offered a more comprehensive composite: "He was our everything, from Lord Buckley to Charles Bukowski to Henry Miller. Warren made someone like Randy Newman even seem normal" (Zevon 2007: 428).

Many of these allusions converge in Zevon's critically acclaimed, self-titled, major label debut in 1976 on nascent media mogul David Geffen's touchstone Los Angeles label, Asylum Records. Not only is *Warren Zevon* a definitive work for Zevon as a songwriter, it also stands as one of the unsung, yet integral records of the substantial California country/folk/rock catalog that was *the* American sound of most of the 1970s. Though overshadowed by the Eagles' bewitching *Hotel California* (same label, same year—Asylum, 1976), *Warren Zevon* is a lurking, literate album that endures as one of the most delightfully dark, demystifying documents of Hollywood desperation and decadence, a record that "bridged the singer songwriter era and the new age of punk's Angry Young Men" (Hoskyns 2006: 247).

Among the distinguished class of the 1970s take it easy, peaceful feeling of the confessional, country/folk/rock school, Zevon was an insurgent. "Warren

---

[1] The "Bronson" reference is Zevon's self-description in corrective response to Browne's "Hemingway" introduction of him during a concert.

was a bit of an unusual character coming out of California because his tone was obviously not a typical Californian unless you went back to maybe Nathanael West," observed New Jersey native Bruce Springsteen. "He had a cynical edge, which was really not a part of what was coming out of California at the time" (Zevon 2007: 147) When singer Linda Ronstadt first met Zevon, she thought he was a "psycopath" (Hoskyns 2006: 245). However, she managed to overlook that first (un)impression to uncover and record one-third of the songs from *Warren Zevon*—"Mohammed's Radio," "Poor Poor Pitiful Me," "Carmelita," and "Hasten Down the Wind," which was further appropriated as the title for her 1976 platinum album, also on Asylum. Beyond his writing and resistance to the country rock sound, even Zevon's appearance was a contrast to the canyon casual of the Laurel and Topanga troubadours. Whether his album cover pose aside a spotlight outside the Palladium or the Asylum Records publicity photo of him reaching into his suit coat pocket (presumably for a firearm), Zevon's look was deadpan, a nocturnal intellect, bespectacled and frequently attired in a black suit, a one-size-fits-all fashion statement that concurrently conveyed pianist, poet, historian, detective, and undertaker.

Zevon paid his dues in and around the Los Angeles music scene during the mid-1960s. He steadily accumulated songwriting, session, and commercial credits that included composing advertising jingles for Boone's Farm (with Harry Dean Stanton), Gallo Wine, and Chevy Camaro. As part of the folk-pop duo lyme and cybelle (a lower case nod to poet e.e. cummings), he released, with Violet Santangelo, a single on the Turtles' White Whale label. Zevon also wrote a few tunes for the Turtle's twin fronts, Mark Volman and Howard Kaylan, "Outside Chance" and "Like the Seasons,' the B-side to the band's 1967 hit "Happy Together." In 1969, Imperial Records released Zevon's first LP, *Wanted Dead or Alive*, an obscure anterior debut produced by Sunset Strip eccentric entrepreneur Kim Fowley. One of the album's songs, "She Quit Me," appeared on the *Midnight Cowboy* soundtrack (1969), re-gendered as "He Quit Me" and performed by Leslie Miller and Garry Sherman. Zevon continued to audition his songwriting skills while touring with the Everly Brothers as their band leader and pianist.

"Thanks always to Jackson"

In the liner notes of each of Warren Zevon's five albums released during the 1980s, the acknowledgment—"Thanks always to Jackson"— is a floating footnote to the credits. Zevon's recurrent expression of gratitude to fellow songwriter Jackson Browne predates his Asylum debut. By the mid-1970s, with the Everlys in disharmony and his own publishing contract lapsed, Zevon considered his career to be at a crossroads. Discouraged, he moved to Spain to reinvent his music pursuits. In the summer of 1975, Browne sent a pleading postcard to Zevon that set in motion his return and a major label record deal.[2] Browne had been an advocate of Zevon's songwriting since they first met in 1968 in Laurel Canyon. He frequently performed Zevon's songs live, and solicited others in the LA music circle, urging them to record Zevon's material.[3] "I didn't think anybody got Warren but me," said Browne. "That's the kind of writer he was—he spoke to your inner cynic. There was a dialogue that went on inside of him that's going on inside of everybody" (Scoppa 2010: 65).

Browne, whose primary allegiance was to hearing Zevon sing Zevon rather than outsourcing his songs, was an ideal benefactor. By mid-decade, Browne had established himself as the archetypal introspective poet in the Los Angeles songwriter sphere. Though born in Germany, Browne's West Coast residency resonated more "native" than other avatars along the sensitive songwriter spectrum such as Joni Mitchell (Canada) and James Taylor (North Carolina). Browne also had credibility and contacts as a cornerstone and wunderkind of David Geffen's Asylum Records. The only artist signed from an unsolicited tape, favorite son Browne's debut was one of the label's initial four releases, along with David Blue, Judee Sill, and Jo Jo Gunne, a Spirit spin-off with the hit "Run, Run, Run." His first three records—*Jackson Browne* (1972, later known as *Saturate Before Using*), *For Everyman* (1973), and *Late for the Sky* (1974)—are arguably as impressive an initial trio of successive albums ever made by any singer-songwriter.[4]

Asylum Records evolved out of a management partnership between Geffen and Elliot Roberts, who founded Lookout Management (named after Lookout Mountain Road in Laurel Canyon). On their way to becoming the most powerful management stable on the West Cast, the duo established a reputation for being trustworthy and artist friendly. Asylum was designed as a songwriter refuge. The name "Asylum"—its iconic logo a heavy wooden door floating on clouds and

---

2   The postcard read: "Warren, Too soon to give up. Come home. I'll get you a recording contract. Love, Jackson" (see Mehr 2008: 3; Hoskyns 2006: 246).

3   Two Browne compositions appear on the Eagles debut, the hit "Take it Easy" (co-written with Glenn Frey) and "Nightingale." He also co-wrote "Doolin' Dalton" for *Desperado* (1973), after unsuccessfully pitching two Zevon songs to the Eagles for the album, and being rejected by the Byrds for their Terry Melcher-produced "reunion" album on Asylum in 1973.

4   And, I would not hesitate to include Browne's fourth record, *The Pretender* (1976), with the streak. This subjective suggestion is, of course, arguable, and likely off-putting to some. But in the words of Tom Petty, "I won't back down." Granted, Dylan's *Freewheelin'* (1963) through *Blonde on Blonde* (1966) is an epic run. Neil Young, has been much more uneven, if not erratic at times, from record to record, alternating between folk country acoustic strumming and Crazy Horse jams. And Springsteen certainly has put together some nice trifectas. I'm just saying, Browne's first three (or four) albums more than hold their own against anyone's records. In an essay in *Paste Magazine* (July 2008: 28), Andy Whitman's perspective on Browne's poetics may be more pronounced than mine: "In fact, it's hard to imagine an album like Dylan's *Blood on the Tracks* without those first three Jackson Browne albums."

blue sky—reflected a unique corporate philosophy of "benevolent protectionism" that buffered artists from the media and music industry. The localized scene of the Troubadour and Laurel Canyon communities converged into a formidable Asylum subculture (Hoskyns 2003: 231-37). The record label was thriving and its artists prolific, with most on an album-a-year release pace throughout much of the decade. The Eagles' string of albums between 1972 and 1976—*Eagles, Desperado, On the Border, One of these Nights, Hotel California*—featuring a radio-friendly Crosby, Stills, Nash and Gram Parsons country rock sheen, was emblematic of the quality, consistency and productivity of the Asylum roster.[5]

Browne negotiated a contract for Zevon. The deal was minimal, with no money up front and a limited recording budget. Browne would produce the project.

> The last thing on my mind was how to make a hit record; I just thought people needed to hear him. So we'd make the best versions of his songs we could. Geffen had the feeling I was just making a record for a friend—doing somebody a favor. It wasn't until after the LP was done that he really heard it for what it was, especially when the critics hailed it. (Scoppa 2010: 65)

Browne recruited an impressive cast of L.A. singers and sessionists to contribute instrumental backing and vocal harmonies on Zevon's 11 piano driven compositions: Phil Everly, Fleetwood Mac's Stevie Nicks and Lindsey Buckingham, Bonnie Raitt, Beach Boy Carl Wilson, Billy Hinsche of Dino, Desi and Billy,[6] Rosemary Butler, J.D. Souther, Eagles Glenn Frey and Don Henley, David Lindley, Jorge Calderon, Waddy Wachtel, Bob Glaub, Bobby Keys, Jai Winding, Ned Doheny, and the Sid Sharp Strings.[7]

Recorded between October 1975 and February 1976, the resulting album released in June was atypical Asylum, its view and tone divergent from most of the label's notables such as Browne, Ronstadt, the Eagles, Mitchell, Souther, solo-Poco Richie Furay, and Byrd Chris Hillman.[8] The lone exception was perhaps

---

[5]   With its 22 million copies sold, the Eagles' collection, *Their Greatest Hits (1971-1975)* (Asylum 1976) has long maintained its place as the best-selling compilation of all time; is tied for top-selling US album, with Michael Jackson's *Thriller* (Epic 1982), which received a significant spike following his death in 2010; and ranks among the top albums with international sales at 42 million.

[6]   Hinsche's participation may be attributed in part to his sister being married to Beach Boy Carl Wilson.

[7]   According to Browne, Zevon had the "wrung out jaded string musicians who had been on every *Lassie* date since 1957, cracking up, laughing" during the first string date of the recording sessions. Zevon wrote some jokes specifically for the session "to get them to play well" (Zevon 2007: 111).

[8]   I vividly recall being considerably deflated after the first listen to *Warren Zevon*. (George Stuart, whose extensive record collection reflected his good music taste, was the first in our college dorm to have a copy of the album.) It was a set-up. The Asylum brand,

street beat poet Tom Waits. "It sounds as though Zevon is out to demolish every cliché in the Asylum bin," wrote *Newsweek's* Janet Maslin (1976: 72).

Zevon's songwriting stood out, exhibiting qualities that were literary, cinematic, romantic, and comically detached; with preferences for noir to neon; gloom to glamour's glow; shadows to shimmer; the loneliness of locals, down on their luck losers and low lifes to the lifestyles of the luminaries. Zevon shared a similar vision with F. Scott Fitzgerald as a chronicler of excess, hedonism, hidden desperation, and the dissolution of dreams.

"I was more interested in contemporary writing than in pop music. I wasn't a great rock and roll fan," said Zevon.[9] "What Norman Mailer or John Updike had to say seemed a lot more interesting than what was going on in pop music in the early 1960s" (VH1.com). Among Zevon's ideals were Raymond Chandler and Ross Macdonald (Ken Millar), author of the Lew Archer detective mysteries. Part of Zevon's novel nature was also linked to his identifying with fictional characters, particularly the kidnapped kid in Macdonald's *Zebra-Striped Hearse* and the rock star protagonist who suffered from the delusion his father was Jesse James in Thomas McGuane's *Panama*.

Midnight Writer

In the view of prominent producer Peter Asher, Zevon was writing about "a different LA" (Hoskyns 2006: 246). *Warren Zevon* is, in part, a geomusical neighborhood novella, a misguided tour that roams an Angelino axis from the Whiskey A Go-Go to the Rainbow Bar and Grill where the Sunset Strip ends to the notorious Continental Hyatt House—a rock star refuge referred to as the "Riot House"[10]—on to Echo Park and the Pioneer Chicken stand on Alvarado Street, then from Topanga Canyon to the Tropicana Motel, ending at the Hollywood Hawaiian Hotel on Yucca and Grace before exiting down Gower Avenue.

Zevon's point of view is double vision as detached observer and passionate participant. By his own admission and with ample evidence, Zevon "chose a

---

Jackson Browne producing, and a supporting cast of familiar singers and players created fairly specific melodic "California" expectations. However, *Warren Zevon* was markedly different in sound and tone. I eventually saw the dark light and grasped its remarkable qualities. It has long been my favorite Zevon album, and one of my favorite records period.

[9] During the course of his career, Zevon accumulated a lengthy list of literary collaborators, among them Dr. Hunter S. Thompson, Mitch Albom, Carl Hiassen, Paul Muldoon, and Thomas McGuane. He also performed briefly in the bard band, Rock Bottom Remainders, with Stephen King, Amy Tan, and Dave Barry.

[10] Michael Walker's chapter "The LA Queens" in his *Laurel Canyon : The Inside Story of Rock and Roll's Legendary Neighborhood* (2006): 179-196, is a very insightful, entertaining account of the decadent Sunset Strip scene, particularly its hotels and hangouts.

certain path and lived like Jim Morrison" and "was the most fucked up rock star on the block" (Gunderson, 2002).

Zevon shapes an antihero atmosphere brimming with outlaws and outcasts on the outskirts, from the late 1880s American West frontier to 1970s Hollywood hangouts on the strips and boulevards. The album is bracketed by the same melody. The piano notes that open "Frank and Jesse James" reprise ten songs later in a string arrangement on the closing "Desperados Under the Eaves." Cinematic, but short of epic, the two comprehensive bookend narratives, the album's longest at 4:33 and 4:45, demonstrate Zevon's proficient piano playing with allusions to his classical training.[11] The compositions are inspired by the cowboy choreography of Aaron Copland's 1942 ballet *Rodeo*. "Frank and Jesse James" features a sophisticated do-si-do bridge, with David Lindley's banjo and fiddle adding authenticity. The piano bandit ballad summons a specter of the Allman Brothers "Midnight Rider" from earlier in the decade, as well as more obvious Old West outlaw echoes from Billy Joel's "The Ballad of Billy the Kid" on *Piano Man* (1973) to the conceptual Western Americana themed albums—Elton John's *Tumbleweed Connection* (1971) and the Eagles' *Desperado* (1973), with "Doolin-Daltons" among its gunslinging songs.[12] There is also a Peckinpah presence that evokes the maverick director's films *The Wild Bunch* and *Pat Garrett and Billy the Kidd*. Forty years later, Zevon's sibling legend would have been a suitable soundtrack theme for the film *The Assassination of Jesse James by the Coward Robert Ford* (2008). While the song may be a kindred historical homage that links brothers James and brothers Everly (Phil sings harmonies on the song), it announces the arrival of the desperado Zevon, a Midnight Writer, writing offbeat into the Sunset Strip.

Zevon's lyricism maintains an oblique biographical undercurrent throughout. "Mama Couldn't Be Persuaded," livened further by Lindley's fiddle, is a parental portrait from Zevon's perspective as a kid "stuck in the middle" of a precarious courtship and union of his Scots-Welsh Mormon mother and Russian-Jewish immigrant father, a gambler-gangster-prizefighter. "Backs Turned Looking Down the Path" is also personal; Zevon's reflection on being "caught between the years" and getting his "outlook fixed" after abandoning California dreaming for Spain. Zevon considered the song to be one of his simplest, best and most overlooked (Zevon 2007: 90).

The warmth of "Backs Turned Looking Down the Path" eases into tenderness on "Hasten Down the Wind," in which Zevon renders a withering dialogue. The he/she seesaw begins with a proverbial premise: She thinks she needs to be free; he doesn't understand. Nothing is working out as they planned. The gentle ache of Lindley's slide guitar, Everly's sweet harmony, strings, and a twinkling piano

---

[11]   Zevon is an accomplished pianist who studied under composer Robert Craft. At age 13, he met his hero Igor Stravinsky. Samples of Zevon's unfinished *Symphony No.1* appear as interludes on *Bad Luck Streak in Dancing School* (1980).

[12]   The facial resemblance between Zevon and the young Elton John image on *Tumbleweed Connection* is mildly intriguing.

complement the emotional state with an appropriate tone and texture for the waning relationship. The love song establishes another strand of Zevon's versatile songwriting, evidence that he could do West Coast mellow and melancholy, and be as sensitive and poetic—"hanging on to half a heart / he can't have the restless part"—as any of the LA songwriting romantics, from Browne to Karla Bonoff and J.D. Souther.[13]

The tender tone twists into darker shades and debauchery, beginning with the hedonistic excess in "Poor Poor Pitiful Me" and continuing through to the album's completion. Zevon's unruly Sunset Strip saga portrays a self-indulgent rock star bemoaning "these young girls won't let me be." Zevon's account is mischievous, highlighted by a clever couplet that rhymes "gender" with "Waring blendor." The Rainbow Bar cruising climaxes at the infamous Hyatt (Riot) House in a night of masochistic sexcess. Zevon refuses to reveal the dirty details. Instead, he delivers a silencing run-on mutter—"I-don't-want-to-talk-about-it"—to end the song in brutally funny fashion.[14]

In "The French Inhaler," Zevon provides a poor, poor pitiful "Piano Man" portrayal of the late-night-into-early-morning miseries at a Hollywood bar. Except there are no "la-lala diddy-das" of Billy Joel's East Coast lounge loser lament. These are friends, phonies and wannabes "with no home to go home to." The song builds to Zevon's last call observation that is brutally blunt. When the lights come up, he catches a glimpse of a pretty face, now wasted, devastated, looking like "something death brought with him in his suitcase." The simile is stunning, a lyrical punch with fatal blow impact. The elegant texture of the Sid Sharp Strings and immaculate harmonies from Henley and Frey are intriguingly incongruent with the acerbic scene. Though soothing, the melodies do little to alleviate the pain, loneliness, futility, and frustration. The choral fade into "So long, Norman" implies the narrative is about Norman Mailer and his failed marriage to Marilyn Monroe, an interpretation Zevon rejected for years. It was not until 2004 that Zevon's son, Jordan, revealed that his mother, Zevon's first wife Marilyn Tule Livingston, confessed on her death bed that the song was bitterly biographical, a kiss-off from Zevon after learning of her tryst with a fellow musician after their marriage ended.[15]

"Mohammed's Radio" is a Halloween hymn. Despite its refrain, "Don't it make you want to rock and roll / All night long," the song is, in the view of critic John

---

[13]   The posthumous collection *Reconsider Me: The Love Songs* (New West 2006) features 13 romantic ballads culled from the Zevon songbook, with a touching introduction in the liner notes by his daughter Ariel.

[14]   Ronstadt's hit version of the song (from *Simple Dreams* (1977)) inverts the gender and modifies Zevon's Rainbow Bar and casual S&M sex at the Hyatt to "Yokahama ... please don't hurt me Momma."

[15]   Livingston died from breast cancer on March 3, 2004, six months after Zevon's death. She was also the subject of Zevon's "Tule's Blues" on *Wanted: Dead or Alive* (reissued on *Preludes* (New West 2007)) and presumably "Hasten Down the Wind."

Rockwell, a "dirge like anthem, a rolling, inexorable attestation to the darker, more passionate side of life" (1979: 218).[16] The ambiguous spiritual subtext approaches hymn, heightened by the Buckingham/Nicks harmonies that crescendo in the chorus. The "someone singing, sweet and soulful on the radio" signals deliverance for the restless and desperate. The song originated, in part, from Zevon's peculiar observation of a Halloween parade in Aspen in 1973. Among the costumed locals was a developmentally challenged man dressed in Arab sheik holding a radio up to his ear. "I remember exactly the look on Warren's face watching that—something changed in his face, and what it was is he was making mental notes and writing 'Mohammed's Radio' in his head," said studio drummer Eddie Ponder (Zevon 2007: 79). Zevon translated the surreal scene into some of his typical remarkably bizarre lines: "In walks the village idiot / And his face is all a-glow / He's been up all night listening to Mohammed's radio."[17]

Zevon's sardonic sensibility is in full display in the deranged, piano-pumping pledge, "I'll Sleep When I'm Dead," which appeared to be a personal reckless rough draft and self-fulfilling prophecy in progress. The song materialized during a dawn in Spain as his wife Crystal was trying to get the up-all-night Zevon to bed. He disobediently snapped "I'll sleep when I'm dead." The retort defused the situation into laughter, and ignited an impromptu songwriting session. Together they proceeded to generate a litany of odd lyrics around the hook line, most of them referencing Zevon fixations—prescription medicine, a .38 special, and "drinking heartbreak motor oil and Bombay gin." The catchy title became Zevon's self-sabotaging signature, as evidenced in its fitting designation of the posthumous oral history compiled by Crystal Zevon in 2007.[18] The song was grim foreshadowing of Zevon's diagnosis-to-death "Deteriorata Trilogy" beginning in 2000—*Life'll Kill Ya', My Ride's Here*, and the Grammy-winning *The Wind*—leading up to his death from mesothelioma in September 2003.[19] Such preoccupations with demise and depravation were central to the Zevon's sneering songwriting. "Old Velvet Nose," a smirking, cigarette-dangling, frequently bespectacled skull grins from the covers, corners, and liner notes of Zevon's records like a skeletal Nike swoosh, sibling of Edward Munch's woodcut *The Scream*. The trademark bears

---

[16]   Rockwell prefers Ronstadt's version on *Living in the USA* (1978) to Zevon's original, citing the production values, hard-edged, weighty ferocity of the arrangement, and Ronstadt's illuminating vocalism (1979: 217-18).

[17]   Warren Zevon, "Mohammed's Radio," Zevon Music, BMI (1976).

[18]   The phrase has slipped into the popular culture vernacular, uttered occasionally as a line of dialogue by television and film characters.

[19]   With apologies for the self-promotion: for a detailed chronicle of this period of Zevon's life and death, please see the chapter "Die Another Day: Warren Zevon's Desperado "Deteriorata" in my *B-Sides Undercurrents and Overtones: Peripheries to Popular in Music, 1960 to the Present* (2009: 173-94).

a resemblance to Zevon: at once a self-portrait, mirror image, X-ray, mask, and alter ego.[20]

The character study in "Carmelita" is detailed and casually despairing. The heroin addict, strung out on the outskirts in Echo Park, is sinking to the depths. With no methadone or welfare check, the desperate junkie is "playing solitaire with a pearl handled deck." Suicidal, he pawns his Smith Corona typewriter and goes to meet his dealer who is hanging out at the Pioneer Chicken stand on Alvarado Street.[21] The Tex-Mex acoustic arrangement reflects the "Mariachi static on the radio," its tubes glowing in the dark, while the chorus implores "hold me tighter."[22]

"Join Me in LA" is a sinister antecedent to Randy Newman's sunkissed satire "I Love LA" from *Trouble in Paradise* (1983). Zevon's treatment of "join me in LA" as a shadowy invitation rather than a slogan promoting tourism is blatant in the song's ominous leading lyric—"Well, they say this place is evil." The black magic mood conjures a canyon cult. At "midnight in Topanga" the DJ warns "there's a full moon rising," and a "dark and sultry" voodoo vibe fitting for the HBO vampire series, *True Blood* (the "LA" conveniently converts into the abbreviation for "Louisiana"). Despite the foreboding nature, Zevon is staying. He engraves the noir narrative with a resounding précis on the soul-selling illusion of the Hollywood dream—"'Cause I found something that'll never be nothing." The music and vocals provide a supernatural silhouette for the nocturne. Bobby Keys's saxophone wails in unison with the soulful vocals of Bonnie Raitt and Rosemary Butler that resound in the chorus, whisper "wake up, wake up," and moan "Ohhhs" of pleasurable pain that solely sustain the song's final minute.

The song cycle builds to a magnificent finale, "Desperados Under the Eaves," a striking composition, both lyrically and musically, that is Zevon's magnum opus. "Warren was obsessive, so he worked on the order of the songs, how it would sound, how it would come off, for a long time," said Crystal Zevon. "The ideas of what it needed to be were almost part of the writing. He was classically trained so he always thought of things more in terms of finished work" (Mehr 2008: 7).

---

[20]   Or a haunting homage to Zevon's Uncle Warren. Zevon's ideal as a child was "a dead man—with my name, looks and career intentions. A dead warrior who'd been waylaid by his heroism ... I grew up with a painting of an uncle, Warren, who looked just like me. He was a military man, a golden boy, an artist. He'd been killed in action ... Uncle Warren was sort of the dead figurehead of the family, and I was brought up to follow in his footsteps. I guess that kind of background gave me the idea that destroying myself was the only way to live up to expectations" (Nelson 1981: 33).

[21]   Perhaps paying additional homage to the firearm afficianado Zevon, Ronstadt's version substitutes "Smith and Wesson" for "Smith Corona" on *Simple Dreams* (1977). Zevon also uses "Smith and Wesson" in some of his live and demo versions of the song.

[22]   "Carmelita" was considered Zevon's "personal calling card" as it was always among the first songs he auditioned for peers, family, and friends, among them Waddy Wachtel and Crystal Zevon (Mehr 2008: 11, 12).

The outlaw spirit of the James brothers rides full circle from the album's frontier overture through its underbelly travelogue into its conclusion. An orchestral echo of the piano melody that commenced the album sets a melancholy tone for the doomed protagonist holed up at the shabby Hollywood Hawaiian Hotel, the embodiment of Nathanael West's "dream dump" (Mehr 2008: 12). The scene is part biographical, a glimpse of Zevon's struggles with alcohol—"still waking up with shaking hands," "staring in an empty coffee cup," determined to "drink up all the salty margaritas in Los Angeles."[23] The view is bleak, a glowering gaze—"the sun looks angry through the trees" and "the trees look like crucified thieves"; the fatigue heavy—"trying to find a girl who understands me"; and the spirit relinquished—"except in dreams you're never really free."[24]

The song features what may be Zevon's definitive quatrain:

> And if California slides into the ocean
> like the mystics and statistics say it will
> I predict this motel will be standing
> until I pay my bill.[25]

Zevon's emblematically droll dread is fatalistic foreshadowing of the Eagles iconic "Hotel California" lyric: "You can check out any time you like / but you can never leave." Though the Zevon view is faintly merciful: "Heaven help the one who leaves."

The final verse finds him "listening to the air conditioner hum." He describes the sound: "It went mmmmmmm ..." The hypnotic humming continues, then flows into a concluding sea chantey choral arrangement by Beach Boy Carl Wilson, a hymn-like murmuring medley of "Dixie" and "Battle Hymn of the Republic." The wondrous whirr of the Gentleman Boys (Wilson, Hinsche, Winding, Browne, Zevon) harmonizing in unison with the Sid Sharp Strings is no purring precursor to the Crash Test Dummies' clumsy cute single "Mmm Mmm Mmm Mmm" in 1993. The haunting coda is a sublime songwriting moment, one that is stunningly acute and astute, an anthemic drone that rises to sheer orchestral and harmonic

---

[23] In addition to first hand documentation in Crystal Zevon's posthumous oral history (2007), Paul Nelson's cover feature, "Warren Zevon: How He Saved Himself from A Coward's Death, *Rolling Stone* 19 March 1981:28-4, 70) is a stunning account of Zevon's continuous struggle with alcohol.

[24] Warren Zevon, "Desperados Under the Eaves," Warner Tamerlane/Darkroom Music, BMI (1976). Madeleine Peyroux delivers a delicate, moody gender inversion of the song on *The Blue Room* (2013).

[25] Ibid. The hotel scene is based in biography. Zevon left without paying his bill, exiting via a fire escape to an awaiting getaway car. Guilt-ridden, he eventually returned to settle his debt, with management requesting only autographed albums. (Yes, Zevon uses "hotel" and "motel" in the song.)

splendor as the record's fading processional down Gower Avenue, equal parts Orleans parish jazz funeral and Western sunset ride-off.

Something That'll Never Be Nothing

> I thought of him [Zevon] as one of the aliens. I think he captured the spirit of that time. His tormented soul was like a deeper expression of what was going on than anybody else was even thinking about, let alone writing about.
>
> —drummer Eddie Ponder (Zevon 2007: 74)

Warren Zevon was a premonition of the decadent zenith for the unrelenting vagaries and self-gratification in the West Coast music scene. Zevon's sordid seclusion under the eaves of the Hollywood Hawaiian captures the mood of the panicked rock fraternity in the mid-1970s. His scene, though solitary, is a vision of desperados turned vagabonds, like everyone else, huddled together in apocalyptic dread of the seismic shift from eden to dystopia, "thinking that the gypsy wasn't lying."

"Despair was ubiquitous in Los Angeles in 1976," writes music historian Barney Hoskyns. "The first epoch of rock and roll was drawing to a close. An inertia had set in just as a new generation was rising up to slay its musical fathers" (2006: 248). When Dylan, Young, Mitchell, Clapton, Muddy Waters, Van Morrison, and others gathered to perform on Thanksgiving Day for the Band's "The Last Waltz," the Winterland wonder event marked a symbolic spectacle exalting the exiting golden age of rock. According to Ned Doheny, "The whole scene got a lot more desperate," with artists increasingly uncomfortable with the personal and professional outcomes of their immense successes. Hints surfaced in song. The sweetness in the Eagles' hit "New Kid in Town" veiled its star paranoia subtext. "We were writing about our own replacements," revealed Henley/Frey co-writer J.D. Souther (Hoskyns 2006: 249)

In the face of the foreboding, the centennial year marked a pinnacle for the melodic, country/folk/rock genre that was the "California sound" and Asylum Records. *Warren Zevon* initially sold 80,000 copies, slipping into *Billboard*'s Top 200 at #189, figures that were far surpassed by several albums released the same year by his fellow Asylum roster mates. Browne's *The Pretender* charted at #5; *Hasten Down the Wind* became Ronstadt's first platinum record, reaching #3 (rock/pop) and #1 (country); and the Eagles' *Hotel California* remained at #1 for eight weeks, well into 1977, and subsequently rose to multi-platinum sales, Grammy recognition, and rock classic eminence.[26]

---

[26] Among *Hotel California*'s many distinctions, several are on *Rolling Stone*'s "500 Greatest" Lists. The album ranks #37 while the song is at #49.

Zevon was connected to all three records, perhaps most obviously as a continuing song source for Ronstadt and producer Peter Asher. Browne, having gone directly, the day after, from producing *Warren Zevon* to his own recording sessions,[27] acknowledged that his atypical lyric on "The Pretender—"I'm going to be a happy idiot"—was influenced by Zevon.

The most curious correlations surface when juxtaposing *Warren Zevon* with *Hotel California*. Beneath the albums' thematic resemblance, there are intriguing distinctions between the two that are more subtle shades than stark contrasts. Released in December 1976, six months after Zevon's debut, the Eagles present a last resort rendition of the pitfalls of paradise and pretty people as prisoners of their own device. While Henley, Frey, Don Felder, Randy Meisner, and Joe Walsh were thinking to themselves "this could be heaven or … hell," Zevon's Pacific portrayal is a purgatory of pity and penance, a poetic portent of the desolate, haunted hotel in King and Kubrick's *The Shining*, where ghosts gather for Unhappy Hour.

Hotel California was clearly more conceptual than *Warren Zevon*. The album embodies the romantic rock and roll mythology and fast-lane lifestyle—the land of blue jeans and cocaine, mirror shades reflecting palm trees, blond hair flowing from convertibles on freeways that led to the ocean. In Henley's view, a love/hate existence that was "a whore" and "a fertile mother" (see Hoskyns 2003: 279-82; 2006: 246-50; Eliot 2005: 147-53).

While the Eagles were living it up, Zevon was living it down. The noir narratives on *Warren Zevon* are infused with more desperation and less of the contemptuous coked-out arrogance that characterized the Eagles' manner and method, extravagance encouraged by their manager and Geffen nemesis, Irving Azoff. Despite dealing with his own demons and disorder, Zevon still swerved from the starlight, spotlight, and sunlight, "refusing to give the rock and roll mythology of California any credence at all" (Hoskyns 2003: 281).

The extent of creative reciprocity between Zevon and the Eagles, whether deliberate or inadvertent, is limited to their commonalities of desperado themes and collaborations with Browne.[28] However, the timing of their 1976 records is noteworthy. The Eagles began recording *Hotel California* in March, one month after *Warren Zevon* was completed. Zevon loiters like a phantom presence in *Hotel California*. The Eagles' sprawling (7:30) closing denunciation of artificial paradise, "The Last Resort," resonates Zevon's "Desperados Under the Eaves." Perhaps more conspicuous is the string arrangement on the brief (1:30) "Wasted Time (reprise)." Whether blatant borrowing, trendy orchestration or resourcefulness, the

---

[27]   Browne began recording *The Pretender* on March 1, 1976; *Warren Zevon* was completed on February 29.

[28]   Crystal Zevon described Warren's relationship with Don Henley as "strange." While discussing whether or not he wanted a funeral following his mesothelioma diagnosis, Zevon said, "I just don't want to spend my last days wondering whether Henley will show up" (Zevon 2007: 439). (Henley did not attend the ceremony.) The balance between sardonic and serious in the comment is difficult to decipher, perpetuating the mythology.

Eagles recruited Sid Sharp, who had contributed significantly to *Warren Zevon*, as their *Hotel* "Concert Master." Considering Henley's and Frey's participation in the Zevon sessions, the intersections between their albums, though negligible, may be dually construed as mere coincidence or subconscious, curious carryover. The parallels and proximities invite whispering intimations of influence, homage, creative conspiracy, and competitive undercurrent.

A subtle sense of "squatter's rights" lingered over the two albums' mirroring similitudes. The back cover notes on the digitally remastered version of *Hotel California*, reissued in 1999, perpetuate the mythology. The tone is as territorial as it is self-congratulatory, as if the Eagles appear to be staking their claim as the key chroniclers of the LA scene: "Meticulous craftsmanship of all phases of the recording was preceded by more than a year and a half of reflection and writing." The passage boasts that the album's three thematically unified #1 singles—"Hotel California," "Life in the Fast Lane," and "New Kid in Town"— "contributed to the group's growing reputation for writing masterful editorials on the singular state of mind called Southern California."

Bob Mehr makes a similar case for *Warren Zevon* in his liner note essay for the album's remaster(piece)ed, double-disc reissue (Rhino 2008), more than 30 years after its initial release. Mehr boldly broadens the discussion beyond the Henley and Frey *Hotel*, stating that Zevon "should rank among Southern California's greatest chroniclers, placing him in a continuum somewhere between early LA historians like Carey McWilliams and contemporary sociologists such as Mike Davis" (Mehr 2008: 13).

Warren Zevon was not destined or designed to rival the Eagles. "Zevon is on Asylum, a famous home for self-pitying narcissists; [including] Don Henley and Glenn Frey of the Eagles," wrote Greil Marcus. "The people who inhabit the commercial context in which Zevon makes his music aren't merely integrated into the system [they were] out to fuck up, they *are* the system" (1978; qtd. in Eliot 2005: 145).

Asylum's limited investment in Zevon's debut record translated into minimal commercial expectations. Sales were secondary, at least on the surface, to Browne's primary purpose of exposing Zevon's songwriting talents. While there is certainly merit in Bonnie Raitt's view that "There's no way the mainstream could be hip enough to appreciate Warren Zevon" (Zevon 2007: 426), there were other factors that may have sabotaged the album's wider appeal and accessibility. Musically, Zevon was a mutineer who resisted fully committing to the predominant country/rock genre resounding in LA's idyllic canyons, strip and boulevards. He preferred to remain on the fringe with a piano-fighter presence rather than deliver an album that conformed to a melodic, radio-friendly sound. Nor was Zevon's voice a prominent feature. In Browne's view, Zevon had "a limited instrument as a singer," his vocals a basic baritone at best, with an ominous Eric Burden bend, but without the gravelly allure of Tom Waits.

There were a number of other Zevon songs written and available for his first album, among them the cavorting "Werewolves of London," which became his biggest hit in 1978 at #21, and the unruly, macabre "Excitable Boy." Both displayed the strand of Zevon's writing that Browne characterized as a "berserk quality" (Boucher 2002). Browne insisted those two songs be saved for Zevon's second album rather than be included on *Warren Zevon*, fearing that, if they replaced the more fitting "Frank and Jesse James," "The French Inhaler," and "Desperados Under the Eaves," those three songs might become lost and never recorded later. "There was a literary quality to those songs and I felt it was better to get them established and out there first and then come out with the record that had 'Werewolves' and 'Excitable Boy' on it. On the other hand, his first album might have been and much bigger hit had it had those songs," said Browne (see Scoppa 2010: 65; Zevon 2007: 112).

Browne's instincts not to compromise Zevon's compositions for commercial appeal proved correct. *Warren Zevon* would have been a dramatically different record had there been any song substitution. The lone exception may have been Zevon's misbegotten, broken down car lament, "Studebaker," which was not released until the posthumous *Preludes* (2007).[29] Zevon's son, Jordan, whose own record debuted in 2008, endorsed Browne's judgment. He also expanded the case, suggesting that his father's subsequent success on his next album, *Excitable Boy* (1978), which reached #8 on the charts, ironically undermined the brilliance of *Warren Zevon*:

> I have such affection for that record because it does have so much of Dad in it. If none of his other records had done anything or if it was the only record he made and he pulled a Nick Drake and kicked off early, I think it would have been hailed as genius. But he had the success of "Werewolves of London" hanging over his head on his next album, and I think that overshadowed how great this record really was. (Mehr 2008: 13)

Zevon's popular follow-up album, and the superior record sales and status of his songwriting peers may have been deflections, but they do not diminish the significance and singularity of his Asylum Records debut. The *noir*ratives that comprise *Warren Zevon* impart an incisive, inimitable shadowy observation of the underside of an era, locale, and lifestyle. The album is an iconoclastic triumph displaying masterful maturity and composition and literary attributes devoid of pretension.

---

[29] The booklet that accompanies the deluxe edition of *Warren Zevon* (Rhino 2008) contains a photograph of a notebook open at a page with a hand-written set of songs neatly printed in capitals, presumably being considered and sequenced for Zevon's debut album. "Studebaker" is on the list, along with three eventual *Excitable Boy* songs, and "Working Man's Pay," released on *Preludes*. Jordan Zevon recorded "Studebaker" first on the tribute record *Enjoy Every Sandwich: Songs of Warren Zevon* (2004) and then on his own debut, *Insides Out* (New West, 2008).

More than any quality, it is the writing that distinguishes *Warren Zevon* from the Asylum Records catalog, more broadly from the prolific 1970s LA songwriter sphere, and more specifically from the classic *Hotel California*. The debut album revealed an abundant songwriting palette and lyrical depth that was sophisticated, intelligent, detailed, dark, romantic, poetic, psychological, geographic, historical, sly, and sardonic. *Warren Zevon* facilitated a precedent for vivid literary locality, a songwriting seam that stretches to regional rock chronicles such as Springsteen's somber acoustics on *Nebraska* (1982) and *The Ghost of Tom Joad* (1995), and the abiding drawl of Lucinda Williams' Louisiana-Mississippi essay, *Car Wheels on a Gravel Road* (1998).

Zevon's prodigious, albeit tormented, talents introduced on his Asylum debut uniformly enthralled critics, as well as his contemporaries and compatriots within and beyond music. *Warren Zevon* inaugurated characterizations and comparisons that continued throughout his career to posthumous praise, ranging from actor/musician Billy Bob Thornton's "mad magical poet" to novelist Carl Hiassen's "a genius in the truest sense." Author/playwright Gore Vidal's assessment is among the most authoritative: "There was simply nobody else writing like Warren Zevon at that time. He was one of the most interesting writers of the era, and certainly ahead of his time" (Zevon 2007: 429-33).

Within Zevon's abundant 20-album discography over a 40-year period, *Warren Zevon* enduresas a masterpiece, the quintessential document of Zevon's brilliance as a songwriter and composer. Renowned music manager and producer Jon Landau, perhaps best known for anointing Springsteen "the future of rock and roll," was an interested bystander who witnessed the Zevon work in progress. Though not directly involved in the recording process, Landau, in anticipation of producing Browne's *The Pretender*, frequented the *Warren Zevon* sessions, enough to earn an honorary "shadowboxing" credit on the album.[30] Landau's observations provide further commanding, credible testament to the virtuosity of *Warren Zevon* as a debut:

> As the record was going by, I kept thinking to myself, once again, how masterful it was. The songwriting was just state of the art. It is in reality, one of the truly great first albums. I don't know how many artists ever creatively kicked off things like Warren did. (Zevon 2007: 114)

---

[30] Browne was scheduled to play Zevon's completed record for Joe Smith, head of Elektra/Asylum. However, when Browne's wife suddenly died, he asked Landau, who knew Smith, to present the record to the company chief, which Landau did (see Zevon 2007: 114).

Chapter 12
"Chasing after vengeance": Elvis Costello's Initial Aim

David Janssen

As we all know, when it comes to significant relationships, first encounters matter. It often seems the case that impacts "at first sight" are in fact less significant than the narratives we ascribe to them after the fact. Yet, the cliché does exist, that wham-bam moment of epiphany when, awestruck, we realize our course of life has just been altered. For me, the latter was the case when I first heard Elvis Costello's voice. To borrow another cliché, I don't remember what time it was when I first heard Bob Dylan, Joe Strummer, Paul Westerberg, or any other of my most significant others in the musical realm, but I distinctly recall the moment when I first heard Elvis Costello.

I believe I was 17, sitting in what passed for the home, a trailer actually, of my high school English teacher. Once a month or so he would invite a few of us nerdy boys over to drink a beer, play epic games of Risk, and listen to music. He had an impressive vinyl collection, pearls as new and exotic as my father's box of 45s once was. One night he put on *My Aim Is True* for a spin. From the first moment, my head reeled. I no longer cared about maintaining my stronghold on Australia; I just wanted to hear that voice. The exact moment that got me was the third line from "Welcome to the Working Week": "all you got to tell me now is WHY, WHY, WHY, WHY!" That line just *summed* me up. A typical geeky kid I guess, the only role that seemed fitting was that of the misfit. Unlike my fellow Risk geeks, I played on the football team. It seemed that I was *in* every high-school social clique, but not *of* any of them. I got good grades, and I truly loved my English classes, which put me on the outs with the jocks, but my sports credentials made an uneasy match with the brainiacs as well. I had some vague desire to go to college, but my heart and soul was in my bedroom with my records and my cheap guitar, which I struggled to learn. The only thing I was sure of was that I wanted *out*; I did not want to wind up working at the lumber mill; I still feel that dread. It was 1982, a small logging town in the Pacific Northwest. That petulant voice that demanded to know WHY could not have been further from me, if you consider how time scurries in both the teen and pop realms; truly, this was a song from 1977, so it should have been nearly as distant to me as "My Baby Left Me." Yet, both arrived for me exactly on time. It was a good time later that I figured out, after studying it, that "Welcome to the Working Week" is about a girl in a magazine, about sexual frustration, about what Costello termed "emotional fascism," but the first time I heard it, that song was about me and my dread, my own "WHY" that dogged my coming of age.

My Aim Is True is not the first Costello record that I purchased; that honor goes to *Imperial Bedroom*, Costello's 1982 release. I had decided to get the new one, and what a shock when I got it home. This almost sounded like music that parents would listen to, not my parents, but it did not speak to me; that one sat for years until I had matured enough to appreciate its colors and moods, a completely different world from *My Aim Is True*, a copy of which was quickly procured by our teen protagonist who was reassured to find that the first arrow was directly on target.

When I consider the difference between the worlds of *Imperial Bedroom* and *My Aim Is True*, I am reminded of the very quality I love most about Elvis Costello: his muse doesn't like to step in the same stream twice. It might be said, in fact, that *Imperial Bedroom* is a kind of logical consequence of Costello's debut. As he sang on "(The Angels Wanna Wear My) Red Shoes," "That's what you get when you go chasing after vengeance." Beginning with "Beyond Belief," *Imperial Bedroom* has the sound of world-weariness, resignation, contrition, and yes, the maturity of someone who had caught what he was chasing just a few years ago. Like Dylan and Bowie before him, Costello also revels in marking his artistic evolutions with distinct changes in persona and look. The persona of *My Aim Is True*, however, is certainly a first impression that continues to resonate in his music and with his audience. It was almost too effective. It is worth exploring the genesis of that image.

What's in a name, indeed! Over the years, I had often assumed that the name *Costello* had been selected with the same sort of intent as *Elvis*, that the vengeful geek on the cover of *My Aim Is True* was a calculated mixture of Elvis Presley and comic Lou Costello. The facts expose my naivety, but I still insist that it's an apt pastiche. The truth is that Costello is a family name. As biographer Graeme Thomson explains, Declan MacManus's father Ross, a successful and well-known jazz musician in England, "caused a minor stir with a version of The Beatles' 'Long and Winding Road', released under the name Day Costello, the surname taken from Ross's maternal grandmother" (Thomson 2004: 21). It is somewhat tempting in that case to wax theoretical about the paternal connection, but that seems to me a dead end because, although *My Aim Is True* may be all about payback, we're not in Oedipal territory here. That all too obvious, yet problematic first name, however, gets us there in ever more interesting ways.

Harold Bloom's incorporation of the family romance in his grand narrative of the Western poetic tradition is instructive here. As he argues, a poet, in order to become a *poet*, must overcome a poetic father:

> A poet ... is not so much a man speaking to men as a man rebelling against being
> spoken to by a dead man (the precursor) outrageously more alive than himself.
> A poet dare not regard himself as being *late*, yet cannot accept a substitute for

the first vision he reflectively judges to have been his precursor's also. (Bloom
1975:19)

Of course, on its surface, this is an absurd juxtaposition. Costello would no doubt
bristle at the suggestion that he is a poet. Songwriters tend to hate that. I find myself
bristling at the conception of Elvis Presley as a poet. Yet, Bloom's idea of the poet
intentionally "misreading" the foundational precursor in order to achieve a sense
of artistic identity *works* in this case. The very nerve of claiming rock's crown by
taking "The King's" name is itself a fantastic rock and roll move. It's important
to remember that *My Aim Is True* debuted in 1977, just as the short, sharp debut
of punk was on its wane. Much has been made of the rather awkward fit between
Costello and punk, but calling himself "Elvis" may be his most "punk" gesture.
The alias itself was something of a punk staple: Johnny Rotten, Poly Styrene, Rat
Scabies, John Doe, etc. The fact that MacManus chose *Elvis* as his nom de plume/
guerre encapsulates the similarities and differences between him and punk rock.
Both share the attitude of vengeance, but Elvis also links Costello to rock tradition
in ways that most punks would not or could not stomach. Thomson explains that
taking the name of the King was not even Costello's idea: "The legend states
that the change of name took place during a drunken meeting in a restaurant on
the Fulham Road early in 1977, [with Costello's manager] Jake Riviera bursting
into the studio and shouting 'Elvis! That's it. Elvis!'... It was risky" (Thomson
2004: 78). Reminiscing on this change of identity in the liner notes to Rhino's
2001 reissue of *My Aim Is True*, Costello recounts: "I'd been given a new name:
'Elvis Costello.' It sounded like a dare. People had weirder names than that in
those days. I didn't give it another thought again until August 1977" (Costello
2001). Characteristic of Costello's elusive allusiveness, the writer expects us to
get the reference to the death of Elvis Presley.[1] The album was released in the
UK in July of 1977; King Presley died in August. When the news broke at the
offices of Stiff Records, the indie record company that had just unleashed Elvis
Costello upon the world, there was much concern. As Costello fans are well aware,
though, accidents will happen, and this turned out to be a fortuitous one: "Far from
being damaging, Presley's death only helped to secure Elvis's growing status as
a homegrown darling of the music press, as if somehow the mere presence of this
skinny, acidic, seething young man had helped kill off the bloated, embarrassing,
Las Vegas circus act that Presley had become" (Thomson 2004: 98-99).

The initial visual image of Elvis mach II is of course crucial to the distinction
that Thomson is painting in his rather melodramatic version of "The King is
dead. Long live the King," an image equally as calculated as the moniker. Yet,
the "misreading" here is brilliant in its contrast. The bespectacled twerp who leers
at us on the cover of the album is the Anti-Elvis; it is a great punk joke. Costello
admits that the creation of that image took some manufacture: "It also seemed that
the squarer I looked the better the camera liked it. The cover image of this album

---

[1]   For an interesting discussion of Costello's allusive penchant, see Griffiths (2007).

was one of the few usable frames as the rest of the session reveals how comical the whole knock-kneed stance seemed to the photographer and subject" (Costello 2001). A glimpse of some of the outtakes of that session confirms his bemusement; in some of them he looks downright handicapped. It's clear, though, that Costello's Stiff backers had their finger on the punk zeitgeist because just a dash of deformity certainly does the trick, which is why the over-size glasses work as well. Stiff co-founders Dave Robinson and Jake Riviera get the credit for "squaring" Elvis: "[Robinson] said, 'Can you try these on?' So he put them on, he was wearing some funny grey suit, we looked at him, and thought 'Elvis Costello!' And he didn't tell us to fuck off, he just said, OK … Jake was behind him, shouting: 'And don't fucking take them off!'" (Thomson 2004: 80). One of the promo posters for release of the album features the cover photo, with the following parody of Voltaire's famous quote about God: "Elvis Costello: If he didn't exist, someone would try to invent him."[2] The real punch line here, though, is that, to a great extent, Stiff did just that. So, in the beginning, Elvis Costello was an invention, a pose; this is no great find in and of itself. What is truly remarkable about this story is the absolute commitment with which Costello wore this persona.

Costello's discussion of his "muse" with Nick Kent, just after the release of *My Aim Is True*, highlights the lengths he was willing to go to give this invention a unique identity: "The only two things that matter to me, the only motivating points for me writing all these songs, are revenge and guilt. These are the only emotions I know about" (qtd. in Thomson 2004: 76). This provocative statement makes my list of top ten rock and roll quotes of all time. It is jarring, ballsy, dangerous. Five years after making that statement, Costello sat down with Greil Marcus for a historic (at least to a student of rock) *Rolling Stone* interview called "Elvis Costello Repents." The context here is the infamous *Armed Forces*-era brawl with Bonnie Bramlett in which, among other drunken inflammatory statements, he called Ray Charles a "jive-ass nigger." It was Costello's very own "we're more popular than Jesus" moment. Incidentally, I had vowed not to even discuss that incident in this article on Costello's debut, but I have come to the conclusion that, in one form or another, it is a logical result of playing the role Costello chose for himself with such utter conviction; it's "what you get when you go chasing after vengeance." In fact, it is probably safe to say that a quest for vengeance is a rather quick find in this low world.

In their discussion of his "repentance," Marcus refers back to those "two things that matter": "Those words have been endlessly quoted—I've quoted them, they're irresistible. Now you're describing that as venom—as if your artistic venom, what you put into your music, had taken over your life." I love Marcus's word "irresistible" here; it certainly sums up my own attraction (pun intended) to Costello's early phase. Costello's response to Marcus reveals his own sense of being hoisted on his own petard: "it had become a problem for me to incorporate

---

[2]   This poster is featured in Liner Notes to *My Aim Is True*. Rhino Entertainment Company. 2001.

the wider, more compassionate point of view that I felt; I was trying to put that forward in some of the songs, and it was so much at odds with the *preconception* of the image" (Marcus 1993: 233). It is not hard to see how such a powerful "preconception" would eventually become an albatross, though I would venture to wager that Costello today has moments of gratitude for his nasty little encounter with Bramlett, which helped prompt him to chart new artistic waters and modes of expression. The main reason that *My Aim Is True* matters is because it formed the irresistible concept in the first place, for it wasn't just the brilliant package that Stiff formed around the album. All of that helped to get our attention, but what won us over were the 13 songs that convinced us that he meant it, that his aim was indeed true.

That title, of course, is the refrain of "Alison," perhaps the best-known song from this debut. She is one of the eponymous great girls of rock and roll. In many ways, the song feels out of place on this "guilt and revenge" manifesto, except that one can feel the multiple dimensions of those "sneaky feelings" on this song better than any of the others. The refrain itself is a bit tricky. Is this the true aim of faith and devotion, or is it a more sinister gesture altogether? The problem with trying to answer such a question is that it's not one or the other; it's a good dose of both. The complexity of this song lies in its "compassionate point of view," certainly at the forefront of this dejected tale of a lost ideal. Yet, easily missed is the target of the singer's aim, who laments in his refrain, "I know this world is killing you." Tap on that assertion, though, and it becomes clear that the singer is the one who is dying here, at least a piece of him, a classic case of projection. As far as we can tell, Alison is as happy as Alison can be. Remember that the only thing that the singer knows for certain is that "it isn't mine." Brilliant word—"it". Costello could have used the easier "you" for that line. The singer does not attempt to demean her with that shift in pronoun, though in fact it may do just that. What he gives away in that moment is all that she could've, would've, should've been if not for stark reality's victory over his Romantic Ideal of her. And in that loss, he *feels* a complexity of emotion disturbing in its naked honesty. The way that the music stops just before the singer admits his desire to "stop [her] from talking" punctuates the sensation of, yes, vengeance that he is experiencing, and when he calls for something, anyone to "put out the big light," we realize that, in an emotional sense, this is an apocalyptic event for the singer. These are the moments of guilty vengeance that, so fluidly composed and passionately conveyed, set the template for what became a preconception that eventually needed debunking.

My reading of "Alison" is very much in agreement with John McCombe's thesis of his great essay "'A Complete Loser': Masculinity and its Discontents in Elvis Costello's *My Aim Is True* and *This Year's Model.*" In a nutshell, McCombe argues that the Elvis Costello's ultimate target is Elvis Costello, that the early phase of Elvis Costello is "marked by fear and *self*-loathing" (McCombe 2009: 193). He makes the salient point that, more than anything, Costello endeavored to supplant what had become the typical male archetypes in rock by representing the "complete loser" in the first-person. McCombe does not focus on "Alison," though a careful reading of the song confirms his central concept—that the singer is choking on the very venom he is inveighing.

In sum, "Alison" is a great soul ballad with a brilliant lyric, though in wrapping up this revisitation of *My Aim Is True*, I have to admit that I don't think all of the songs on this debut stand the test of time quite as well. Some of them, such as "Pay it Back" and "Sneaky Feelings," still contain a veneer of the "pub rock" sound of mid-1970s England that was D.O.A. by the time of the album's release and that never really translated to America. Yet, there are a handful that, like "Alison," became touchstones for many of us in the '80s. Along with "Alison," "Watching the Detectives" was a near "hit" for Costello. The song was written with a conscious design to tap into the punk zeitgeist. Costello explained, "I spent a lot of time with just a big jar of instant coffee and the first Clash album, listening to it over and over. By the time I got down to the last few grains, I had written 'Watching the Detectives'" (Costello 2001). The clever ruse of this moody song is that the blue-tinged surface of the detective show, in all its familiar violence, serves as a perfect objective correlative for the singer's frustrated and thwarted desire. "She's watching the detectives," we're told again and again, as he sits with her, stewing in his own abandonment.

Amidst all the talk of anger and vengeance, it's easy to miss one of Costello's great strengths as a writer; he can be wickedly funny. The dark humor of "Watching the Detectives" can be found in the disjunction between the song's menacing sound, which is very nearly a *noir* parody, and the mixture of ennui and unrequited desire in the viewing room, where there is no action. Costello's gifts as a humorist are well displayed on the last cut of the album as well, "Waiting for the End of the World," where Costello exploits the mundane frustration of trying to get home on the train by hyperbolizing it as an apocalyptic death wish. At times, Costello is a slapstick artist, with the humor usually aimed back at himself, as in the hilarious couplet from "(The Angels Wanna Wear My) Red Shoes: "I said I'm so happy I could die / She said, 'Drop dead' and left with another guy." Yet, the "guilt and revenge" thesis seems to work best when mixed with a good dose of satire, as it does to stinging effect on "Less Than Zero," a song that effectively demonstrates Costello's willingness to take aim beyond crimes of the heart with its acidic portrayal of "Mr. Oswald" Mosley, a prominent British Fascist of the 1930s, enjoying a 1970s resurgence in the media. Very nearly a "protest song," the singer concludes that "everything" has been compromised and reduced by the complicit acceptance of this public whitewashing that the singer witnesses.

Mentioning those songs brings me back to my first encounter with Costello and the fact that, even though "Welcome to the Working Week" resonated with me in a visceral way, I clearly didn't "get" it at first. When it comes to Costello, I am certainly not alone in this regard. How many listeners, Americans in particular, truly "got" "Less Than Zero" on first listen? Cultural difference has something to do with that, of course. Many listeners heard "Mr. Oswald" and thought JFK, which prompted Costello to pen "Less Than Zero (Dallas Version)" (Thomson 2004: 84). More than that, though, Costello's lyrical gifts demand our attention.

He's not interested in making it easy on us; it's too important, and "it" here is whatever he's singing at the moment. Of course, Costello's penchant for word play sometimes can seem a bit out of control. As Thomson puts it in his discussion of *Armed Forces*: "[The album] also revealed Elvis as both master and maniac of the word game, throwing puns, double entendres, double-bluffs and non sequiturs into the air like confetti, almost like a form of textual Tourette's" (2004: 132-33). My personal favorite example of "textual Tourette's" in the Costello canon is a line from "Strict Time," off *Trust*, his fourth album: "Try to look Italian to the musical valium." I am really not sure what that means, and I won't even try to contextualize it within the song, though I adore that tune; the line has in fact occurred to me in certain situations and is part of my lexicon. So, I celebrate the verbal mania, even when it baffles me. What I find most irresistible about Costello, though, is that his voice, in all its conviction and emotional depth, convinces me—most of the time. An artist who takes risks is going to miss sometimes. We can debate the merits of *Almost Blue* (country Elvis) or *The Juliet Letters* (classical Elvis), but it's safe to say that all Costello fans can find particular phases and stages of his artistic development and genre-hopping that don't quite do it for them. There are Costello records I prefer over *My Aim Is True* on most days, but even after 30 years, when I return to it, he still has me at "WHY?" True aim indeed.

Chapter 13

Alive on Arrival from Meridian to Manhattan: Steve Forbert as Huck Finn, Tom Sawyer, and the Next "New Dylan"

George Plasketes

That kind of youthful energy, you've got to take advantage of it.

—Steve Forbert (2011)[1]

In his rollicking, rhyming, self-appraisal, "What Kinda Guy?," Steve Forbert pronounces positively "I'm Mississippi, got the New York blues."[2] The exuberant declaration encapsulates the spirit, scope, and rite of passage perspective in Forbert's appositely titled debut album *Alive on Arrival* (Nemperor 1978). The critically admired, ten-song, folk-rock sequence provides a troubadourian tale of transition from adolescence to adulthood, from the Deep South to New York City during the mid-1970s. Forbert's youthfully familiar "follow your dream" narrative is a conceptual, autobiographical big city quest that elicits parallels extending from Chuck Berry's "Bye Bye Johnny" to the hustling premise of *Midnight Cowboy*, James Leo Herlihy's novel adapted into an Academy Award film in 1969, to an inevitable installation on the "next new Dylan" totem.

While critics conveniently invoked the Dylan deity in response to Forbert's precocious presence and talent as a songwriter, guitarist, and harmonicat, they also recognized his steadfast spirit. Forbert arrived in New York City from Mississippi on a musical mission, a wide-eyed 21-year-old idealist, heroically displaying "Huck Finn's savvy tempered with Tom Sawyer's sense of purpose" (Considine 1983).[3] In make-a-wish, law of attraction fashion, Forbert preordained his eventual

---

[1] Unless otherwise indicated, all of Steve Forbert's quotes in this chapter are from my personal interviews/conversations with Forbert (September 30 at Eddie's Attic, Decatur, Georgia) and via telephone (October 4, 2011 and January 24, 2012). Thanks to Sue Schrader at Blond Ambition PR/Blind Ambition Management for the arrangements and access. And I am endlessly, deeply grateful to Steve Forbert for his graciousness, time, thoughtful conversation, and gifts of music and song.

[2] I appreciate Steve Forbert's kind consent to quote from the lyrics of his songs on *Alive on Arrival* throughout this chapter. All songs written by Steve Forbert, Welk/Rolling Tide Music (ASCAP).

[3] Bill Flanagan also employs the Huck Finn analogy in his insightful liner note profile in *The Best of Steve Forbert: What Kinda Guy* (Nemperor/Epic Legacy 1993).

debut album's optimistic, resolute title more than a year before being signed to a record label. "I took it for granted that I got record deal and it was well received because that's what I was hell bent on doing," said Forbert. "In my mind that was reality. I was just going to have to take the time, put in the effort and go to the places and write the songs and make the right choices, which I got lucky on a lot of those choices, to make it a reality."

Alive on Arrival's covers provide revealing glimpses of those traits. The front image is a head and shoulder shot of a boyish, fresh faced, cool coifed Forbert, layered in t-shirt, open dress shirt, and blue jean jacket (see Figure I.1). The poster-like portrayal is fitting for a contemporary hip clothing retailer, a simple but stylish look that is rural South, urban and Liverpudlian, with Forbert bearing a slight resemblance to a young Paul McCartney, circa pre-Quarrymen. On the back jacket (Figure 13.1), Forbert is approximate duple Elvis—a rigid rockabilly Presley pose, firmly gripping his Gibson guitar, similar to, but a more steadfast six-string stance than, a gawky Costello on *My Aim Is True* from a few years earlier.

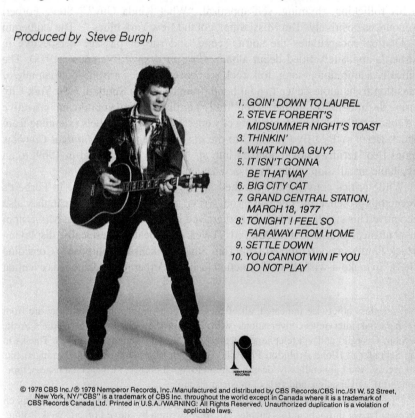

Produced by Steve Burgh

1. GOIN' DOWN TO LAUREL
2. STEVE FORBERT'S MIDSUMMER NIGHT'S TOAST
3. THINKIN'
4. WHAT KINDA GUY?
5. IT ISN'T GONNA BE THAT WAY
6. BIG CITY CAT
7. GRAND CENTRAL STATION, MARCH 18, 1977
8. TONIGHT I FEEL SO FAR AWAY FROM HOME
9. SETTLE DOWN
10. YOU CANNOT WIN IF YOU DO NOT PLAY

Figure 13.1   Steve Forbert's *Alive on Arrival* back cover.

Rainbow Dreams

Forbert shares the same hometown with Jimmie Rodgers, "the Father of Country music." In 2002, Forbert's tribute to Rodgers, *Any Old Time,* earned a Grammy nomination in the Contemporary Folk category. Their common origins in Meridian—currently the Magnolia State's sixth largest city, located 90 miles east of the capital, Jackson—are not the proverbial Mississippi musical roots. Forbert explains:

> Mississippi carries a lot of negative connotations. Musically, people go 'Wow, then you must know so and so, and drank the same water as Elvis. No he's from Tupelo, a couple hours away. But if you want to talk about Jimmie Rodgers, yes. Many of course, associate it with the Delta Blues, but that's a world away, other side of state. And, of course, a completely different life experience that I'd never been subjected to.

Forbert did not engage in a prolonged round of geographical musical chairs between other music hubs within closer proximity to Meridian—Memphis (230 miles northwest), New Orleans (200 miles southwest), Nashville, and Austin. "I went to Atlanta a year or so earlier. But I just wasn't ready to take root anywhere. I looked around, went back to Mississippi, and year later I was ready to make the move."

Among the more distant destinations on the musical map, Los Angeles did not appeal to Forbert, despite being a well established singer-songwriter paradise. In tune with the East Coast/West Coast contrasts, Forbert was unwavering in his conviction that New York's villages, rather than California's canyons and the Sunset Strip scene, epitomized his "Promised Land." Musical exploration in New York's vicinity appeared boundless between 1973 and 1977, with many modern styles simmering and surfacing—punk, hip hop, salsa, disco, Minimalist downtown composers, and Lower Manhattan loft jazz (see Hermes 2011). In Forbert's view:

> There was no comparison. Patti Smith, the Ramones, Television, that's very exciting. It was new, fresh, exciting stuff. The remnants of the most important folk world was in Greenwich Village which is where I was coming from, and lot of other stuff really interesting and happening. To me, LA at that time was kind of Eagled out musically. I never considered it.

Predictably, New York was initially overwhelming to Forbert, who recalls being homesick by the time his train from Mississippi reached the northeast corridor. The city's infrastructure was crumbling and the crime rate high, but rent was cheap. Forbert would not leave his guitar in his apartment overnight or during afternoons for fear it would be stolen. "I knew I wouldn't have to have a car if I was in New York City, so that was great," said Forbert. "It was one expense I could get around. If you could get there and get an apartment, then if you needed to you could sing on the streets. You can't sing on the streets in LA. I expected it might come to that."

And it did, almost immediately. Busking on street corners, in train stations and subway platforms became a defining dimension of Forbert's New York newcomer narrative. He documents the experience in detail on one of the album's centerpiece songs, "Grand Central Station, March 18, 1977." Elizabeth Koda-Callen's watercolor illustration of Forbert singing in public that accompanies Paul Nelson's lead record review of *Alive on Arrival* in *Rolling Stone* (July 26, 1979: 57) further reinforced the street-singer image. "I didn't hate having to do that, I simply saw it as a challenge," said Forbert.

Forbert gravitated to Greenwich Village and its flourishing club circuit. He religiously lined up for hoot nights at the renowned Folk City, and at the seminal punk rock den, CBGB's, where he landed prime opening slots for bands ranging from Berlin Airlift and the Shirts to Velvet Undergrounder John Cale and New Wave trio the Talking Heads (Chris Franz, Tina Weymouth, and David Byrne, before Jerry Harrison joined). As the "resident folkie," Forbert was comfortable in the predominantly punk environment, absorbing some of its attributes into his acoustics.[4] During afternoons, Forbert frequently "auditioned" his own songs, recording solo material with the club soundman, Charlie Martin, which he would play back, listen to and self-critique. After noticing the energetic edginess of Forbert's folk-rock sound during performances at the club, Ramones managing partners Danny Fields and Linda Stein adopted him as a client.

Forbert found more-folk friendly venues along Bleecker Street, among them The Other End and Kenny's Castaways, where he was offered his first paying gig. Eighteen months into New York City residency, Forbert's quest for a record contract received significant impetus when venerated *New York Times* music critic John Rockwell attended one of Forbert's solo shows at Kenny's Castaways. Forbert recalls:

> He wrote this glowing review that kicked everything off. I was still an unknown I hadn't proven anything except to one guy, with some influence, who liked the show. It was the *New York Times*. It was John Rockwell. It was right on my home turf and all the record companies were in New York, and they read it and the next day they were curious. It was enough to get record companies interested immediately, that's what it did.

Beyond his hooky "next new Bob Dylan" lead, Rockwell praised Forbert as "wonderfully talented and assured ... the kind of performer who makes you realize his worth the minute he begins to sing," and for having the "ability to transcend the folk genre into something broader and more massively appealing" (1977). Almost exactly one year later (22 December 1978), Rockwell again leaned

---

[4]   Forbert dismisses the suggestion that his aggressive acoustic guitar playing is "anti-punk" or "folk punk."

on the "next Dylan" brand in another Forbert review, but placed the comparison in the conclusion rather than the lead.

The endorsement from such a prominent critic and publication proved pivotal for Forbert. "It carried a lot of weight, more than demos," he said. "I did demos forever, did tapes for people who turned me down that I met later who wanted to sign me. That review alone was a year worth of work or nine months of slugging it out, done overnight. It would have taken longer had Rockwell not written that article."

After considering several record company offers, Forbert signed with Nat Weiss and Nemperor Records, a division of the Epic label. Working with producer Steve Burgh, Forbert fastidiously shaped 10 songs into his debut. The album was not conceived as markedly "Side One: Mississippi/Side Two: New York City," yet there is what critic Paul Nelson identifies as a "rare affecting wholeness and unity of mood" (1979: 58). "It's conceptual in the sense that we wanted to keep it unified: 'kid comes to the big city and these are his reactions, period,'" said Forbert. "Only a few songs made the transition to New York from Mississippi."

The first five songs on the retro release of early Forbert recordings, *Young Guitar Days* (2001), were culled from the *Alive on Arrival* sessions. Among the notable outtakes is "House of Cards," Forbert's poignant, bittersweet response to hearing the news of Elvis Presley's death during the summer of Son of Sam in New York City.[5] Just as "House of Cards" would have, in Forbert's view, "been too much of a distraction and detour" on the debut, songs that wound up on Forbert's second album, *Jackrabbit Slim* (1979)—notably the #11 hit single "Romeo's Tune"—clearly did not fit *Alive on Arrival*'s conceptual framework either.

Alive on Arrival was recorded totally live with no overdubs. The sparse, but tight production resourcefully retained the restless vitality of Forbert's live solo performances that "suggest a wider range than the pious intimacies of folk" (Rockwell 1978: C33). Though chosen "out of the blue" by Forbert to be his producer, Burgh proved to be acutely attuned:

> Steve Burgh took what I was doing live in the clubs and brought in the right players, the right engineer and he made it all sound believable. He didn't lose anything in the translation from the studio and putting it on tape, mixing it, and the entire process of making it into a record. Steve shepherded that whole project through really well. Everything was focused and very much in the here and now. I think that's what came through on that record.

The well-crafted tunes are guided by an effortless sense of melody framed by a simple, organic sound and a conspicuous vocal style. Forbert's dexterous guitar-playing is a crisp acoustic mode, both strumming and aggressive, complemented

---

[5]   Liner notes to *Young, Guitar Days* (Rolling Tide 2001) include Forbert's concise recollections of his early New York City days.

by arresting, harmonica solos, beginning with the album's opening quiver and threaded throughout as hooks, lengthy bridges, textures, and accents.

The raspy, Rod Stewart resonance of Forbert's voice exudes a wispy innocence that floats firmly, with an occasional whisper. His distinct delivery and "vigorous phrasing" are marked with " irresistible vocal winks"—teasing, slight hesitations, extensions and pronounced syllabic accentuations on hard consonants such as "b"s, "t"s and "k"s (see Rockwell, 1977; Nelson 1979: 57). The unique technique routinely punk-tuates and momentarily prolongs verses. "Flash" and "cash" stretch into "Flassshhh" and "Cassshhh." In "Going Down to Laurel," the postponement is perfectly placed: "They tell me this great life can always ... (BEAT) ... end." Forbert's singing style is natural, not affectation:

> It's not something you ever want to think about. [Critic] Bill Flanagan pointed out to me in 1988 or so, "You often say the last word of a line and delay it." I never even noticed this. I don't think about it. Furthermore, you don't want to think about it or dwell on it. It becomes self-conscious. I would hate to think that Billie Holiday really thought about singing.

Big City Cat and Rat Trap Towns

> I'm supposed to be happy
> I'm here where it's at
> I'm a face in the crowd
> I'm a big city cat
>
> —Steve Forbert, "Big City Cat" (1978)

Alive on Arrival has a journal-like quality, each of the ten songs an entry loosely linked into a narrative that is more observational than overwrought confessional. Nor is Forbert's early twenties tale burdened with brooding introspection and epiphanies; the point of view is precocious without being pretentious. The lyrics are pleasingly earnest, yet proactive, with overarching themes such as the trials and tribulations of transition and the bittersweet world of growing up. There are doses of disillusion without despair, and twinges of loneliness and yearning. Idealism and innocence, aspirations and disappointments intermingle.

The opening song, "Going Down to Laurel," launches the album with steadfast ease. The homespun hook is enticing: a harmonica flutters, followed by four percussive taps—a muffled echo of the single concussive gunshot snare that initiates "Like A Rolling Stone"—that cue a simple lead guitar chord progression, pedal steel strands, and sturdy backbeat to frame Forbert's hoarsey vocals.[6]

---

[6]   The quivering harmonica in "Going Down to Laurel" was a frequent alarm clock for me early in graduate school, courtesy of my roommate John Lang, who routinely cued

Youthful buoyancy abounds as Forbert heads down the road, one hour south of his hometown. He is "glad to be so young, talking with my tongue, careless, taking chances, crazy in my day." There is New York foreshadowing in the Laurel trip, with "everything so loud and fast," but determination that defeats distraction in the "dirty stinkin' town": "But me, I know exactly what I'm going to find."

"Steve Forbert's "Midsummer Night's Toast" may be more a parting shot than a tribute, a (not so) fond farewell, time-to-move-on, *American Graffitti* moment. Among those Forbert has a "Here's to" nod for are: "the shitty jobs that I despise, pretty women made for cash, dashing daddy's son who's such a flash, the filthy rich, lucky dogs, his sister's drag job, regrets, and debt." While "singing and sulking, sitting and listening with a young man's ear to all the rainbow dreams," including his own, Forbert has grown weary of the "rat trap town" and is "trying to get over where the wall breaks down." (Four songs later, in "Big City Cat," Forbert uses the same Meridian modifier—"rat trap town"—to characterize Manhattan.)

Beyond the album's initial Mississippi melodies, a subtle sense of transition and introduction ensue. "Thinkin'," is a strumming, psychoanalytic ode, in which Forbert cautions that excessive analysis of life's options will leave you "stranded behind, losing your mind." It is ambiguous whether the meditation is a mirrored inner dialogue—"I look in your eyes and see shackles and chains"—; a ditty of self-doubt—"you're chasing some notion you've misunderstood"—or an other-directed, universal observation of someone "flashing madness all over the place." Forbert provides analysis—"There's so many depressions all plowed in your brain / trace them too far, and they'll drive you insane / You're twisted so tight now you hardly can talk"—and prescribes a simple, self-help solution: "Get out in the daylight and go for walk."

The rockabilly, Buddy Holly hiccupy "What Kinda Guy?" is a lighthearted litany of personality traits, an introduction of sorts that plays like a catchy, lyrical precursor to a contemporary social network profile. Among the series of qualities that Forbert rattles off are "love some turkey but don't eat lamb; no sweet potato but I do like ham; don't wear pajamas and don't sniff glue; kept my jacket but lost my tie." He further confesses: "I'll tell you truly / That I sometimes lie."

The core of *Alive on Arrival*'s chronicle lies in the four-song sequence of New York scenes that follows. There is a noticeable shift in tone to a more somber sensibility, beginning with the loss of innocence contemplation, "It Isn't Gonna Be That Way":

> You've traveled so far
> the wind in your face
> thinking you've found the one special place

Alive on Arrival for breakfast. It was John who introduced me to the album, proud of the fact that he and Forbert were from Meridian. John claims that his sister, Leah, dated Forbert briefly. I find that believable, but not his other assertion that the "Johnny" in Forbert's songs are referencing him.

> where all of your dreams will walk out in line
> and follow the course you've made in your mind
> Hey, it isn't gonna be that way. It isn't gonna be that way.

The parable is painfully forthright:

> I came on my own and felt much like you
> I thought I was king and knew what to do
> but everything burned and fell from my hand
> I had to turn back or build a new plan.

Forbert accepts that he is not a god who can walk out in time where no one has been and reveal what he sees. The caution continues to closing:

> You'll just have to live and see what you find
> and take it from there and follow the signs
> You think you can live and dream your own fate
> and think you can wish and walk through the gate
> It isn't gonna be that way.

While Harry Nilsson's version of Fred Neil's "Everybody's Talkin'" murmurs as an undercurrent throughout *Alive on Arrival*, the Joe Buck theme song ascends to a more audible echo in "Big City Cat." Forbert's vivid cityscape is a *Midnight Cowboy* montage cluttered with sights and sounds—buildings, people, weary old stairway wobbly and worn, motors, racket, traffic, horns, hissing heaters, banging pipes, dogs barking, babies crying, all-night screaming and laughing—and an "eye for an eye, tooth for a tooth, sigh for a sigh" attitude. Forbert is deep in the well of the edgy, rat trap town, where "everyone's looking, but who really cares." He is "getting skinny, walking on eggs, climbing on thread," worst of all, cannot even pee because of the lunatic following him down by the john. David Sanborn's lively alto saxophone provides a curious and contrasting celebratory shade to Forbert's face-in-the-crowd frustration.

"Grand Central Station, March 18, 1977" is an equally lucid diary of a cold winter day, with crowds and trains coming and going, and Forbert down near a doorway busking:

> Howling out words and banging out chords
> think what you will, laugh if you like
> it don't make no difference to me
> I open my case and might catch a coin
> but all ears may listen for free.

The autobiographical tune is an allusion, an East Coast companion composition to Joni Mitchell's "For Free" from 1970. "It was totally impulsive and from experience. I came home and wrote the song," recalls Forbert. "It's the other side of the mirror, and happening to live other side of that scenario. It wasn't conscious. It's just like an answer to that song." Resolve resonates in Forbert's station sidewalk solo:

> I took my chances and luck saw me through
> stayed until I'd finished
> played what I pleased
> and poured out my sound.

The aching "Tonight I Feel So Far Away From Home" lives down to its title, sinking deeper into distance and despair. "I saw a man break down today / break down into tears." However, the tenor recovers on the album's closing two songs, rising into acceptance and arrival with "Settle Down,"—"if I seem a little crazy / it's just because I am … my wheels are mainly on the track"—and punctuating positively with the piano-driven moral of the journey on "You Cannot Win if You Do Not Play." The song has sustained as a ceremonial closing tune of Forbert's live performances.

Beyond Dylancarnate

> Evoking the young Dylan has become a cliché for artists of this sort, but, in this case, Mr. Forbert deserves the evocation.
> —*New York Times* music critic John Rockwell (1978: C33)

> Nobody is the new anybody.
> — Steve Forbert (Zollo 1991: 154)

Alive on Arrival was not considered a commercial hit, settling in toward the lower end of the Top 100 chart for several weeks. However, the cream of the critic crop, particularly the New York-based music journalists—Rockwell, Nelson, Robert Christgau, J.D. Considine, Bill Flanagan, Robert Palmer—were captivated with Forbert's auspicious debut. Despite his peculiar dismissal of the second side of the album, Nelson was adamant in his *Rolling Stone* review: "Because nothing, nothing in this world, is going to stop Steve Forbert, and on that I'll bet anything you'd care to wager" (1979: 59).

Alive on Arrival earned an honorable mention on Rockwell's *New York Times* "Top 10 for 1978," a prestigious list highlighted by the Talking Heads, Rolling Stones, Steve Reich, Neil Young, Ian Drury, Bruce Springsteen, Linda Ronstadt, Blondie, Wendy Waldman, and Warren Zevon (1978: C21).

Rockwell's appreciation sustained from his earlier reviews of Forbert's live performances, in which he proclaimed the yet unsigned Forbert "already a star." It was Rockwell who initiated the Dylan allusion with Forbert, though he qualified the convenient comparison, conceding its duality: "How tired Bob Dylan must be to hear young performers compared to him, and how tired young performers must be to encounter that totemic invocation" (1977). One year later, *Alive on Arrival* further reinforced the merit of Rockwell's initial assertion of the Dylan duality (see above epigraph). In a 1980 profile by Palmer in *Rolling Stone*, Forbert explained that his approach was purely pragmatic more than it was about being a Dylan derivative:

> I'm not trying to be the new anybody ... I wanted to do my own material, I didn't have any money to hire a band ... and I think I was right in assuming that Greenwich Village would be the best place to perform my own material and possibly get some attention, move on to making records and all. It wasn't an effort to be *like* anyone; it seemed to me like the most practical way to go about getting things my way. (Palmer 1980: 8)

Forbert comprehended the critical cliché. He was not deterred or distracted by the Dylancarnate designation and its accompanying blessing/curse dichotomy:

> I had to expect some of it. I'm in Greenwich Village—I'm playing a harmonica and acoustic guitar and I'm leaning heavily into lyrics. Come on, what am I going to say?—"You're crazy." It was just like, you know this is coming and I had to be prepared for that if things took off and I had any recognition—which might not have happened—but it did. But that had happened to other people as well. Everybody knew who had been paying attention that it was cliché already. I knew that it was a cliché, too. But I didn't take it literally or feel like, "That's right, I am 'the new Dylan.'" It wasn't something I had to live up to. I just wanted to be up to being a good songwriter and make some good records.

Timing was also a factor that shaped *Alive on Arrival*'s production. During the late 1970s, the imminent synergy of the music marketplace continued to accelerate toward the onset of music video with aesthetic and commercial consequences for artists and their approach to music. Forbert considered the context and the transition into the MTV era:

> I caught the tail end of a time when you could go in, set up with some talented musicians and a good engineer in a good studio and record live. First three records I did had absolutely no overdubs. And you could get it on the radio. But records began to get more crafted after that, needless to say when electronics sound started to become common place—Soft Cell and Human League—the whole landscape changed. And then suddenly you had to conceptualize videos and think that way, and look, adapt, perhaps loosely act and become more visual in a massive new way. Never before, I mean, Fred Astaire and Ginger Rogers, Bing Cosby, they were in a lot of movies, but most musicians weren't. Big Joe

Turner ... is he in any movies? I caught the tail end when I could do a natural recording. Live, just the same as Sam Phillips had done it.

But that was over by 1983. And everybody had to react to that. Then you couldn't just *record* records you had to *make* them. There were certain people that had always *made* records—the Beatles, Phil Spector—they constructed and were very meticulous. But that became the thing. You could still be a Gordon Lightfoot or America. But attitude, image, presence, that became a lot more of a factor. I had some attitude that made up for *Alive on Arrival*. But we got into a thing where attitude become much more a contrived part of a person's act.[7]

In the aftermath of his debut at the cusp of the 1980s, Forbert recorded three albums for Nemperor over the next four years. In 1983, his proposed fifth album was rejected, triggering a prolonged, complicated contract dispute with Columbia that lasted until 1987. Suspended in legal limbo, Forbert relocated from New York City to Nashville.[8] He emerged from the entangled exile on Geffen Records' roster, releasing two gems, *Streets of This Town* (1988, produced by E Streeter Garry Tallent) and *The American in Me* (1992).[9]

In the two decades since, Forbert has continued to be an unwavering folk rock troubadour. His impressive body of recorded works—16 studio albums, four compilations, three live sets and nine website exclusives—confirms his consistency and conviction living up to, if not exceeding, what Forbert said he wanted to do from his early days playing in Greenwich Village, simply to "be a good songwriter who makes some good records."

The spirited, steadfast Huck Finn/Tom Sawyer qualities that Forbert demonstrated while moving toward his debut destination during the 1970s persist. Forbert remains road relentless, predominantly playing in clubs and mid-level venues, which are well suited for his engaging, energetic, one-man-band basics—acoustic guitar, harmonica and boot-stomp plywood panel percussion. Though the "next Dylan" divination remains unfulfilled—as it has been, and will be

---

[7]   Forbert's "MTV moment" is a cult curious cameo as Cyndi Lauper's boyfriend, wearing a tuxedo jacket and carrying a bouquet of flowers as he enters the door of an apartment party, in the pop feminist "Girls Just Want to Have Fun" video in 1984. Forbert's promotional fill in the video stemmed from his admiration for Lauper when she fronted the band Blue Angel before she became a colorful MTV sensation. "I thought she was modern day Brenda Lee. I saw a lot of their gigs and they knew I was a fan," said Forbert.

[8]   Keith Urban ("Romeo's Tune") and Roseanne Cash ("What Kinda Girl") are among artists who have added some country credibility to Forbert's catalog with their cover versions of his songs. On a more abstract level, Willie Nile, whose self-titled debut was released in 1980, might be considered the "next Steve Forbert" as his sound, style, and career course bear some resemblance to Forbert's.

[9]   The most detailed and presumably accurate account of Forbert's record label limbo can be found in Bill Flanagan's interview for *Musician* magazine (October 1988). In addition to Geffen, Forbert has released records on Giant, Rolling Tide, Palladin, 429, and Koch, and via exclusive downloads on his website.

perpetually and predictably for any singer-songwriter—the distant imprint persists to permanence, an indelible, mythical mark on Forbert. Over the course of his 36-year recording career, there are few interviews, articles or citations (this essay obviously included) that do *not* contain a requisite reference to Forbert's one-time status as a "next" or "new Bob Dylan."[10] The constant rewind commonly elicits a polite, articulate, well-rehearsed recitation from Forbert, delivered with script-like consistency. Forbert securely dismisses frequent critic and loyalist laments that he deserves a bigger following. Nor does he consider characterizations such as "underappreciated" or "unsung" pertinent prefixes. He prefers plainly—"singer-songwriter."

Steve Forbert's debut record may not have announced a "Second Coming," but it marked an arrival with enduring qualities for both artist and album. Late 2011, *Alive on Arrival* received the meritorious "deluxe edition" treatment as an expanded, two-record set with a remastered original, demos, outtakes, and live versions. Reflecting on his debut, Forbert is content with his debut album's legacy:

> *Alive on Arrival* wasn't a "big" record. It was still an underground thing, not Top 40. But it was promising. It was a good record and I'm proud of it. But that wasn't a thing that would really distort your outlook where suddenly you're looking through a fish eye lens. I was fairly comfortable with it. I expected it. It wasn't too weird. Things blew a lot wider and became noticeably different when "Romeo's Tune" became a hit on my next record. A debut generates a lot of promise. At least it did back then. Today may be more live or die on the first record.
>
> It's still the best record I ever made. To listen to one of my records, I don't hear a lot of things I would change, and I'm very critical of myself and anything I listen to. That one is pretty pleasant, even yet to listen to. That, to me, must mean something.

---

[10]   Perhaps more coincidental than cosmic, the connection continues as Forbert's *Over with You* and Dylan's *Tempest* were both released on September 11, 2012. In January 2013, the video for Forbert's super storm single "Sandy" has a glaring subterranean subtext. The no-budget shoot at the Asbury Park, NJ boardwalk, directed by Guy Daniel, features Forbert turning a stack of white notecards with "Sandy's" handwritten lyrics. The video conjures Dylan's "Subterranean Homesick Blues," from the visuals and props to intimations of "don't need a weatherman to know which way the wind blows."

Chapter 14
Ready for the House: Jandek's Inert Unveiling

Nicole Marchesseau

There it was in my hands: a CD of Ready for the House, *one of the university's five nearly untouched Jandek albums I borrowed from the library's audio stacks. I awaited the half-crazed, deranged musical anomaly that Irwin Chusid had described in his chapter devoted to this supposedly quintessentially outsider artist in* Songs in the Key of Z: The Curious Universe of Outsider Music *(2000). And after listening to Jandek's first album I had been drawn into something; I just wasn't sure what it was.*

"Naked in the Afternoon," the opening song of Jandek's 1978 debut, *Ready for the House*, is classic Jandek, establishing the tone for the rest of the album as well as the next several decades' worth of recordings.[1] From the onset we hear jangly acoustic guitar, its warbling stretched-tape sound summoning images of a beaten-up, untuned pawnshop discard. Sameness quickly sets in. A wispy voice enters, shuffling gently, synchronized loosely with the guitar:

> I got a vision, a teenage daughter
> Who's growing up naked in the afternoon
> I know a brother close to his mother
> Who stays out late in the evening time
> I keep repeating, it takes a beating
> To grow up naked in the afternoon
> You are a cowboy if you wear those boots
> You are a cowboy when you wear those boots
> Big time in the city
> I got a letter
> I read in the paper
> It said a man was shot to death
> It said a cow gave poison milk[2]

---

[1] *Ready for the House* was originally released by The Units. The band name was changed to Jandek after threats of litigation by a California band that had already laid claims to the former name.

[2] Countless transcriptions of Jandek lyrics appear on Seth Tisue's website, Guide to Jandek, http://tisue.net/jandek/. Tisue has relayed that many of the transcriptions were

The unrelenting sound of instrument's open strings continues for nearly the entire album. Although musical stasis overwhelms at times, a sense of purpose emerges as *Ready for the House* progresses.

"First You Think Your Fortune's Lovely," the next track, is much like the first. Specific lyrics stand out: Jandek's sentiment, "I feel so lonely, my rapture's painted on the floor," resonates with the dirge of the guitar. More often than not the voice chants on a central pitch, dipping from time to time to the flattened tone below and occasionally rising to a minor third above. Music is guided by incanted words. It seems blues- or folk-derived, though these blues are suspended in the absence of harmonic progression.

Dynamic levels fluctuate throughout the album, at times peaking into distortion. Consonants sibilate and pops occur where words are pushed out more forcefully. Careful listening reveals barely perceivable digital noise, perhaps partly attributable to the numerous transfers of the album: from reel-to-reel to record to CD.

Midway through *Ready for the House* Jandek's rhythmic trudge grinds to a halt at the conclusion of "They Told Me About You," yielding to the stronger (if fluctuating) tempo of "Cave In On You." "European Jewel"[3] closes the album and contrasts with all previous songs: exclusive open-string playing is left behind; an electric guitar is used instead of the ghostly acoustic; and a more conventional open-string major chord tuning flavors the track. While still far from mainstream expectations, "European Jewel" upholds a comparatively normative state. This reprieve only lasts so long though—the song ends abruptly, mid-word, after nearly five minutes. Did the reel run out of tape? Was the recorder switched off abruptly? Regardless, "European Jewel's" sudden choke is no mistake; it serves as a sign of a story that has only begun.

Cover art for *Ready for the House* consists of an out-of focus photograph of a living room. Jaundice-yellow blinds conceal a portion of a large picture window. The space, with the exception of rose-colored molding and window casing, is adorned in shades of teal—dark for the floor, muted for the couch, and a softer, lighter hue for the walls. A book with a blurry face on its jacket leans against the window. Two others prop up one end of the sofa. There is a small table adorned with a garish red silk flower arrangement and two more unidentifiable books. The room is orderly. A sense of visual balance is achieved in the photograph's standard 'rule of thirds' composition. Neither "Jandek" nor the album title is found on the cover. All we see is the photograph.

---

collaborative (email message to the author, September 22, 2011). Lyrics from "Naked in the Afternoon," *Ready for the House*, Corwood Industries, 1978 (CD 0739), courtesy Corwood.

[3]   Marked as "incomplete" on the *Ready for the House* version of the song.

Figure 14.1   Jandek's *Ready for the House* cover art: blurred and anonymous

The university needed their CDs back and I complied with their recall requests. Bitter cold winter weather prompted me to place one of the iridescent discs on the tip of my finger before exiting the house so I wouldn't need to fumble for it in the car. I bustled out holding with what felt like a thousand things under my arms and made it down the concrete steps then across the slippery sidewalk. But before reaching the car I lost my footing and fell down hard onto the ice. The CD cracked badly when I went down.

Who or what is Jandek? Judging by the first three albums—*Ready for the House* (1978), *Six and Six* (1981), and *Later On* (1981)—Jandek is the nom de guerre of a DIY singer-songwriter making music inspired by folk and blues traditions. However, the project transforms itself with *Chair Beside a Window* (1982), when other musicians are heard, though their full names are never disclosed, save for their appearance in song titles like "Nancy Sings" or "John Plays Drums." Over the years, musicians (of varying degrees of musical aptitude) enter and then leave the Jandek world. Their transience, along with Jandek's lyrical content, contributes to sense of the project as one that is autobiographical. If this is so, much of it is filtered through metaphor. Even more is simply left out, although over the course of the project's development some of these gaps are filled. Perhaps strategically or maybe just incidentally, Jandek reveals only enough to intrigue, not enough to satisfy.

Still adhering to once-common tape-culture practices of the 1980s, all Jandek albums are available by mail-order through Corwood Industries, a label based in Houston, Texas, that handles Jandek albums exclusively. The company is run by Sterling Smith, also the presumed central performer of the project. Jandek and/or Smith has repeatedly declined interviews. In fact, there were no live performances until 26 years after the release of *Ready for the House*, when in 2004 Jandek first appeared at the Instal Festival in Glasgow, Scotland. Despite the decades-long disinclination to play live, since 2004 there has been a boom of performances worldwide. Sonic and video documentation of these performances is available for purchase through Corwood Industries. Live CDs and DVDs bear titles such as *Glasgow Sunday* (recorded 2004, released 2005), *London Tuesday* (recorded 2005, released 2008), and *Hasselt Saturday* (recorded 2005, released 2009). On stage and in fan and reviewer discourse Smith is often referred to as "The Representative from Corwood Industries" or more simply as "The Rep," or "Corwood."[4] In performance, there is little to no acknowledgement of the audience, nor is there any eye contact. After the concert's final number, The Rep and the other musicians involved leave the stage without further word to the audience, and (despite enthusiastic response from the crowd) there are almost never any encores.[5]

Although Corwood has largely avoided journalists, there have been two exceptions: in 1984, *Spin* writer John Trubee recorded a telephone interview with Smith; and in 1999, journalist Katy Vine tracked down "the person believed to be Jandek" for an informal conversation, forming the basis of an article which was later printed in *Texas Monthly* (Vine 1999). In 2004, a documentary, *Jandek on Corwood*, was released. The film explores Jandek through the eyes of his observers, and features interviews with a host of authoritative parties, including

---

[4]   There are distinctions between The Representative from Corwood Industries, Corwood Industries, Jandek, and Sterling Smith. Jandek appears to be the name of the musical act, The Representative of Corwood Industries is the name of the performer, Corwood Industries is the business name, and Smith is Corwood Industries' proprietor. Although these distinctions became clearer over time, often the different names are still commonly used interchangeably.

[5]   Jandek performed the only known encore at a hometown concert at Rudyard's in Houston, Texas, April, 2009 (see http://blogs.houstonpress.com/rocks/2009/04/aftermath_ jandek_at_rudyards.php (accessed November 2, 2011)).

reviewers, a radio programmer, and Vine herself. Filmmakers Chad Friedrichs and Paul Fehler aim, at least in part, to humanize the person behind Jandek in the film,[6] but not without exploring the "mystery man" aspect of the project. In what was surely not a coincidence, Jandek's first live performance happened within months of the completion of the documentary. The concert came unannounced. Most fans only realized that the event had taken place afterward, when photographs of the show began surfacing online—the images taken of the live performer bore an uncanny, albeit aged, resemblance to the pale figure appearing on many earlier album covers. Indeed, in one lyric from the Glasgow concert Jandek declared that he had "made the decision to get real wild" (*Glasgow Sunday* 2004).

The library's lost or damaged materials replacement cost was so exorbitant it prompted me to acquire the CD myself and give the library the recording directly. Luckily this was an option. The price for twenty Jandek CDs directly from Corwood was eighty dollars, a comparable price to the replacement cost of one damaged library item. And so I composed my request for a mixed box which would include a replacement for the damaged disc and made out my first check to Corwood. Two weeks later, the box arrived. Twenty-one CDs were neatly lined up (Corwood Industries sent an extra to replace the library's recording) within the brown paper covered box. In between two of the jewel cases there was a Corwood catalogue and a short note.

Jandek's world is a weave of interrelated and self-referential lyrical, musical, and visual motives. Throughout the project, lyrics from albums crop up later as album titles. On *Ready for the House*, "First You Think Your Fortune's Lovely" contains the words "staring at the cellophane," a line later reincarnated as the title for a 1982 release. On the same track from *Ready for the House*, occurs the phrase "chair beside a window," which became another 1982 album title. The trend continues: further on, we hear the line "somebody in the snow," words which resurface as the title of a 1990 release; and in "They Told Me I Was a Fool," we hear "follow your footsteps," the title of a 1996 album. Jandek's borrowing of lyrics for future releases extends consistently beyond *Ready for the House* as well; likewise, the self-referencing goes well beyond appropriation of song lyrics for future album titles.

Fast-forward 22 years after Jandek's debut, and we find Jandek reversing the former practice of using song lyrics for album titles. On "It's Your House," the second track of the spoken-word release *Put My Dream on This Planet* (2000), Jandek confirms that he is indeed "ready for the house." Reciting in a typical shuffle blues cadence (but without musical accompaniment), he describes the building's structure in detail:

---

[6]   Phil Milstein, interview with the author, September 26, 2011.

You know, I'm ready for the house
Let me build my house
I got a dream
Of granite rocks
And iron bars
Let me build my house of rock and steel
Let me build my house
Let me build my house
I got this dream
Of rock and granite
Black flecks in the gray stone it's granite
It's heavy rock
It's heavy rock
It's cast iron
Cast iron and heavy rock
Don't got no glass
Don't got no wood
Don't got no synthetic fiber
No foil products.[7]

These words, taken from the middle portion of the poem, are only a small segment of the track, which clocks in at over 22 minutes. Of course the *Ready for the House* reference is obvious; but the poem is full of revisited and reworked lyrical themes from throughout his oeuvre. "Granite," "iron," and "rock," for instance, also resurface in different lyrics along Jandek's journey. We hear about "granite rocks" and "iron spikes" in "Ten O'Clock Shadow" on another spoken-word album, *This Narrow Road* (2001). On *London Tuesday* (recorded 2005, released 2008), a live recording of one of the few solo acoustic Jandek performances, we hear another reference to "iron."

Other lyrical motives are also resurrected on *London Tuesday*. The characters first introduced in "Naked in the Afternoon" re-emerge: the teenage daughter, the cowboy, and the cow that had previously given poisoned milk. A reference to "the castle" suggests the house/fortress planned in "It's Your House." The following excerpt is from "Part Three" of *London Tuesday*:

The innocence is lost
The king took a vacation
Left all the subjects to their own
They sabotaged the castle
Iron chains they pulled down
The teenage daughter smitten to the core

---

[7]   Lyrics from "It's Your House," *Put Your Dream on This Planet*, Corwood Industries, 2000 (CD 0706), courtesy Corwood.

The boots the cowboy wore
Leather torn and spurs broken
The cow in the pasture
Didn't come home last night.[8]

Jandek's self-appropriation extends to sonic aspects of the project as well, "European Jewel" being a fine example. Beyond the incomplete version on the debut, the song resurfaces three more times on *The Rocks Crumble* (1983). These later versions have seemingly arbitrary numbers appended to them—613, II, and 501. As previously mentioned, the *Ready for the House* rendering is the first Jandek song with near-standard guitar tuning, though the open strings are pitched somewhat higher than usual and the instrument's highest string is slightly flat.[9] "European Jewel" is also the first Jandek song to include motivic material: a descending bar chord riff. The song is strophic. Initially, we hear the opening riff, then Jandek settles into a verse-alternating-with-guitar-riff pattern. After each riff, the guitar rests on an open string chord while a verse is sung. This continues for nearly five minutes.

Each version of "European Jewel" on *The Rocks Crumble* is reworked, though we still hear variations of the riff on the first incomplete version. On "613" the major chord tuning is replaced with tuning in fourths. We still hear the descending chord motive but pitches are altered due to the change in tuning. Slackness in the instrument's sixth (lowest) string makes the pitch less predictable: it often growls roughly a semitone below. This results in a muddier, rougher-sounding resting chord, lending an ominous feel to the song. Adding to the darker atmosphere is a slower, drawn-out tempo. All three renditions of "European Jewel" on the 1983 album appear consecutively. "II" features haphazard, mostly arrhythmic drumming, as though the drummer is paying no heed to the guitar and vocals. As on "613," the tempo is slower than on the incomplete version. Drums plod on again on "501," and likewise show a flagrant disregard for rhythmic regularity. The relentless guitar riff remains present and the lyrics are restated, the tempo winding down towards the end of the song. This last version has a burnt-out feeling; the journey has come to a close, and the "European Jewel" microcosm is now completely encapsulated within the larger Jandek meta-story. The wrapping-up of "European Jewel" leaves the impression that the song and the larger Jandek project are connected by an aesthetic that goes beyond lyric cross-referencing.

---

[8]   Lyrics for *London Tuesday* 2008 (CD 0793) transcribed by fan Nate Wilson, posted on the Guide to Jandek archives, http://mylist.net/archives/jandek/2008-October/005127.html (accessed September 22, 2011). Courtesy Corwood.

[9]   It is unclear as to what the original tape might have recorded as far as the tunings were concerned. Raised pitches may be a result of altered tape speed. This possibility was suggested by Milstein in the interview with the author. The tuning indicated in this essay represents what is heard on the most recent CD release of *Ready for the House*.

Thematic development serves the purpose, in part, of filling gaps within the Jandek narrative. As with the musical and lyrical developments explored above, visual threads contribute to Jandek's project. In *Jandek on Corwood* (2004), Amy Frushour Kelly comments on the use of negative space:

> He takes pictures that are all about negative space. Negative space is ... when you have a sculpture and say the sculpture has two hands and it's like this [creates an "O" shape by connecting thumbs and index fingers of both hands]. The space right in between the two hands, where there's nothing there—the void—that's negative space. And I find it significant because his storytelling very much has to do with negative storytelling, leaving out very important parts.

Such an aesthetic is at work on the cover of *Ready for the House*. Much of what we see is fragmented. Only part of the sofa is in view, a portion of the window is cut off, and there is a stray chair leg from an otherwise out-of-frame chair. In keeping with the gap-filling that Jandek does musically and lyrically, in subsequent cover art we are allowed visual access to the other rooms and objects within the house. However, again, the viewer is usually not privy to all objects in their entirety. For instance, indoor photographs show almost whole guitars (*Staring at the Cellophane*, 1982; *Living in a Moon So Blue*, 1982), and incomplete drum sets (*The Rocks Crumble*, 1983; *Interstellar Discussion*, 1984; *On the Way*, 1988). Other cover art features images of The Rep himself (*Foreign Keys*, 1985; *Nine-Thirty*, 1985). He is outside, often in front of a white siding or clapboard-clad house though sometimes in front of a brick wall (*Modern Dances*, 1987; *Blue Corpse*, 1987). His facial expressions can be contemplative or occasionally blank, but often he is smiling. More white houses are revealed, as are more portraits—of instruments and Jandek.

One particular photograph points to the theme of decay or disillusionment, paralleling in that respect the lyrics explored above in *London Tuesday*. On the front of *I Woke Up* (1997) is a couch which could well be the one seen on *Ready for the House*. The sofa is now outside, clearly having been exposed to the elements for an extended period of time. Ivy grows down its back and the once teal upholstery is now torn and sun-bleached. Behind the couch are familiar white houses. The cover of *I Woke Up* serves to fill the negative space left by the passage of time since *Ready for the House*. Jandek's creations at once fill in the project's existing voids and create new ones, thus contributing to its ongoing sustainability.

Listening to the 60-plus Jandek recordings that I had amassed through numerous orders placed with Corwood Industries was far from effortless. Some of them were easier than others to listen to. Ready for the House *and the several releases that followed were not too hard on the ears, but the same could not be said for the likes of* Khartoum *(2005) and* The Humility of Pain *(2002)—I admittedly could only get through the latter once. Eventually I had to ask myself, "was I a fan of Jandek?*

Did I actually like Jandek?" It appeared to be more of a fascination than anything else.

In 1983, the first known review of *Ready for the House* appeared in *Op* magazine, one of the then primary but now defunct tape-culture outlets for independent music in the United States. The author was Phil Milstein, who, in a later interview with me, mused that Jandek's sonic and visual art was perhaps game-like to its creator. Though unprovable, Milstein's idea works well with the deliberate branching out of the project: Jandek begins as a solo musician who eventually acquires a hodgepodge band of coming and going performers; he experiments with playing the piano, the harmonica, and fretless bass; and releases spoken word albums. In 2004, Jandek performs his first live show. This happens shortly after the release of a documentary about him in which we never see any footage of Jandek himself (except for still shots of the album covers), though we are privy to samples of correspondence between the filmmakers and Corwood. Screenshots of handwritten phrases like "You may not get all the answers you want it's better that way [*sic*]" appear at various points during the film. Milstein's thoughts that the Jandek project is a deliberate unfolding "game" contrasts somewhat with writer Danen Jobe's ideas concerning Jandek. Jobe, author of an upcoming work of fiction concerning a character based loosely on Jandek, regards the project as the story of a man passing through life, as documented through music and photographs.[10]

Jandek has not been overlooked by enthusiasts of music situated on the edges of genre and taste. Reviews published in *Op*—including those which followed Milstein's—marked only the beginning of a wider interest in Jandek. WFMU radio programmer Irwin Chusid devoted a chapter to Jandek in his publication exploring the musically bizarre, *Songs in the Key of Z* (2000). On a more cursory level Jandek is mentioned in relation to Kurt Cobain's record collection in a 1993 article about Nirvana appearing in *Spin*. The rocker ironically declares that "He's not pretentious ... but only pretentious people like his music" (Steinke 1993: 49). In more recent years, Jandek has performed with respected musicians worldwide, including long-time fan Thurston Moore of Sonic Youth. Distribution of Jandek recordings has also expanded: though Corwood Industries continues to make CDs available through mail-order by cash or check, independent online record stores Aquarius Records and Forced Exposure now also carry Jandek recordings. Reissues of early vinyl are also available through Jackpot Records, the label that promoted the show with Moore. While getting the word out through larger distribution channels has facilitated acquisition of Jandek albums, media discourse associated with the widening of Jandek's world has also contributed to a parallel extension of the project. Although there is still some mystery shrouding the artist behind Jandek, the passage of time has resulted in the unveiling of the story through interconnected visual, lyrical, and musical motives, gradually building a coherent

---

[10]   Danen Jobe, e-mail messages to author from 2008 to the present. Jobe is the author of *Niagara Blues* (forthcoming 2013).

whole while also contributing to the project's forward trajectory. Jandek, whose wayfaring ramshackle blues hobble first unveiled itself in near musical stasis in *Ready for the House,* continues to work carefully and deliberately, revealing only enough to maintain interest and carry momentum.

Chapter 15

Rickie Lee Jones: "Acquired a Cool and Inspired Sorta Jazz"

George Plasketes

At first glance, Rickie Lee creates an effect; at second glance, she creates an impression; and on the third pass, this lady creates a stir.

—music journalist Timothy White (1981: 39)

On April 6, 1979, two weeks after the release of her self-titled debut album on Warner Bros. Records, Rickie Lee Jones was booked as the musical guest on *Saturday Night Live*, the NBC broadcast network's popular late-night satire. The iconclastic variety show, in its fourth season, provided an influential two-song showcase for musical artists inserted between the Not Ready for Prime Time Players comedy sketches and Weekend Update faux news segment Following the customary introduction by the week's guest host—actor Richard Benjamin— Rickie Lee Jones commenced with her catchy hit single, "Chuck E.'s in Love." Jones, wearing her signature crimson red beret and cradling her acoustic guitar, fronted a large backing ensemble that included a horn section and a trio of interracial background singers swaying and finger snapping in street corner doo wop jive. For a 24-year-old who had been thrust into sudden notoriety and had limited live performance experience, Jones displayed striking poise and stage presence before the in-studio and national television audiences. She later admitted how uncomfortable and out of control she felt on the show, though it was not evident (see White 1979: 43). Jones deftly hit camera cues and sang with self-assurance; her sidewalk savvy seamlessly translating with slight swagger and soul to New York's Rockefeller Center's Studio 8H stage (Figure 15.1). The surrounding set design may have offered some sense of security for Jones. The urban iconography presented small-scale street corner spectacle that reflected her background, image, music, and lyrics: a lamp post, flame breathing industrial barrels in the foreground; the stage floor strewn with paper particles, hubcaps, steering wheels and miscellaneous auto parts. (In her subsequent live shows, Jones often incorporated a parking meter on stage, which she would load with change to time her set.)

The live, unedited scene was vibrant, a revelatory glimpse of Jones's conspicuous sound and sassy sketch of a street character named "Chuck E."

Figure 15.1   Rickie Lee Jones, *Saturday Night Live* performance, New York City,
            April 1979.

and his fabled love affair with a cousin.[1] The three-and-a-half-minute song, "with roots halfway between Van Morrison's 'Domino' and Lowell George's 'Dixie Chicken'" (Flanagan 1987: 395), had curiously infiltrated the era's Top 40 airwaves alongside Donna Summer, Supertramp, the Cars, Bad Company, Blondie, and Journey. Later in the late-night, for her second song, Jones delivered an intimate, torchy "Coolsville," despite the show's producers' preference for the upbeat "Danny's All Star Joint." The totality of Jones's charismatic *Saturday Night Live* performance—the music, lyrics, vocal and visual styles—was a first impression that emitted an aura echoing Jon Landau's Springsteen prophecy— "I saw rock and roll's future"—from five years earlier, only this vision was a less grand, jazzier variation with a Boho vibe.

"Cool" instantly became the requisite critical catchphrase affixed to Jones, a tag reinforced by the album cover image depicting her in a red beret dragging on a cigarillo. One month later, *Time Magazine* (21 May 1979) hailed Jones as "The Duchess of Coolsville," the title for the news weekly's feature by Jay Cocks. *Rolling Stone* (31 May 1979) followed with a Stephen Holden profile, "Rickie Lee Jones in the cool world." Despite Jones's desperate attempts "to avoid the whole LA rock star trip" (Holden 1979: 9), the critical groundswell continued in conjunction with the debut album's impressive chart position, sales, and sold out shows for Jones' performances. In August, the cool climaxed with Jones's appearance on the cover of *Rolling Stone* (9 August 1979). The headline—"Rickie Lee Jones: The Story of a Runaway Success"—contained biographical and career connotations that were presented in a six-page interview with Jones by one of the era's pre-eminent music journalists, Timothy White. The arresting cover image

---

[1]   When *Rolling Stone*'s Timothy White asked Rickie Lee Jones, "Who was Chuck E. (Weiss) in love with?", she blushingly replied, "His cousin. I mean that's what I heard." She explains: "There was this phone call from Denver one day and it was Chuck E. And (Tom) Waits hung up the phone and said, 'Chuck E.'s in love!' I just made the rest of the song up" (White 1979: 43). The "mystery lover" in Jones's "Chuck E.'s in Love" resembled— without matching the magnitude of—the lingering intrigue surrounding the narcissistic "probably think this song is about you" identity in Carly Simon's "You're So Vain" from 1972. Rumors and hints—many spurred by Simon herself during interviews—evolved into an unsolved mystery that featured letter clues, backward recorded whispers, and contests. The lengthy list of candidates includes Mick Jagger, Warren Beatty, David Bowie, David Cassidy, Cat Stevens, Nick Nolte, Howard Stern, Watergate source Mark Felt, David Geffen, and Simon's love interest and guitarist Danny Armstrong. A slightly lesser degree of identity inquisitiveness accompanied one of Dan Fogelberg's most popular songs, the excruciatingly sentimental ballad, "Same Old Lang Syne." Fogelberg readily admitted the account was autobiographical, but he always refused to name the high school sweetheart who was the subject of the song. Following Fogelberg's death from prostate cancer in 2007, Jill Greulich (formerly Anderson), revealed that she was the "old lover at the grocery store" that Fogelberg ran into on a snowy Christmas Eve in the mid-1970s. In 2008, the site of the song—Abington Street in Peoria, Illinois where the convenience store was located—was designated "Fogelberg Parkway"in honor of the singer.

portrayed newcomer Jones in a guarded, crouched pose with one arm crossed and the other extended, a racy enchantress wearing a black bra, lace skirt, white heels and a beret. Jones characterized her "look" as "a stripper and German cabaret dancer" (Maiscott 2011). Jones's style and manner projected a forward glance toward Madonna, Cyndi Lauper, and MTV's videogenics on the horizon, two years away, and extending well beyond to Lady Gaga decades in the distance. Jones further foreshadowed the onset of music video with a twelve-minute, three-song film/video in which she is depicted as an innocent city girl walking the streets with her friend, while a sleazy Tom Waits look-alike is stalking them from his car.

Rickie Lee Jones (Warner Bros., 1979) is routinely recognized as one of the most auspicious debuts not only of the 1970s, but of all time. Anchored by a jazzy bop hit single "Chuck E.'s in Love" (#4 *Billboard* Hot 100) and the snappy "Young Blood" (#40), the album was a success both critically and commercially. In addition to its platinum sales status and a place in the Top Ten (#3), the album earned five Grammy nominations—Record of the Year, Best Pop Vocal Performance, Best Rock Performance, Song of the Year, and Best New Artist, the lone category that Jones won.

Paul Zollo, editor of *Song Talk* magazine, the journal of the National Academy of Songwriters, wrote that Jones's debut was "unparalleled in popular music" (1991: 133). "Unparalled" perhaps, but also unlikely. Rickie Lee Jones's arrival was somewhat of an anomaly. The hipster, neo-Beat, jazz cool that defined her debut were improbable sources of such widespread success and acclaim during a period when New Wave and Disco were the prevalent sounds in the music marketplace. In 1978, the *Saturday Night Fever* soundtrack, a double album of disco and multiple hits from the Bee Gees, now transformed from their Beatlesque beginnings, stayed at #1 for an astounding 24 weeks, or approximately six months. The thriving singer-songwriter genre, particularly the prosperous California strand, peaked mid-decade, with many key artists leveling off or in transition within a shifting music scene. Among some of the most distinguished female artists, Carole King's *Coming Home* (1978), notably the song "Disco Tech," exemplified the unsettled state.[2] After seven straight gold-selling, Top 20 albums, King's album failed to reach the Top 100. Vocalist Linda Ronstadt sustained with Peter Asher produced formulaic interpretations of the pop rock "oldies" and material from relatively unknown songwriters such as Kate McGarrigle, Warren Zevon, and Karla Bonoff. Protégés such as Bonoff, Wendy Waldman, and Nicolette Larson, a backup singer for Neil Young, managed flashes of short-term successes.[3] Following *Court and*

---

[2]   For a concise discussion of Rickie Lee Jones and the generation of women artists coming of age in the late 1970s within the context of singer-songwriter and punk movements, see Gardner (1997).

[3]   Larson's hit version of Young's "Lotta Love" did not impress prominent critic Dave Marsh, who wrote, "Larson epitomizes the worst of LA Seventies pop rock. So laid-back it's a wonder she can stand up. Her debut is a certified snore ..." (Marsh and Swenson 1983: 288).

Spark (1974), Joni Mitchell's gravitation toward jazz persisted with *The Hissing of Summer Lawns* (1975), *Hejira* (1976), and *Mingus* (1979), a tribute album on which she wrote lyrics for jazz composer Charles Mingus's melodies. In addition, Mitchell continued to diversify her artistry, easing her painting further into the foreground as evidenced in the *Mingus* album cover.

"Rickie Lee in some ways filled the hole left by Joni," suggested longtime California music scene figure Ron Stone, who later managed Jones, among many other artists (Hoskyns 2006: 254-55). Jones did not embrace that premise, and was brazenly outspoken about her fellow female songwriters, particularly Mitchell and her lack of authenticity as a jazz artist.[4] "It's a genuine place where I'm coming from when I write or sing my songs," said Jones. "They're certainly more lyrical and genuine and less full of crap than any of the other girls I see singing songs these days in their disco wetsuits or whatever" (White 1979: 44). Jones's influences were more rooted in Coleman Hawkins, Betty Carter, Peggy Lee, Sarah Vaughan, and Van Morrison than they were Joni Mitchell, Carole King, and Linda Ronstadt. Of her female contemporaries, Joan Armatrading and Laura Nyro were among artists she most closely identified with. Jones's street poet image, style and "Billie Holiday on a rock bender" presence on stage countered the prevailing music industry gender codes for appearance and manner:

> I thought, Janis Joplin drank on stage, why can't I ... I was probably like Amy Winehouse ... too bawdy too raucous. The way people saw me, the singer-songwriter, the expectations of behavior—I wanted to defy that right away, that's why I went for that stripper look. I wanted to open it up. [Rather than] this is how we dress, this is how we act. I'm gonna get up and dance. (Maiscott 2011)

Rickie Lee Jones was more hip than hippie, more Sunset Strip scenester and Santa Monica Boulevard lass than lady of the canyon and its confessional clique. Jones's self-described "lower-middle class hillbilly hipster" background is a vagabond narrative checkered with drifters, rounders, and traveling vaudevillians. A frequent runaway and teenage hitchhiker whose spirit evoked Sissy Hankshaw, the lead character in Tom Robbins's novel *Even Cowgirls Get the Blues*, Jones's restless rebel resume includes episodes of being expelled from school, stealing a car ("in the name of romance, so it was all right" (Holden 1979: 12)), hopping freight trains, living in hotels, and sleeping under the Hollywood sign.

Jones adapted the proverbial "walk on the wild side" into her own sphere—"'the jazz side of life'—the other side of the tracks, it's a real insecure constant improvisation" (White 1979: 44). Jones inherited the resolute jazz identity from her father, Richard Loris Jones, an amateur jazz musician, who taught his daughter

---

[4]   For Jones's critical assessment of her contemporaries, particularly Mitchell, see White (1979): 44. It is also astounding that Jones is excluded, without a word or reference, from Gillian G. Gaar's *She's A Rebel: The History of Women in Rock & Roll* (1992).

her first songs—standards such as "Bye Bye Blackbird," "The Sunny Side of the Street," and "My Funny Valentine."[5]

After back and forths between Chicago and Phoenix, and then Olympia, Washington, Jones settled in Los Angeles in 1973 where she could "be the teenager I always wanted to be" (Holden 1979: 12). She hung out with a street bohemian crowd, and eventually began performing in bars, inns, theaters, and clubs in Hollywood and the Venice Beach vicinity. Her repertoire included rhythmic spoken-word monologues, interspersed with jazz and show tune standards, racy covers, and some original songs. Jones allied with hepcat Tom Waits and local musician Chuck E. Weiss. Together they formed a trio of Troubadour regulars and Tropicana Motel residents. Waits and Weiss were family figures to Jones—"real romantic dreamers stuck in the wrong time zone" (White, 1979: 43). The kindred spirits provided a nucleus of outsider sources, shades and scenes, both real and imaginary, who inhabited Jones's songs as close cousins to Waits's hobo saint characters. On his album *Blue Valentine* (1978), the back cover and inner sleeve depict Waits and the then-unknown Jones—"the mysterious blond"—posing as lovers on a Thunderbird hood, and Weiss on the other side of the car in the inner sleeve shot.[6]

Waits became the artist Jones was most frequently associated with. Her jagged street scenes, shadowy figures, and underbelly attraction are analogous with Waits's hard-luck tales. The seedy glamour of late-night bars, dives, and diners, and the antiheroes hanging out within, further suggest that Jones frequents the same noir neighborhoods in Los Angeles that Warren Zevon revealed on his self-titled debut in 1976. "My writing is all from a particular neighborhood, I can pick any person on this street or the next and just be them," said Jones (Holden 1979: 13).

In critic Timothy White's view, Jones's songwriting:

> evokes is the disarming determination of certain stratum of the American underclass—The Great Disconnected, a network of restless runaways, hobos and disenfranchised strivers who have resolved to reinvent their shattered lives rather than be beaten down by prevailing values. They are gentle eccentrics and hardened hooligans who have nothing to lose and no desire to compromise. (1981: 39)

---

[5]   "The Moon is Made of Gold," a lullaby written by Jones's father in 1954, has long been a part of her live sets. Jones performs the song (along with "Autumn Leaves") on Rob Wasserman's *Duets* (1985) and recorded a newer version of the song for her album *Balm in Gilead* (2009).

[6]   One of the most thorough, engaging composites of the personal and professional interrelations between Jones, Waits, and Weiss is chronicled at www.tomwaitslibrary.com/extras/rickieandchuck.html.

Sidewalk Charlemagnes—Bragger, Sal the Weasel, Kid Sinister, Old Black Cat, Cecil—loiter in alleys, barrios, and on street corners, "dancin' in the welfare lines / actin' like some jerk off fool." Some are "in the wrong end of behind the eight ball black," another "in a half-way house on a one-way street, a quarter past left alive." A desperate mother seeking deliverance, petitions, "Swing Low, Saint Cadillac."

Warner Brothers was among several record companies interested in Jones's four-song demo cut under the auspices of A&M Records and circulated by her manager at the time, Nick Mathe. Allegedly, it was the song "Easy Money" that sealed a record deal for Jones. A friend of hers, Ivan Ulz, sang "Easy Money" over the phone to Lowell George. After hearing Jones sing her own rendition in Topanga, George recorded the song for his post-Little Feat solo debut, *Thanks I'll Eat It Here*, which premiered the same month as *Rickie Lee Jones*. (Two months later, on June 29, George died at age 34 of an apparent heart failure.[7]) George claimed that it was his recording of "Easy Money" that swayed Warner Brothers to listen to Jones and sign her to a contract. Both Jones and Warner producers discredit George's account. "It's not true. It's a nice story, though," Jones told music critic Bill Flanagan (1987: 358, 397).

Warner vice-president of A&R, Lenny Waronker, followed up the demo and "Easy Money" intrigue by going to hear Jones perform during "Hoot Night" at the Troubadour. Waronker, whose father Si founded the Liberty Records label, was one of the most fruitful, artist-friendly producers of the era, and a vital figure in cultivating "the (Burbank) California sound." He had been a part of the Warner-Reprise transformation from AOR/pop into a hip Hollywood entertainment empire. The quintessential LA record company, overseen by Mo Ostin and Joe Smith, was at the forefront of the proliferating Laurel Canyon scene in the late-1960s, competing with David Geffen and Elliot Roberts's Asylum label for the surplus of singer-songwriters. Beyond its roster that featured Joni Mitchell, Neil Young, James Taylor, Gordon Lightfoot, and Van Morrison, the Warner label established a reputation for its willingness to take chances on "backroom talents," developing atypical LA artists such as Randy Newman and Van Dyke Parks, both Waronker recruits, and tulip tiptoeing Tiny Tim (see Hoskins 2003; 2006).

Once offered a contract, Jones's stipulation for signing with Warner Brothers was that Waronker, along with his longtime production partner, Russ Titleman, would produce her record. Waronker was more tolerant of Jones's eccentricities than most of the other Warner executives. According to Jones, the producing duo appreciated her "wild and unusual personality" and gave her "complete space" (Cocks 1979, May 21) "She came in with this massive attitude, to the point where you were kind of intimidated," said Waronker of their first meeting (Hoskyns 2006: 254). "Rickie Lee was fairly wild, but you knew you were in the presence of

---

[7]   Ironically, or fittingly, George is eulogized in the Rickie Lee Jones cover issue of *Rolling Stone* (9 August 1979: 9, 22-23, 25). A thin black banner—*Lowell George 1945-1979*—looms above the *Rolling Stone* logo and Jones's image on the cover shot, announcing the lengthy tribute inside the issue.

something special," added Titelman. "The sessions were spontaneous, explosive; she never done this before, she was just a kid with a guitar, but she knew exactly what she wanted. At the end of the session, we played through the album and she sat there and asked, 'Is that me?'" (see White 1992; "Chuck E. Weiss and Rickie Lee Jones" in www.tomwaitslibrary.com).

There was no commercial calculation by Waronker and Titlemen on Jones's debut. Together with Jones, they shaped a record with a sound that is gracefully oldtime. The studio approach personified Jones's affection for "playing rooms and finding those old clubs ... like shows used to be, to make people feel that they went out and a really special time" (Holden 1979: 13). The album's 11 songs of well-groomed bop—a jazz fusion with folk and rock—are a harmonically rich blend of West Coast melodicism and East Village hip, highlighted by unique song structures, jazz ambience, shifting rhythms, nocturnal shades, a Beat sensibility, and intermittent cabaret sentiment. Crisp acoustics, funky frets and plucky bass lines anchor the production, with horn arrangements that feature Tom Scott and Chuck Findley. Moods in the song sequence shift without being uneven or interrupting continuity. The jubilance in "Chuck E's in Love" and "Danny's All Star Joint" contrast with the wistful reflections in "Company" and "On Saturday Afternoons in 1953." There is dreamlike distance in "Night Train," a shadowy lullaby about a mother and her baby running from the devil, out of reach of the law. Urban snap in "Young Blood," accented by the inimitable, ubiquitous background vocals from Doobie Brother Michael McDonald.[8] Spectral longing, humor and metaphor in "The Last Chance Texaco." Street corner solitude in "After Hours."

The unifying facets of the album's striking sound are Jones's distinctive delivery and vocal style. The range of Jones's musky, nasal, little girl intonations are delicate and forceful, rising from faint moans to full throated high notes and occasionally plummeting to deep jazz groans as evident in the low line that concludes "Coolsville." The airy textures of Jones's supple vocals and syncopated phrasing are a sweet and sentimental, rough and tumble confluence that concurrently conveys maturity and innocence, sophistication and awkwardness, breathlessness and power. Her voice slightly slurring in an anguished alto, Jones lithely shuffles, swoops and slides across her lyrics, scatting in between phrases and eliding words in vintage hipster, speed speak (see Cocks, 1979, May 21).

Jones's vocal delivery emphasizes the sound of words more than enunciation, which often obscures the rich language of her cool cat lyricism. "It was more important to round it out than to make sure you knew what I was saying," said Jones. "Singer first, speaker second" (Maiscott 2011). When asked about one of Jones's songs during the debut's recording session, Randy Newman, who

---

[8]   An episode of the animated comedy *Family Guy* (Fox) pays humorous homage to McDonald's frequent background vocals, as (an animated version of) McDonald is enlisted by lead character Peter Griffin to repeat all of Peter's lines of dialogue by singing them during a scene.

contributes synthesizer on the record, replied, "Can't tell. Couldn't understand a word" (Cocks 1979, May 21).[9]

True to her own characterization of Chuck E.'s walk, Jones' lyricism and sound reflect "a cool and inspired sorta jazz" with cinematic and show tune shadings. Beat language emerges in the album's very first line, as Jones's character wonders why Chuck E. "don't come and p.l.p. with me." (Loosely translated, 'p.l.p.' means, "public leaning post," as in leaning on a friend.) Couplets emerge from improvised rhyming exercises set to finger-snapping rhythms, with pure sound superseding literal sense. The jukebox at "Danny's All Star Joint" goes "doyt-doyt" (which Jones intended to rhyme with "joint"; see Holden 1979: 13). Fragments of poetic phrases accent the exotic incongruity of the musical vignettes, complementing Jones's syncopations: "white boy's cool," "under-riders on the boulevard," "barefoot cruise," "forty weight hard," "chippyin' your little kiss," "Winston lips of September."

Despite its artistic and commercial accomplishments, *Rickie Lee Jones* did not instigate a wave of jazz pop rock into the 1980s. Perhaps the album's most enduring artistic attribute lies in Jones's distinct, sinuous vocal stylings, which routinely echo influence in songs by a litany of female artists that followed, among them Edie Brickell, Jill Sobule, Mary Margaret O'Hara, Sheryl Crow, Victoria Williams, Jewel, Angie Hart (Frente), Karen Peris (Innocence Mission), Feist, Corrine Bailey Rae, and Regina Spektor.[10] Jones's post-debut Grammy recognition is also singing specific. In 1989, Jones's duet with Dr. John, "Makin' Whoopee," was awarded a Grammy for Best Jazz Vocal collaboration. Her cover collection, *It's Like This* (2000), also received a nomination for Best Traditional Pop Vocal Album.

The follow-up to Jones's debut, *Pirates* (1981), defied her own assertion that "following an incredible debut is impossible" (Zollo 1991: 136). The album was equally bold and arresting, promptly demonstrating that *Rickie Lee Jones* was not a novelty, accident, or contrived, bawdy Bohemian pose, as a few critics suggested. *Pirates* went Gold, reaching #5 on *Billboard* with charting singles "Lucky Guy" (#64), "Pirates (So Long Lonely Avenue)" (#40), and "Woody and

---

[9]   (Fortunately) Jones's vocals are deciphered in print in the album's liner notes, which reveal the album to be a good read. In addition, Jones's stripped-down, live acoustic set on *Naked Songs* (1995), which includes five songs from the debut album, lives up to its title as it provides a pure aural glimpse of Jones's vocals and lyrics.

[10]   Jones appears to be keenly aware of the vocal imitators and soundalikes, whether they are inadvertent or intentional. Her responses range from being flattered to feeling ripped off. "Jewel doesn't bother me at all because she's a little kid and you can really go 'Wow. She just really really … that's the specific time and place—Me. And then it became her and now she's doing it the way she sees it. Sheryl Crow's older and should have known better. She's a professional singer who decided to do other people. Jewel was just really really influenced (see http://1001-songs.blogspot.com/2011/06/in-more-than-30-years-since-chuck-e.html).

Dutch on the Slow Train to Peking" (#31). Like its debut predecessor, critical praise, several five-star reviews, and another provocative pose by Jones on the cover of *Rolling Stone* (6 August 1981) and an accompanying feature by Timothy White, highlighted *Pirates'* achievement.

Jones's 15 records over three decades have consistently remained true to the jazz roots, atmospheric textures, and idiosyncrasies displayed on *Rickie Lee Jones* in 1979. There is little obligation to commercial or mainstream market appeal in Jones's discography, which, in part, may account for her catalog being spread across seven different record labels. Jones's uncompromising romanticism, old club sensibility and counter-celebrity posture persist:

> I don't want to sell it to you and I won't do it. I'll show up so you know I'm here.
> And I'm really tired of people going, "Are you still making records?" Because
> yes, I'm still making records. I didn't sell it then and I'm not going to sell it now.
> I still think if you make a beautiful piece of music they might not all run to it in
> the first six months but they will find it and that's what you came to do. ("Rickie
> Lee Jones Interview" 2011: 1)

Chapter 16
Metallica Kills
Deena Weinstein

Metallica's electrifying debut, *Kill 'Em All*, ushered in more than just a new band — it was the debut of a new metal subgenre: thrash. The album was far and away the most exciting release from the now ultra-famous mega-selling band. It is also their best album, even if it was their worst-selling effort. It is their best to those who seriously appreciate excitement, and it was exciting to those metalheads with a taste for speed who heard Metallica's debut when it came out.

There is a world of difference between a band's debut album and their first album, even though the music is the same. The debut stands for itself; the first album is the beginning of a series through which it is heard. Listening to *Kill 'Em All* after hearing the band's subsequent work, especially after their major label breakthrough, *Master of Puppets,* in 1986, and certainly after their massive hit *Metallica* (aka *The Black Album,* 1991), is an archeological experience. Coming upon *Kill 'Em All* when it came out in the summer of 1983 was a jaw-dropping event. In contrast, I found their subsequent releases to be disappointing. None were as exciting; several were simply execrable.

Debuting the Band

Debut albums are branding tools—and possibly none is more so than *Kill 'Em All.* It branded the band by its logo, sound, and words. And the band's name was also a brilliant branding move: Metallica arrogates to itself the significant part of the genre's name, metal, a literal semantic cue associating the band with the style of music and audience (Androutsopoulos 2000). No well-paid branding consultants could have done better (Colapinto 2011). The band's co-founder, Lars Ulrich, a would-be tennis pro from Denmark who had moved to California while in high school, had a variety of ideas for that crucial piece of creative work, naming a band that did not yet fully exist. Among his alternatives were "Blitzer, Grinder, Helldriver, Thunderfuck, as well as 'Lars Ulrich' spelled backwards" (Quintana, "San Francisco Heavy Metal"). In the fall of 1981 he spoke with his San Francisco-based friend Ron Quintana, a metalhead DJ. Quintana was going to start a metal fanzine and was trying to come up with a name for it. Two of his proposals were "Metal Mania" and "Metallica." Ulrich told him that "Metal Mania" was the better of the two. Possibly it was, but his advice might have been motivated by wanting to use the other name for his yet-unnamed band (Quintana).

The band's logo was another early band creation that served as a visual brand. It was created by April 1982 when Metallica recorded its first demo to send to venue bookers in an attempt get gigs. It was also printed on the band's business cards sent with that tape. The card also contained the contact phone number and the term "power metal"— a phrase thought up by the original bassist, Ron McGovney, to describe their sound.[1] The logo spells the band's name in a chunky sans serif font. The first and last letters are distinctive, larger in size, in a different italicized font, and sporting wickedly sharp serifs. The center letter A is slightly modified too. The band's subsequent demos, concert fliers, album covers, and t-shirts maintain that logo.

The debut album's proposed title was supposed to have a similar meaning as the band's name: *Metal Up Your Ass*. However Jonny Z. (Zarzula), their manager, co-producer, and label honcho, put the kibosh on that title. This was going to be his label Megaforce's first release, and he had his own business concerns.

Kill 'Em All may have been the band's debut, but it wasn't their first recording. That honor, such as it was, belongs to a track on a compilation album of LA metal bands titled *Metal Massacre*, It was released in June 1982. Metallica's contribution was the song "Hit the Lights." *Metal Massacre* was also a debut, the first release of a new indie metal label, Metal Blade, started by 21–year-old Brian Slagel. A metal fan who worked as a buyer for a metal record store in Los Angeles, Oz Records, Slagel also put out a 'zine, the *New Heavy Metal Revue*.

I remember picking up that 'zine at the same store in Chicago where months later I'd first hear *Kill 'Em All*. The issue had a cover story on metal guitar-god Michael Schenker (many seemed to worship his work including Lars Ulrich, Slagel, and a guitarist up in San Francisco, Kirk Hammet). A friend of Slagel met Ulrich who was wearing a tour shirt from a then-obscure British metal band, Saxon, at a Schenker concert. Slagel recalls that:

> The next day, the three of us went around LA, trying to scrounge all the European imports we could find. Ulrich was a record collector. We would laugh, because we would go over to his house and he would have a drum set sitting in the corner, not even put together. He was always like, "I'm gonna put a band together!" And we were like, "Yeah, sure you are, Lars!" (Epstein 2009)

Ulrich had been introduced to James Hetfield and to his roommate, friend, and bass player Ron McGovney, by Hugh Tanner, former guitarist in Hetfield's band. McGovney remembers that:

---

[1]   McGovney said that he thought the term "had a nice ring to it," adding that Lars was not amused: "I can't believe you did such a stupid thing!" The term stuck, at least for the name of the first demo, recorded in April 1982 (McGovney 1997, cited in http://www.ilikethat.com/metallica).

[when] he and Lars first jammed, I thought Lars was the worst drummer I had ever heard in my life! He couldn't keep a beat … he just couldn't play. So I told James, "This guy sucks, dude". And I told them to do whatever they wanted to do and I was just gonna stick to photography, at the time I was taking pictures for bands like Mötley Crüe" (O'Connor 1997)

Hetfield wouldn't disagree with that assessment. "Certainly the first time Lars and I got together for a jam, [forming a band] didn't happen, there was no vibe," he admitted. But he overlooked that defect when he learned that there was an offer to make a recording: "At that time in my life I wanted to play music, I didn't want to work" (Hetfield, *Kerrang!*).

Ulrich got Slagel to include his not-yet-a-band's effort in the compilation. The song "Hit the Lights" was recorded in late 1981 on a Fostex tape machine. Hetfield's friend, guitar teacher Lloyd Grant, played lead guitar. The song was recorded several other times before the debut album. "Hit the Lights" was originally written in Hetfield's and McGovney's prior band, Leather Charm. Soon after recording the song for the compilation, Ulrich placed an ad in a local rock magazine that was answered by Dave Mustaine, who became the band's guitarist. Mustaine spoke to me about his part in Metallica's origins:

When James Hetfield, Lars Ulrich and myself had met there was the New Wave of British Heavy Metal and there was the punk scene. There was also my belief about how a guitar should be played, Lars' belief about how a song should be created, and James' belief about how riffs should be patterned. The three of us came together and started writing songs and the nucleus of Metallica was born. (Dasein 1992: 16)

In April 1982, their song "Hit the Lights" was on their first demo tape, commonly called the Power Metal demo. It was also recorded on their "No Life 'Til Leather" demo produced in late 1982. All of that demo's seven songs appeared, in more or less revised form, on the debut album. (The song was also re-recorded for a second printing of *Metal Massacre*.)

Slagel, Quintana, and Zarzula were among a host of mediators who were critically important to Metallica's emergence. All were defiantly indie, not connected with mainstream media companies. And all were committed metalheads. Bassist McGovney served as a mediator too in his role as photographer. It was through his contacts that he got Metallica a prime slot, their second live gig—at the Whiskey on Sunset in LA. Then there were the numerous tape-trading fans who also worked as music distributors, paying to do so rather than making money. Metallica's demo tapes, made in garages and at live gigs, were copied and sent around the world. They were the major advertisers for early Metallica.

One tape-trader brought a Metallica demo recorded at a show at the Mabuhay in San Francisco to Jonny Zarzula's stall in a New Jersey flea-market. As Zarzula recalls:

> It wasn't very well recorded, but to me it was like the most perfect sound I'd ever heard. We hustled together $1,500 for them to rent a van to come out to the East Coast and play some shows. When they got here, it was like, "We have no money to get back, no place to stay—we're livin' with you!" (Epstein 2009)

Shortly after nearly burning down Zarzula's house, the band relocated, living and playing in a grimy rehearsal room in Queens, New York that the thrash band Anthrax suggested.

Thrash metal wasn't actually started by Metallica; like all good cultural creations, it has many ancestors. Thrash was a made-in-America product which was fashioned from raw materials imported from the UK. Its decidedly British roots were in heavy metal and especially in the so-called New Wave of British Heavy Metal (NWOBHM)—bands like Venom, Diamond Head, and Iron Maiden. And then there is Motörhead, a band begun when metal and punk were just coming into their own in the mid-1970s, which combined elements of both of those genres. Motörhead is at least thrash's godfather, although if suitable DNA tests were available, one could slap a paternity suit on them. Ulrich, before forming Metallica, had been president of the Motörheadbanger's fan club.

The members of the early thrash bands in the US were big fans of those British bands. As Ulrich put it, "Yeah, I know people regard *Kill 'Em All* as the start of thrash, but I give full credit to Venom. *They* started it all. Their first album *Welcome to Hell* was so f**kin' unique when it first hit. And Metallica were obviously influenced" (Ulrich and Dome 1988: 31).

The best-known thrash scene erupted in San Francisco. It had key mediators. One was Rampage Radio, the metal specialty show on University of San Francisco's KUSF radio. Then there were the various venues like the Stone, Ruthie's Inn, the Old Waldorf, and the Keystone, where newly minted thrashers like Exodus, Testament, and so many others played. 'Zines, like Quintana's *Metal Mania*, connected fans and bands, both inside the Bay area and beyond.

Other areas such as New York City, where Anthrax erupted, were also in on the thrash action from the beginning. What these sites had in common was a strong metal fan base, a variety of mediators, and a thriving hardcore punk scene. Chicago, where I lived at the time, had these features too.

Although Metallica began in Los Angeles, the band seriously came together in San Francisco. Their first visit was thanks to Brian Slagel, who was publicizing the *Metal Massacre* compilation there with a show with some of the bands that appeared on the album. Metallica was not one of those invited to play, but one band canceled and Slagel called on them to fill in at the last minute. Bassist McGovney took his father's old Ford Ranger truck, rented a trailer for the gear (and drum riser!). McGovney described the show:

> We had no idea that our *No Life Till Leather* demo had gotten up there, they knew all the lyrics to our songs and everything. People asking us for our autographs, it

was a trip, we couldn't believe it. When we played in LA with bands like RATT, people would just stand there with their arms crossed. (O'Connor 1997)[2]

A decade later a rock journalist looking back described that concert: "a large platoon of rabid metal fans, all of whom owned the *No Life* demo and knew Metallica's music riff-for-riff. Assaulted with cries of ... 'Mustaine is God!' the other *Metal Massacre* bands could hardly finish their sets. The 'Bay Area Bangers' had adopted Metallica as their own" (Doughton 1997: 5). One might argue that the "Bay Area Bangers," an audience created in part by a late-night radio show playing a heavy dose of metal, especially from NWOBHM bands, was the source of thrash metal.

San Francisco also contributed half the members of the band that recorded the debut album. Bassist Cliff Burton, from Trauma, replaced McGovney, and lead guitarist Kirk Hammett migrated from Exodus.

Hearing the Debut

Kill 'Em All was so very exciting for several reasons. For one, it was raw. Missing were the so-called production values, which studio wizards, aka producers, intervene in the band's creative process. Lacking such sheen gives the impression of "authenticity" or hearing the band naked. Then, too, some of the musicians, especially the drummer, weren't very good.

Rawness was also a result of songs that were not created organically but were a patchwork of sounds more or less crudely stitched together. Many musicians contributed parts, some were in the band, others were once in the band, and some didn't know that their work was a contribution.[3] Too many cooks may spoil the broth, but the host of musicians contributing to this opus made for a really tasty stew.

"Hit the Lights" was written in Hetfield's earlier band (possibly by guitarist Tanner). Cliff Burton's "(Anesthesia) Pulling Teeth" came from his previous group. Mustaine contributed much of "Phantom Lord," "Jump in the Fire," and "The Four Horsemen." The latter song's music was created prior to his joining Metallica (vocalist James Hetfield rewrote the lyrics). While recording "The Four Horsemen" for a demo after Burton joined as bassist, Mustaine admitted that he "was being a jerk" when he inserted a riff from Lynyrd Skynyrd's "Sweet Home Alabama" (NA 2011). When Mustaine was summarily fired from the band on the way to the East Coast where they would record their debut album, Hammett, his replacement, kept that riff.

---

[2]   The spelling of "Till" in the title of the demo is the way it was originally spelled on the demo tape, written by Ulrich, although O'Connor omits the initial apostrophe. Most writers have used the more conventional spelling, "'til".

[3]   Pieces of songs by Lynyrd Skynyrd and Queen seem to have been included.

Since the pieces patched together to make these songs shared a similar sensibility, the result feels like it has integrity and coherence. The precise term may be what Claude Lévi-Strauss (1962) called a bricolage: constructing something from existing diverse objects rather than engineering the parts to create it. The bricolage method does not produce a polished product.

Raw is appropriate for an introduction to a new, and tough, sub-genre. Metallica's subsequent releases became more and more polished, far more cooked than raw, reaching the zenith, or more precisely, the nadir, in the *Black Album*.

Speed was another reason for *Kill 'Em All*'s exciting sound. It wasn't just a hallmark of Metallica and the other young thrash bands. Fast was in the musical zeitgeist of the time—popular styles included punk, hard-core punk, and the rockabilly revival. Most significant were the NWOBHM bands, such as Diamondhead and Blitzkrieg. Ulrich had lived and toured with Diamondhead for some months prior to creating Metallica. At least as important was Motörhead, a band whose name referenced its speed, and its drug of choice. "We kept on looking for music with faster beats," Kirk Hammett said of his previous band, Exodus. "We kept telling our drummer, Tom Hunting, 'Faster beats, man! The faster, the better!' And then when we saw Metallica, we were like, 'Oh, my God—this is the American version of all the bands we've been listening to!'" (Epstein 2009). And on their debut, as opposed to some of their other albums, Metallica had no ballads.

Kill 'Em All's lyrics created as much excitement as the band's music. Taken together, the words of the songs on the album form a single theme. It is a concept album that heralds the breakthrough of a new subgenre of metal, its fans, and its leader, Metallica. It is a celebration of metal. It is a call to arms to a new generation of metalheads, many of whom were already armed and ready.[4] The album's message proclaims that the thrash revolution is now underway and Metallica is leading the army of headbangers, the metal militia.

Preaching to the converted—after all who else heard the album?—both invokes a community and creates it. Exhorting people to become who they already are, that is, the converted, is like shooting fish in a barrel. And hearing those exhortations is a most exhilarating experience. At least it was for those who heard the album when it was released in the summer of 1983. It was absolutely thrilling. Those who heard the album later, as merely the band's first release, didn't get the excitement. As metal blogger Cosmo Lee put it: "So at this point, Metallica's lyrics were basically sloganeering" (2011). The same could be said about the words of any leaders—including those in politics, religion, or some social movement.

The band's subsequent albums were also themed. Their second release, *Ride the Lightning,* is about death. Death is what Heidegger called our own-most possibility—it is what uniquely belongs only to the individual. Their next, *Master of Puppets*, examines a variety of ways that one person, not a group or category, is manipulated. In contrast, *Kill 'Em All* is for all headbangers, for the community of metal fans. It is aimed at a group with a sense of collective identity, what Marx

---

4   Much like the Who's "My Generation" was to the youth of 1965.

might call a class in itself and for itself. The last track, "Metal Militia," underscores this solidarity: "we are as one for we all are the same, fighting for one cause"— fighting for the cause of metal.

And each song is aimed at inspiring this militia, from the opening track, "Hit the Lights." That song's first line, from which the title of the "No Life 'Til Leather" demo was taken, references metal's leather garb. (It is reminiscent of another song about the metal community's sartorial fabrics, NWOHM band Saxon's "Denim and Leather.") The song brags about the band's "enthusiastic" "insane," fans.

Leading the metal militia in its thrash charge are the four members of Metallica, celebrated in the band boast "The Four Horsemen." The song is Hetfield's rewrite of the lyrics of Mustaine's "The Mechanix," that replaced the original's sexual content with reference to the four horsemen of the apocalypse. It is an allusion, albeit modified, to the New Testament's Revelation of St. John. In the Biblical account, the four horsemen were conquest, slaughter, famine, and death; whereas Metallica's quartet is time, famine, pestilence and death. It doesn't seem likely that this deviation was an error. Both Hetfield and Mustaine were well versed in Christianity, each having been raised in very religious families, although affiliated with sharply different denominations.

Hetfield's parents were devout Christian Scientists, who believed that God would take care of everything, including any health problems. When his mother developed cancer, the family did not consult doctors, and she died from it when Hetfield was in high school. Mustaine's mother was a Jehovah's Witness, a denomination in which signs of the apocalypse play a prominent role, and she took her son with her as she went door to door trying to convert others to the faith.

Several songs on the album celebrate the fans' values and practices. "Whiplash" exults in headbanging, a defining feature of metalheads, invited here to bang their heads "against the stage." Even the track without lyrics, the bass instrumental "(Anesthesia) Pulling Teeth," is a salute to key values of the community—a demonstration of virtuosity and powerful low-pitch sound.

The shortest song, the only one under 4 minutes in length, "Motorbreath," extols burning one's candle at both ends, totally going for it, rather than being safe and boring. Safe and boring are the reverse of thrash values. And if thrash fans have one enemy, it is poseurs, epitomized by the glam metal—soon to be called hair metal—scene, that dominated the Los Angeles area. "Seek and Destroy," the album's longest song (almost 7 minutes), expresses that antagonism. Nothing unites people as easily as a common enemy.

"Jump in the Fire" is a call to "join us." Innovatively written as a recruitment pitch from Satan, it conforms to the hellish religious metaphors that have always permeated metal, from its origins with Black Sabbath and Judas Priest.

As a debut album that set the standard for a new genre, hearing *Kill 'Em All* when it first came out was as exciting a musical experience as one could imagine. The new when it is great is unparalleled — it brings to a peak forces that are waiting to be released and puts them together in an integral form. Once a genre has been established, later listeners can never feel that "shock of the new." As a first album for Metallica, *Kill 'Em All* is heard through its succeeding oeuvre. For metalheads, certainly for me, everything after *Kill 'Em All* falls flat.

Chapter 17

"I know someday you'll have a beautiful life": Pearl Jam's *Ten* and the Road to Authenticity

Marcello Giovanelli

Introduction

Pearl Jam's debut album is a special and important record in the context of both the alternative music *grunge* phenomenon of the 1990s and the band's own growth as important rock musicians and artists in the subsequent 20 years. Indeed for many, Pearl Jam's debut album, together with Nirvana's *Nevermind*, is synonymous with the word grunge itself. The album is a seminal work that marked the mainstream breakthrough of guitarist Stone Gossard and bassist Jeff Ament, the founding members of grunge pioneers Green River and so has an important place in the genealogy of Seattle rock. It remains a commercial and critical success, selling nearly ten million copies, and being certified platinum thirteen times. It regularly features in "best of" lists in the music press and popular journalism[1].

However, the commercial success of Pearl Jam and other bands from the region such as Nirvana, Soundgarden, and Alice in Chains, raised questions about the authenticity of grunge as a musical style since it had initially presented itself as an underground and unreservedly alternative movement that shunned mainstream acceptance. Furthermore, the album's highly polished style and intricate production did not sit comfortably with critics who claimed it was not faithful to a simpler, pared-back "grunge sound." The success and all of its associated trappings pushed the band into a position where they recognized the album as an emblem of inauthenticity. It was this very inauthenticity that later Pearl Jam albums and the band's actions rallied against in subsequent years. The intrigue of *Ten* lies not only in its rich musicality but in its status as a symbol of how the "Seattle sound" was on its way to becoming nothing more than a self-parody. More perhaps than any other album in recent times, it gave the band the perfect opportunity to redefine themselves as one of the most musically and culturally important acts in modern popular music.

---

[1]   See for example Von Appen and Doehring (2006), who compile a meta-list of 38 "best albums of all time" lists from the period 1985-2004. *Ten* is placed at #26.

Seattle: Grunge, Place, and Authenticity

Although Seattle rock and grunge[2] might appear to be phenomena of the late 1980s and early to mid 1990s, the region had a long and rich music history and legacy. As the home of 1960s and 1970s bands such as The Wailers and The Sonics, the city had developed a strong underground punk scene and a vibrant musical community. The reasons given as to why a geographically-isolated location in the Northwest Pacific became a cultural hotspot have ranged from the economic—the fall of Seattle's aerospace economy led to reduced employment opportunities for the city's youth and consequent boredom (Wiederhorn 1998)— to the meteorological—the region's climate is grey and drizzly. Azerrad (1995) claims that the music movement was underpinned by a strong urge to rebel against the suburban middle classes in a city where repressive alcohol laws meant that the movement had to go underground to survive. Given the relative isolation of the city and region, few bands included Seattle in national tours in the 1980s and the music scene primarily relied on self-promotion through amateur fanzines and promotional material. The reluctance of local radio stations to give exposure to local acts, instead choosing established and mainstream artists, was broken only by *The Rocket* magazine and radio stations that began to promote and play alternative and even local forms of music (see Tow 2011: 25-29). Alden and Gilbert (1993) suggest that the city's isolated, claustrophobic position paradoxically allowed for greater artistic freedom since artists were not under any national spotlight and could innovate freely without fear of overt criticism.

From what Mudhoney's Mark Arm termed "the two i's: isolation and inbreeding" (Azerrad 1992) came a shared sense of purpose and a developing movement. These very characteristics established a scene, a *sonoric landscape* (Crang 1998: 92) that fostered a sense of belonging. Seattle as a geographical space becomes a cultural *place*, which provided "an anchor of shared experiences between people and continuity over time. Spaces become places as they become 'time-thickened'. They have a past and a future that binds people round them" (Crang 1998: 103).

For Seattle bands, these shared experiences manifested themselves in the form of an identity that was less concerned with a set of shared musical characteristics and more about being defined in terms of their attitude (Tow 2011).[3] And, central to

---

[2]   Establishing a uniform definition of *grunge* has proven to be difficult since there is little consensus as to either its exact meaning or its genesis (see Mazullo 2000: 713; Tow 2011: 160-70, 223; Yarm 2011: xiv, 194-7. In this chapter, I use *grunge* to refer to a particular kind of music initially from the Seattle/Washington region that had certain attitudinal and cultural characteristics, notwithstanding the fact that the term later became used to refer to bands from other parts of the US and indeed the world.

[3]   Bell (1998) does in fact try to identify a Seattle/grunge sound based simply on loudness and musical honesty. Strong (2011) stresses grunge's socio-political commitments and its adherence to a strict fashion and mode of living, whilst Shevory (1995) draws on

this attitude was the question of authenticity. As Frith (1992) notes, the competing elements of authenticity and commercialism are pervasive in popular music with the tension particularly acute in alternative bands for whom being authentic is a way of defining themselves as outside of a mainstream and an often despised set of norms. For grunge, being authentic was about maintaining a sense of artistic integrity through an alternative style of playing and avoiding the obvious trappings of commercialism. However, once Seattle bands had been signed to major record labels and began to receive considerable national airplay, this sense of authenticity became endangered as they became public property and commercial fodder. Nowhere was this more evident than in "from Seattle" being stuck on the front of records, the marketing of a Seattle/Grunge dress-code by fashion magazines and in the rise of "copy-cat"' bands, often from other parts of the country (see Pato 2009: 320; Yarm 2011: 350). The appropriation of one of its most powerful signifiers of authenticity in its overt dress code, and the metonymic use of the name as a brand harmed not only musical integrity but also spatial and cultural identity. Seattle as cultural place, in Crang's terms, became fragmented and its anchoring elements dissipated to the point where it ceased to stand and recognize its own authenticity, instead merely existing as a set of readily transferrable and potentially profit-making properties. As both Bell (1998) and Wood (2011) show, nowhere was the response to this more evident and tragic than in the reaction of Kurt Cobain to Nirvana's popularity and success and his subsequent suicide.

The Paradoxes of *Ten*

The genesis of Pearl Jam as a band is well documented (for example, see Neely 1998; Pato 2009: 247-48). The spine of the band was the pairing of Stone Gossard and Jeff Ament, who had been musical partners in the grunge pioneers Green River[4] and later, in Mother Love Bone. The original line-up of the band that began performing as Mookie Blaylock[5] was completed by the addition of drummer Dave Krusen, Mike McCready, a lead guitarist with a distinctive blues-rock sound and Eddie Vedder, a vocalist who had auditioned with the band by recording lyrics over three Stone Gossard tracks onto a tape that been sent to him in San Diego,

---

analogies between grunge and punk and defines the genre's primary concerns as being subversion, the championing of the rights of the marginalised, and the occupation of "an emotional terrain in which the need for self-help devolves into the desire for self-annihilation" (1995: 34).

4   Anderson (2007: 24) considers Green River's *Come on Down* (1985) to be the first and prototypical grunge album.

5   The name of the New Jersey Nets' basketball player, Mookie Blaylock, was chosen before the band's first ever show at the Off Ramp Café in Seattle in 1990.The band later changed their name to Pearl Jam in the face of potential legal and marketing problems (see Neely 1998: 63-74).

having initially been introduced by former Red Hot Chili Peppers and future Pearl Jam drummer Jack Irons.

As an album, *Ten* is a series of quite subtle paradoxes. Firstly, as Anderson (2007) suggests, its cover and inner sleeves draw attention to one of several inconsistencies that begin to emerge when the album is considered as an alternative/grunge album. Anderson draws attention to the use of basketball symbolism on the front cover and inner sleeve, where the five band members raise their hands in group unison as though "they have called a time-out and are about to get back into the game" (Anderson 2007: 75). He argues that this deliberate foregrounding of sports imagery deviates considerably from the conventional model of grunge music as incompatible with the type of mainstream behaviour associated with sport-playing. Furthermore, it can be argued that the highly staged and self-conscious nature of the band's appearance both digresses considerably from an established authentic look yet contains nothing of the irony evident on the cover of Nirvana's *Nevermind*. Following Anderson's argument, to all intents and purposes, it looks inauthentic. And yet, read in an alternative way, the image provides a visual symbol of the coming together of a movement in the five hands bound and anchored by the music inside the album. Read in this way, the cover's iconicity highlights the band's position as the natural successor to Green River and Mother Love Bone as the prototype of the Seattle sound.

This potential for plural and often conflicting interpretations is indicative of an album that refuses absolute categorization. Musically, its sound, alternating between the heavy metallic riffs evident in "Once," to the drenched blues of "Deep" to the more plaintive yet equally emotional "Black" and "Release," demonstrates an eclecticism unlike that of any of Pearl Jam's contemporaries. At the same time, Vedder's lyrics and voice, angry at times, soulful and mournful at others, visits a spectacular range of emotions, situations, and thematic concerns; this frequently does not sound like and should not be a grunge album such is the range of content. The focus veers at a dramatic pace from the narrative autobiography of "Alive," to the social commentary of "Jeremy," based on Vedder's reading of a newspaper story about an isolated schoolboy in Texas who committed suicide,[6] to the melancholic "Black" with its focus on unrequited love and the subsequent loss of the cherished other. In addition, the musical complexity with interlaced guitars, innovative bass effects and multi-tracking used to its limit, are representative of a highly wrought and genuinely thoughtful work.

Yet, the album seems strangely formulaic: drums, bass, two very distinctive guitar sounds that could fit quite easily in any 1970s rock classic, Mike McCready's ubiquitous pentatonic solos and a staple diet of catchy verses and choruses. The production sounds suffocating and the effect of vast amounts of reverb applied to

---

[6]   This focus on the marginalized individual became a key recurrent theme in Pearl Jam's second album *Vs.*, for example in "Daughter," "WMA," and "Elderly Woman Behind the Counter in a Small Town."

the tracks in postproduction make the album sound glossy and even mainstream;[7] it feels and sounds like the type of flamboyant rock that the grunge movement was reacting to. And, of course, this particular aspect was not lost on Kurt Cobain, who criticized Pearl Jam's more extravagant musical tone simply as "cock-rock fusion" and questioned the band's claim to authenticity by stating that he found it "offensive to be lumped in with bands like Pearl Jam … They were never part of the underground" (Neely 1998: 123). Robert Roth, guitarist-vocalist of the Seattle band Truly sums up this attitude:

> It wasn't punk rock, it wasn't underground, it wasn't rebellious to me … I mean they imported their singer from San Diego, they had auditions. It just seemed like a weird kind of way to go about it. It wasn't quite the organic, "from the streets" thing that other bands were. (Pato 2009: 258)

Ten's ability to be both a critical and commercial success epitomizes the album's position as both a symbol of a movement and the prototype of a scene and a sound that had been appropriated into a brand. If *Ten* was partly responsible for grunge's arrival into the mainstream, then it also marked the beginning of its end. And, it could be argued that the band quickly sought to distance themselves from what the album came to represent if not from the music itself.[8] The magic of *Ten* therefore becomes not so much in its own sound but the shift in direction that it triggered.

Redefinition and Authenticity

In the backlash and uncertainty that surrounded the commercial explosion of Seattle bands, and later the death of Kurt Cobain, *Ten* became the perfect benchmark from which Pearl Jam could stress their authenticity and in doing so redefine themselves on their own terms. Perhaps, part of this shift was natural since as Mike McCready, reflecting on *Ten* had explained: "we were a band for only three and a half months when we recorded it—but I don't think it's the best we can do" (Gilbert 1998: 78).

However, much of this was a conscious movement away from a grunge *code* and was most significantly evident in their third and fourth albums *Vitalogy* and *No Code*. Here, Pearl Jam deliberately marked themselves as more proto-punk, anti-materialist, and anti-commercial; their refusal to develop and movement away from *Ten*'s initial sound is striking. *Vitalogy* saw the band attack the trappings of

---

[7] The remix of *Ten* released in 2009 was in part due to the band's dissatisfaction with the original sound.

[8] The popularity and longevity of songs from the album is evident in the fact that, according to statistics from the band's official website, the top five songs performed from 1990 to the end of 2011 are from *Ten*: "Even Flow," "Alive," "Black," "Jeremy," and "Porch."

fame through the nihilistic and scathing cynicism of "Not for You," "Nothingman," "Corduroy," and "Satan's Bed." Its raw, aggressive rhythm guitars, and the less refined leads than had appeared on both *Ten* and *Vs.*, served to wipe away the polish of the band's first album with its edgy garage sound. Most striking of all was the 1996 release *No Code*, which turned the *Ten* sound on its head, all the way from the skeletal, opening revelation of "Sometimes" through to the proto-punk and indecipherable "Lukin," to the spoken-word ballad "I'm Open" and the closing lullaby of "Around the Bend." *No Code* — the title itself is an explicit rejection of categorization—is *Ten*'s antithesis, from its collage cover of random Polaroid images right to Stone Gossard's lead vocal on "Mankind," a natural contender for the song that doesn't sound like it could ever be on *Ten*.

The push towards becoming more authentic was not restricted to the band's musical output. They famously stopped making videos, refused interviews to promote tours and records, transmitted *Monkeywrench Radio* from Eddie Vedder's house, including sets from Seattle bands and musicians, and decided, following a series of disagreements with Ticketmaster, to accept an invitation from the Department of Justice and make a formal complaint about the corporation's monopoly of concert ticketing.[9] Perhaps, most tellingly, the sacking of drummer Dave Abbruzzese in August 1994, amidst claims that he was both too careerist and musically divergent from the style that Pearl Jam now wanted to embrace, was a clear move towards positioning the band as more authentic (see Yarm 2011: 474-78). Later, they released live CDs of their shows in a bid to prevent illegal bootleggers from profiting from their fans, and have worked tirelessly and, more often than not, inconspicuously for charitable causes. Their fan club with its international network of rabid followers has redefined the intimate authenticity of the physical notion of space into a virtual internet community. Nils Bernstein, a former publicist for the renowned Seattle independent record label Sub-Pop, crystallizes the work of the band over the past 20 years into an acknowledgement of true authenticity when he suggests that "in a sense, [Pearl Jam] have been the punkest band of any of them" (Pato 2009: 455).

Conclusion: Lifting the Curse

Fast-forward to 2006 and, following a further three commercially and artistically successful albums, two full sets of tour bootlegs, a greatest hits album, a live album, and a collection of B-sides and rarities, Pearl Jam broke further innovative ground by releasing their eighth (self-titled) album on the back of a deal with Clive Davis's J Records. The album, which was critically acclaimed was hugely

---

[9]   Although Pearl Jam ultimately withdrew from their battle with Ticketmaster, it was and still is seen as a battle of artistic authenticity against the "corporate machine."

symbolic in that it represented the band's first release away from a major label.[10] On July 1, 2006, Pearl Jam performed a ten-song set on VH1's *Storytellers*, where, before playing "Alive," Vedder spoke about the song's autobiographical lyrics which outlined his discovery that his father was not the man he had grown up believing him to be. He explained how the pain in the song had over the years been diluted through the fans' transformation of it into a self-powering anthem. "They lifted the curse. The audience changed the meaning for me" Vedder said.

If anything, the story serves as an analogy to Pearl Jam's journey over the past 20 years: the band created the archetypal era-defining rock/grunge album, breathtaking in its musicianship and depth of emotional intensity, only to spend the rest of their careers working against what it came to stand for and instead seeking more authentic connections on their own terms. So, how appropriate to openly acknowledge that part of the band's growth has been in the shared experience between performer and listener as inhabitants of that cultural notion of place: a mark of true authenticity.

---

[10]   J Records was still owned and operated by Sony Entertainment. However, Pearl Jam released their last album, *Backspacer* (2009), on their own Monkeywrench label.

Chapter 18
LeAnn Rimes's *Blue*: A Country Star in the Making

Sarita M. Stewart

In 1996, amidst hit songs such as Alanis Morrisette's "You Oughta Know," Seal's "Kiss From A Rose," and Smashing Pumpkins' "Bullet With Butterfly Wings," LeAnn Rimes, a 13-year-old singer from Dallas, Texas, burst into the music marketplace with the release of her debut album *Blue*.

Rimes debut narrative, like many impacting first records, can be framed within the album's label and personnel. *Blue* was released on the country music powerhouse, Curb Records. Mike Curb, the label's founder and owner, was already a legendary hitmaker at the time of Rimes's debut. Curb had experienced early success with his first record label in the mid-1960s, producing movie songs and soundtracks. He eventually merged his company with MGM Records and served as the company's president. In this capacity, Curb oversaw the legendary entertainer Sammy Davis, Jr., singer Petula Clark, and pop sensations The Osmonds. Curb also served as producer for these artists as well as other acts, and was named *Billboard*'s Producer of the Year in 1972.

Following MGM's sale to the music conglomerate PolyGram Records, Curb founded Curb Records as a Curb/Warner Brothers imprint in 1974. The label generated enormous mainstream success with such diverse acts as the pop group The Four Seasons, country music duo The Bellamy Brothers, the rock group Exile, teen idol Shaun Cassidy, and pop singer Debby Boone (see CSUN 2006).

My own career at Curb Records began rather inauspiciously as the company's receptionist in the fall of 1986. At the time, Mike Curb was once again experiencing success with album co-ventures released through the company's major label partners, including projects by The Judds (RCA), Hank Williams Jr. (Warner), Sawyer Brown (Capitol), and Lyle Lovett (MCA) (Pierce 2000). As Curb recalled, he and his management team soon came to realize that "if we ever wanted to properly market our artists-to-be on our label with our own marketing department and our own promotional department, and not form co-ventures with other labels, we would have to move to Nashville" (Pierce 2000: 109). Curb's production company soon morphed into an independent record label, and the company's headquarters were moved to Nashville, Tennessee in 1992.

I had moved up in rank by this time, first serving as a production assistant in the creative department, and then working with Curb's sister Carole Curb Nemoy, who headed the international division of the record label. As Director of

International Marketing, I managed all of the Curb album releases, regardless of music genre, and corresponded directly with the executives representing all the major independent distribution companies worldwide. After completing my MBA in 1994, I was transferred to Curb's label headquarters in Nashville and became one of its two Directors of Marketing.

Curb Records in Nashville

The mid-1990s were exciting times to be employed by a record label. The technological changes that would soon overtake the music industry were not yet fully diffused. There were more than 30 record labels operating in Nashville at the time, making it difficult for new companies to find any office space on "Music Row" or "Music Row 2" (also known as the Cummins Stations building). This, in spite of the fact that country music album sales declined 12 percent in 1996, down from 32.8 millon to 29.3 million units from the previous year (Country Music 1996). Many new artists currently recognized as country music superstars were releasing their debut and sophomore albums, and beginning their climb towards superstardom. Curb Records had been successful in its first efforts as a stand-alone entity with the success of the Hal Ketchum's gold album *Past The Point of Rescue* (Pierce 2000). Still, it was not until the 1994 release of Tim McGraw's second album, *Not A Moment Too Soon*, that the label really began to take off. McGraw's controversial single "Indian Outlaw" had commanded country music's attention upon its release in early 1994 and his new album was a big hit. It eventually sold over five million copies, reaching the top of *Billboard*'s country and pop album sales charts and being recognized as Country Album of the Year in 1994. With the company now managing its own marketing and promotional functions, Curb had reunited with the Warner Music Group in 1995 when influential Atlantic Records became the company's distributor (Warner Music Group 2002). With the additional manufacturing and distribution strength of Warner-Elektra-Atlantic branch distribution system behind the Curb label, the supporting infrastructure was securely in place to help artists to break through to the next level of commercial success.

"Blue" Beginnings

The story behind Margaret LeAnn Rimes's rise to fame is well documented. Born in Jackson, Mississippi in 1982, Rimes was an only child. Her vocal gift was evident early on: she began singing at age two, and performed in her first talent show at five years old. Rimes' long-time friend and fellow artist Steve Holy said Rimes possessed "the greatest natural voice I've ever heard" (Reeves 2011). The family relocated to Texas seeking wider exposure for their daughter's talent. She soon began performing on the local Opry circuit in Metroplex-Mesquite, Garland,

Greenville, and Grapevine (Monthland 1997). At age eight, Rimes became a regular performer on the Saturday night lineup at Johnnie High's Country Music Revue in Arlington, Texas, to local acclaim. She was also a junior champion on the television talent show *Star Search* (Mendelsohn 1996).

Rimes attracted the attention of Bill Mack, the well-known Dallas country music DJ, who had witnessed her performance of the national anthem at a Dallas Cowboys football game. Mack was intrigued enough to go see Rimes perform, recalling, "at 11 years old, it was frightening how unbelievably good she was" (Mendelsohn 1996: 5). Mack was also a songwriter, and had written a song entitled "Blue" for the legendary country singer Patsy Cline in 1958. However, Cline never recorded the song prior to her 1963 death in a plane crash. While other performers had previously recorded "Blue," Mack was still seeking "the right voice" for his song; he sent the song to Rimes when he heard she was looking for material (Stark 1996). Rimes's rendition of Mack's "Blue" was included on her first album, *All That* (1993), which was released on the Dallas independent label Nor Va Jak when she was 11 years old.

Mike Curb first became aware of LeAnn Rimes's talent in 1995. Benson Curb, Director of Sales for the company, had received her cassette demo tape from one of his Texas contacts, and had passed it along to Mike for his review. That weekend, Curb was traveling with his wife and daughters on a family vacation to the Smokey Mountains. While on the trip, the family listened to submitted tapes as per Curb's usual routine in overseeing the company's Artist & Repertoire (A&R) activities. Curb placed Rimes's tape into the cassette deck. "Blue" was the first song, and, as Curb recalls, he said, "this can't be right. This doesn't sound like a thirteen-year-old girl" (Pierce 2000: 111). Curb and his family continued to listen to Rimes's cassette on their way back to Nashville. They stopped at a gas station, where Curb first called Lyle Walker, Rimes's Dallas-based attorney and co-manager, then Wilbur Rimes, LeAnn's father, to tell him how much he liked the tape. The Rimes family left Dallas the next day, and drove to Nashville to meet with Curb. The two families had dinner at a Cracker Barrel restaurant later that night (Pierce 2000). Rimes had received some interest from Decca Records in early 1995, when their Nashville representatives flew to Dallas to see her perform (Stark, 1996). In April 1995, Curb closed the deal as LeAnn's parents signed a recording contract on their daughter's behalf with Curb Records (Reeves 2011).

The Making of a Very Young Star

One of the biggest challenges when beginning to work with any artist is the foundational process of how to begin fashioning their image in ways that allow them to connect with their audience. Predictably, LeAnn Rimes's pre-teen age presented a unique challenge. However, she did have very strong positives— notably an amazing singing voice—from which we at Curb could begin to build her image, and fashion a preliminary marketing plan. While everyone at Curb was in awe of Rimes's powerful vocals, the inevitable Patsy Cline comparisons were a built-in familiarity and marketable reference point.

Meanwhile, the studio production team began to mobilize, led by producer Chuck Howard, who was brought in as the company's Vice President of A&R in 1995. Howard owned his own production company, and worked with a number of top music talents, including country music singers Billy Dean and John Berry. Howard is among *Blue*'s three co-producers, along with Johnny Mulhair and Rimes's father. The process was tedious. Wilbur Rimes reportedly re-mixed the "Blue" single nearly 40 times. As Mike Curb emphasized, "everything had to feel right—the mikes, the echo effects, and so on" (Pierce 2000: 113). Not surprisingly, the "Blue" single had a retro, old-time feel. Some radio programmers felt the single was a bit of an oddity, especially with the yodel that Rimes added in her interpretation of the song (Stark 1996).

Once the music was completed, the marketing team, in conjunction with the radio promotion staff, began to promote, market, and publicize *Blue*. The company had two main record company promotional label imprints at the time. The first was Curb Records, which oversaw recording artists Tim McGraw, Sawyer Brown, and Ronnie McDowell, among others. Rimes's album was assigned to the second promotional team, a new imprint named MCG/Curb, whose roster included Hal Ketchum and Hank Williams, Jr. Carson Schreiber, Vice President of the MCG/Curb label, moved from the West Coast to Nashville to oversee the roster's direction. The two Curb/MCA labels remained in place, including the imprint featuring multi-market artist Lyle Lovett, and the Curb/MCA Nashville roster, which featured Wynonna Judd.

Meanwhile, the marketing department worked under the moniker of The Curb Group. It was our collective job to manage the production and preparation of all recording and supporting materials related to the singles and full album releases of the two Curb promotional labels for the commercial market. In short, my workload was dictated by the demands of the label's active release schedule. As a result of this myopic focus, the commercial releases never seemed "real" until our team was in the three- to six-month promotional phase prior to an album's release. In Rimes's case, even though the family visited the Curb offices whenever they were in town, I didn't really connect with them until we sat together during the 1996 Country Radio Seminar luncheon held in Nashville that March.

LeAnn Rimes's considerable talent was making waves among the radio programmers who came to see her perform in the MCG/Curb hospitality suite. I interacted with LeAnn and her parents within that environment. Her mother was sweet, and father insightful, while LeAnn was seemingly a "normal" teenager. We spoke at length about the international music market, as well as my responsibilities within the company's organizational structure. The connection with the Rimes family later proved to be vital in that they were always quite helpful in accommodating the international press with access to LeAnn as needed for interviews. While we all recognized and appreciated Rimes's immense talent, no one could have predicted the level of worldwide success that she would soon experience. Rod Essig, who co-managed Nashville's leading talent agency, Creative Artists Agency, and who served as Rimes's booking agent noted, "it normally takes two years, three years to develop an act. LeAnn Rimes was six months" (Reeves 2011).

The Explosion Heard Around The World

While the impetus within the company was to get a single out quickly, it took some time to determine whether to designate "Blue" or "The Light in Your Eyes" (Stark 1996). The label selected "Blue" with it obvious throwback to Patsy Cline. The rationale, in part, was that once the listener got past the astonishing teenage-girl singing, they could connect with the song's emotional power. Rimes was often asked during interviews how someone so young and with limited life experience could convey the lyrics with such maturity and emotional authenticity. She explained, "I'm really not that conscious of the maturity of the lyrics ... but I don't think I have to experience a lyric to sing it, and I'm not saying I did experience all the lyrics I sing" (Monthland 1997: 109). In addition, there seemed to be a collective industry "waiting" to see whether Rimes had staying power as an artist or was a one-hit wonder. Rimes drew comparisons to former teen stars such as Brenda Lee and Tanya Tucker (Mendelsohn 1996). Mike Curb addressed the age issue directly, saying "I wanted to sign LeAnn because there hadn't been a teenage artist for twenty-five years and because LeAnn has such an awesome talent ... I knew the odds against a teenager making it big were tremendous" (Pierce 2000: 112).

Meanwhile, the MCG/Curb radio promotion team was getting results. Schreiber had decided to go for official airplay on the new single on May 20, 1996. "Blue" debuted at #49 with a bullet on *Billboard*'s Hot Country Singles & Tracks airplay chart in its first week. Radio programmers across the country were finding that the single struck a strong chord with their listening audience. Many country programmers compared the audience reaction to that of Tim McGraw's "Indian Outlaw" and its follow-up "Don't Take the Girl" single in 1994, as well as Billy Ray Cyrus's infectious "Achy Breaky Heart" of 1992 One program director reported that the "Blue" single generated the station's first email about a record following installation of their website several months earlier (Stark 1996). A commercial single was prepared for release in both cassette and CD formats on June 4, 1996. It subsequently debuted at #1 on *Billboard*'s Top Country Sales chart with sales of more than 21,000 units. The debut album *Blue* followed in July, also marketed in both cassette and CD formats. The album debuted at #1 on *Billboard*'s Top Country Sales Chart, and at #4 on the *Billboard* 200 on July 27.

Figure 18.1   LeAnn Rimes's *Blue*: Teenage talent.

The Challenges of Sudden Stardom

During the era, a record label would normally watch an artist begin to break region by region in their push towards mainstream success. The power of radio airplay was instrumental in Rimes's swift ascent to stardom. The "overnight sensation," while exciting, presents enormous logistic challenges for both the artist and their label operatives. Most artists have a chance to become comfortable with, and gradually grow into, their success. When an artist begins to experience such immediate widespread success, they are often pulled in multiple directions. Whenever promotional activities are scheduled, the artist is responsible for having to fulfill the activity, whether an interview with the press, an appearance at in-store event, or a performance at a venue. A performer will often conduct all of these activities in a given day, depending on their tour schedule. While much of this lifestyle is perceived as, and often is, glamorous, the schedule can be quite taxing on the performer. Rimes case was no exception. She was seemingly everywhere at the same time, which presented overwhelming physical and mental demands, especially on such a young person. Rimes played 107 concert dates in 1995. When *Blue* hit, and Rimes newfound fame followed, demand dictated she remain on the road. Booking agent, Rod Essig, recalled that Rimes's concert earnings increased from $10,000 per appearance to over $100,000 in the course of a week (Reeves 2011). Financially and socially, Rimes's lifestyle was dramatically different from the norms of her age group: she was home-schooled, did not have friends her own age and did not experience "normal" teenage activities such as sleepovers and prom (Mendelsohn 1996).

Rimes experienced success at levels that most artists at any age never reach. She had a gold album by the end of September 1996, as her debut sales reached 500,000 units (Mendelsohn 1996). Rimes also had a high-powered Los Angeles-based public relations team, led by Sandy Friedman and Lori Lousararian at Rogers and Cowan. The public relations team worked double-time to manage the overload of media requests worldwide. Rimes was a high-profile guest on various television shows, including *Good Morning America* and the *Late Show with David Letterman*. She also made numerous appearances on the Wal-Mart Country Music Across America concert tour, with more than 8,000 spectators attending her Amarillo, Texas appearance in August 1996 ("Country Corner," 1996). Rimes made her first official appearance on the world-famous, prestigious Grand Ole Opry stage on September 13, 1996 (Ericson 2011).

Awards and nominations accumulated, verifying the merits of *Blue*. Among Rimes' honors were the Country Music Association's Horizon Award (now known as the New Artist of the Year) in 1997, and "Best Female Country Vocal Performance" and "Best New Artist" at the 39th annual Grammy Awards, also in 1997. Such recognition was a stunning accomplishment for a 13-year-old artist and virtual unknown 12 months earlier.

Bill Mack's "Blue" also won the Grammy for "Best Country Song." While the single "Blue" only spent one week in the Top 10 on *Billboard*'s Hot Country Singles & Track airplay charts, it remained the #1 single on *Billboard's* Hot Country Singles Sales chart for 20 weeks ("Chart Beat" 1996). Other singles from the album, including the #1 hit "One Way Ticket," further showcased Rimes's talent. In January 1997, the Recording Industry Association of America (RIAA) certified *Blue* multi-platinum, with sales exceeding 3 million units.

Rimes's Run

The momentum for Rimes's music continued into 1997. Determined to capitalize on her instant success, Curb quickly released a follow-up, *Unchained Melody: The Early Years*, and a collection of Rimes singing inspirational songs within the next year. The label also packaged an exclusive holiday single with the *Blue* album that was available only at Target retail chain. The song "Light In Your Eyes" was the A-side, with "Unchained Melody" the B-side ("Country Corner: Greatest Gainer," 1996). The single unexpectedly found its way to radio, prompting commercial demand for Rimes's version of "Unchained Melody." In addition to the title cut, the follow-up album also contained several songs from Rimes's pre-*Blue* album *All That*. *Unchained* debuted at #1 on both the *Billboard*'s Top Country Albums and the Top 200 sales charts. Rimes was the only country artist, other than Garth Brooks, to debut in the #1 album sales slot (Chart Beat 1997). This success gave Curb Records additional time to prepare Rimes's third album, *You Light Up My Life: Inspirational Songs*, which featured the "How Do I Live" single, originally intended to be part of the *Con Air* movie soundtrack (Monthland 1997). This album had broad radio format appeal, including pop, country, and Christian, mainly due to the crossover quality of "How Do I Live." *You Light Up My Life* also debuted at #1 on three *Billboard* sales charts in the September 27, 1997 issue—Top Country Albums, Top Contemporary Christian Albums, and the *Billboard* Top 200. Rimes considered this triple crown achievement to be "one of the happiest days of my life" (Evans 1997: 43). By the end of 1997, *Billboard* magazine announced LeAnn Rimes as the "number 1 pop artist, pop album artist, country artist, and country female artist" (Pierce 2000: 113). Curb Records benefitted, as the label was recognized as *Billboard*'s #1 country label for both albums and singles, as well as the #1 country record label according to Nielsen Soundscan.

Beyond *Blue*

The post-*Blue* years have represented a number of predictable peaks and valleys for LeAnn Rimes. She has survived the scrutiny and expectation of the stardom syndrome that set in at age 13, with her personal and professional lives extensively documented in the press, from music journalists to the tabloids. Since her debut, Rimes has released 15 albums, including two *Greatest Hits* collections on Curb, her most recent being, *Lady and Gentlemen* (2011) and *Spitfire* (due in 2013). Rimes has expanded her entertainment pursuits beyond music, writing inspirational books, appearing in made-for-TV movies and as a spokesperson for the Psoriasis Foundation. Ultimately, it is *Blue*'s embodiment of youth, vocal power, and echoes of Patsy Cline that mark, if not define, LeAnn Rimes's chronology.

Chapter 19

Third Eye Blind: Reluctantly Voicing the 1990s

Joshua D. Hillyer

Third Eye Blind is often remembered as a "nineties band," a label that firmly places them in the same category as Limp Bizkit, Smashmouth, and of course, Backstreet Boys. For others the decade is irrelevant; instead, Third Eye Blind is that band with the "do do do" song. But perhaps the San Francisco-based alternative rock group is more than an over-played single on a "Remember the '90s" late-night infomercial.

Third Eye Blind is not a self-made indie success story. In fact, the band sold over six million copies of their debut album (RIAA n.d.), which featured five popular radio singles. The success of their eponymous album is especially incredible in light of the changes that the recording industry faced as rock became rap-rock and music buyers became music downloaders. More important than sales, the album created a loyal following of fans who connected with the songs' enormous hooks and emotional lyrics. But many critics missed the depth and nuance of the album's lyrics, which were penned by the valedictorian of his UC-Berkeley graduating class (Guthrie 2003). Perhaps being misunderstood is the album's legacy; after all, "Semi-Charmed Life" is known for its "do do do" chorus rather than its haunting and quirky tale of drug abuse. Thus, in this chapter I highlight the significance of Third Eye Blind's debut recording by noting its dark and subversive subject matter as well as its unique "acts" structure and lasting (albeit surprising) relevance in the punk and indie community.

Before *Third Eye Blind*

Although Third Eye Blind did not release their self-titled debut album until March 26, 1997 (RIAA n.d.), the band had played shows for years. Like many bands in the 1980s and 1990s, however, the group did not reach a large audience until their demo garnered the attention of major label executives. The demo, which reached industry names as large as Rock and Roll Hall of Fame member Clive Davis, left several labels fighting to release Third Eye Blind's album (Whiting 1996). Even with (or maybe because of) reports of singer Stephan Jenkins breaking a piñata filled with live crickets during a label showcase, it was clear that the band had a memorable and marketable sound. Ultimately, Third Eye Blind decided to sign a recording contract with Elektra Entertainment Group, as a result of the high degree of artistic control that the label promised (Reece 1997). With the major label deal in place, the band was set to unleash its vision for melodic alternative rock to the masses.

The Debut Album

The product of the band's studio time, *Third Eye Blind*, contains 14 songs that describe Jenkins, his views on culture and society, and a decade that was disinterested in accepted behavior and rules. Indeed, the album features dark themes and references to drug use, suicide, and unrequited love. However, bright chords and catchy choruses sometimes overshadow or at least mask the aforementioned topics. Instead, Jenkins's melancholy stories are more likely to be noticed upon second and third listens. That is, the songs contain a level of intrigue that is not immediately noticeable, requiring listeners to pay attention to the words that carefully guide each song to its loud and memorable chorus. Similar to other media from the 1990s that has since been criticized as too "surface level," then, *Third Eye Blind*'s mixture of upbeat music and introspective lyrics is more indicative of the decade in which it was made than of the rock genre to which it belonged.

In describing Third Eye Blind's single "Semi-Charmed Life," Jenkins, perhaps inadvertently, summarized the subversive nature of all of the band's lyrics when he stated: "Underneath that shiny surface there's a storm lurking" (Reece 1997: 20). As noted earlier, though, this depth in his lyrics and the larger significance of the band's music are not likely to be what listeners notice upon their first time hearing "Semi-Charmed Life." Instead, the complexity of the eponymous album and its feelings of love, happiness, loss, and despair are left for those who listen to it as a collection of songs: an album.

Third Eye Blind is an album that can be interpreted as having a three-act structure, with each act containing four to five songs bearing similar tones, themes, and moods. However, identifying the album as having three acts does not mean that it strictly follows the traditional story-telling structure of Hollywood films. Further, I am not suggesting that Jenkins told a story about the same characters' lives from the first to last song. Instead, the three acts simply denote the atmospheric and lyrical similarities of the album.

Rather than establishing characters and setting, Act One establishes Third Eye Blind. It informs listeners of what they should expect from the band—brash, confident, catchy, gloomy, honest, and entirely listenable music. The album opens with "Losing a Whole Year," a song that establishes Third Eye Blind as comfortable with any topic, including references to depression, Internet addiction, and sex. Beneath the serious lyrics, though, the band provided catchy, noisy, and rhythmic music that allowed listeners to approach it without necessarily realizing the gravitas of the song.

The other songs in Act One of *Third Eye Blind* further develop the honest, hyper-negative nature of the band. "Narcolepsy," a song about sleep paralysis, includes an infamous lyric about deceased writers and the fear of never waking up. Unlike the aforementioned noisy opening song, "Narcolepsy" begins with clean guitar tones before later drifting into fast, punk-inspired rhythms with distorted guitars. Perhaps unintentionally, the song demonstrates Third Eye Blind's depth as musicians and lyricists, revealing their ability to write different styles of songs while telling morbidly humorous stories.

Act One concludes with a trio of successful singles, "Semi-Charmed Life," "Jumper," and "Graduate." The significance of "Semi-Charmed Life" to Third Eye Blind's career cannot be overstated, as the band sold over 500,000 copies of the single alone (RIAA n.d.) during a time when the Internet was beginning to emerge as a deterrent to purchasing individual songs. Similar to "Losing a Whole Year" and indicative of the prevailing rebellious attitude of the 1990s, "Semi-Charmed Life" tells a fun yet frightening story of addiction to a drug that became more popular than ever in the 1990s: "speed." On the subject of the tension between the inviting music and dark lyrics of "Semi-Charmed Life," Jenkins explained that "the music that I wrote for it is not intended to be bright and shiny for bright and shiny's sake. It's intended to be what the seductiveness of speed is like, represented in music" (Knopper 1997: 24). Potentially more than any Third Eye Blind song, "Semi-Charmed Life" with its sultry drug story interspersed with "do do do" choruses, illustrates the band's identity as a radio-friendly yet socially-aware rock group.

The final two songs in Act One, "Jumper" and "Graduate," solidify that, in addition to being an entertaining band, Third Eye Blind has a considerable voice on issues that impact young adults. "Jumper" especially positions the band as more important than the average major label alternative act of the 1990s, as Jenkins makes sense of suicide, drawing attention to society's (sometimes unmet) needs to be affirmed or understood by others. Fittingly, the chorus is "I wish you would step back from that ledge my friend; I would understand." "Jumper," then, served as an anthem of sorts for a generation of young people who would have preferred not having an anthem.

The shift between Act One and Act Two, while subtle at first, is considerable upon repeated listenings. Unlike the emotionally poignant yet fun songs of Act One (which were clear choices to be singles), Act Two is marked by conflict and angst, similar to much of the media from the 1990s. The first song from this act, "How's It Going to Be," immediately sets the tone for the middle portion of the album as sad, disappointed, and free. Although Act One also begins with a song about a failed relationship, Jenkins develops its story using self-aware and witty lyrics. In "How's It Going to Be," Third Eye Blind moves away from the morbid humor of Act One and, in true ballad form, laments how quickly love can run its course. Even Elektra executive Greg Thompson felt a connection to the song, stating: "[It] is one of those special songs that's going to blow this band wide open. It penetrates beyond format and demographic" (Taylor 1998: 86).

The dissatisfaction that characterized many of the greatest films of the 1990s continues in Act Two with songs such as "Thanks a Lot" and "Burning Man." Despite "Thanks a Lot" never being released as a single, it perhaps best fit the sound of alternative rock in the 1990s, with its fuzzy post-grunge guitars and metaphorical references to confidently murdering one's confidence. "Burning Man" goes even further into the desire to be free, despite the inherent darkness in all existence. For example, Jenkins sings that "Life is not to fear; life is to enjoy. He'll get you, oh Mr. Death catches all some day." With such strong themes of ambivalence and dissatisfaction displayed in "Thanks a Lot" and "Burning Man," it is difficult not to compare, or at least liken, Act Two to the 1990s film *Reality Bites* and its characters' struggles with identity. That is, *Third Eye Blind* presents itself as a darker version of the film's ever-confused but likeable characters.

Act Two concludes with "Good for You" and "London," both loud and distorted songs about the disappointment and confusion of major life changes and events. Although there are still signs of the confidence that Third Eye Blind expresses in songs from Act One such as "Losing a Whole Year" and "Graduate," these songs describe the band as more exposed and vulnerable. For example, Jenkins sings about simply trying to help someone rather than definitely understanding a friend's problems, like in "Jumper." It is apparent that the songs in Act Two demonstrate the struggles that many experience as they age and enter new stages of life. Similar to the grunge movement from which catchy alternative rock bands such as Third Eye Blind were born, it is not intended to be uplifting. It is intended to be real.

Third Eye Blind concludes with four songs that are slower in tempo and often use quiet-loud-quiet dynamics for emotional effect. These are the album's most moving songs lyrically, as well. This act includes a love song: "I Want You," a story of loss: "The Background," a tale of letting go: "Motorcycle Drive by," and a closing song that describes the ever-changing universe and how humans cope with existence: "God of Wine." These songs, which Elektra never released as singles, are still fan favorites. As recently as 2011, Third Eye Blind opened and closed some of their concerts with "Motorcycle Drive By" and "The Background," respectively. Perhaps, like many things labeled as "alternative," Act Three is beloved by fans because it is theirs to interpret. It belongs to the fans rather than the wider radio-listening public who enjoyed songs such as "Semi-Charmed Life."

Act Three emphasizes honesty and understanding. On "I Want You," Jenkins sings that "there will be no regrets when the worms come, and they shall surely come," demonstrating a level of acceptance that is absent from earlier songs on the album. Despite the next three songs describing different kinds of loss, the band communicates that life continues. The acoustic, then loud-and-acoustic "Motorcycle Drive By" is especially indicative of the aforementioned acceptance sentiment. The song tells a story of a failed attempt at reconnection that ends with a surprising postscript in which the protagonist simply goes surfing. The band concludes the song by acknowledging defeat but realizing that there is still hope and opportunity: "I've never been so alone, and I've never been so alive."

Like the prevailing attitudes of the 1990s, Jenkins sometimes attempted to downplay the moody aspects of his art and instead focused on its more approachable aspects. For example, Jenkins described his feelings on the gloomy elements of the group's album: "I don't think the overall sense [of the album] is dark or depressing. There are reconciliations as well. Music is a form of redemption" (Taylor 1998: 86). Members of Third Eye Blind often speak of the band's music in such grand ways, advocating that the songs take on greater meanings and significance than just being radio singles. And for many fans, that is exactly what happened.

After *Third Eye Blind*

Whether a result of changing tastes in alternative rock music (from bouncy and catchy bands like Third Eye Blind to heavy and rap-oriented bands like Limp Bizkit and Papa Roach) or whether a result of the advent of illegal music downloading services, Third Eye Blind never duplicated its initial success and multi-million sales with subsequent albums. *Blue* (Elektra 1999), sold over one million copies and featured several popular singles such as "Never Let You Go" and "Deep Inside of You." The album received mixed reviews, as the band experimented with different sounds and styles while still attempting to retain the unique lyrics and attitude that made *Third Eye Blind* such a hit. Dellio (1999) summarized the negative reactions that some journalists and fans felt in stating "[I am] not sure what to make of the Bon Scott flourishes on 'The Red Summer Sun,' but as I'm sure, even Third Eye Blind would agree, it's not the kind of thing that needs to be pursued any further."

Third Eye Blind continued to record and perform, releasing their third album with Elektra in May 2003. The album, *Out of the Vein*, was the band's first recording not to sell a million copies, resulting in only one single that received significant radio play: "Blinded (When I See You)." Indicative of the aforementioned challenges Third Eye Blind experienced while releasing music during a season of change in the music industry, the album was the group's last release with Elektra. According to Jenkins, the label "ceased to exist" near the launch window of *Out of the Vein* (Uhelzski 2007). Although Elektra later re-emerged as a record label, the band has not released any new material with them. Instead, Third Eye Blind released their most recent album, *Ursa Major*, on their own Mega Collider Records label in 2009.

Despite tumultuous periods resulting from unexpectedly low album sales and lawsuits from two guitarists, Third Eye Blind has continued to perform for large audiences. Unlike many of their now-defunct alternative rock contemporaries such as Semisonic and Better Than Ezra, the group has potentially remained relevant because of a level of respect and admiration from the influential indie and punk communities. For instance, numerous bands cite Third Eye Blind as a primary influence, including Arctic Monkeys, Panic at the Disco, and Permanent Me.

The aforementioned respect reached a boiling point when former *Spin* editor and current marketer and blogger Sarah Lewitinn published a controversial article on the band. Lewitinn (2009) discussed the reasons that Third Eye Blind's lasting appeal and influence on current bands eludes her (predominantly noting their mainstream success) before marveling at the degree to which the band still matters to so many listeners and musicians. Her article led to responses from the popular music blog AbsolutePunk (whose editors often post about the band and have interviewed Jenkins), where users discussed the band's place in music history (Lally 2009). Even entertainment writers addressed Third Eye Blind's legacy, jokingly explaining that "the huge success of their debut proves what a great band Third Eye Blind is, and their lack of success since then proves what a great band Third Eye Blind is" (Tannenbaum 2009). Despite some writers' dismissive considerations of the group's longevity and influence, the debate drew attention to the weight and reach of the Third Eye Blind phenomenon just as they embarked on a new, independent stage of their career.

Jenkins has made it clear that he is not interested in Third Eye Blind's legacy as a 1990s band (Jenkins 2009). Indeed, it is apparent that the band and their debut album have considerably impacted the current state of alternative rock music and even a new generation of fans, attesting to their significance outside of the decade of *Third Eye Blind*'s release. However, the first impression of the band, with their brash, honest, and surprisingly deep lyrics, effectively summarized the years of change and personal growth that many fans happened to experience during the 1990s. Although these children of the 1970s and 1980s still lived by Kurt Cobain's "whatever, nevermind" mantra, Third Eye Blind's expression of understanding through dark humor was what they actually needed.

Chapter 20

Dap-Dippin' Independent Tradition: The Rebirth of Rhythm and Blues

Andrew G. Davis

In one of the most significant and compelling commentaries on the subject of rhythm-and-blues music, Nelson George lamented the death of the genre in the late 1970's and early 1980's. The demise of R&B, according to George, was brought about by a convergence of factors including, but not limited to: the cyclical assimilation and correlated atrophy of black cultural forms into mainstream (i.e., white) American popular culture; the success of disco as a crossover vehicle for R&B artists; black middle- and upper-class indifference towards (or even outright disdain for) black popular cultural expression, which resulted in a lack of economic support; and, perhaps most notably, the corporate annexation of independent R&B labels that began in the early 1970s (George 1988). It is in regards to this last factor that I frame my discussion of the significance of Sharon Jones and the Dap Kings' 2002 debut album, *Dap-Dippin' with…*

George's view is supported by a number of facts. Before 1972, major labels overwhelmingly (and consciously) kept out of the rhythm-and-blues market (Mabry 1990). Indeed, the development of rhythm-and-blues (as a genre *and* a market) from the mid-1940s through the early 1970s cannot be discussed outside the context of independent labels. R&B was born at live shows, raised by regional black radio, and came of age through independent labels (George 1988)—Aladdin, Apollo, Excello, Imperial, King, Savoy, and Specialty, just to name a few (Redd 1974; Shaw 1970). During the 1960s, independent labels accounted for 76 percent of the decade's *Billboard* Top 25 R&B singles; Motown alone accounted for an impressive 48 percent (Ripani 2006). Intrigued by the industry success of the independent labels Motown and Stax, Columbia Records Group commissioned the Harvard School of Business in 1972 to conduct a study on the potential profitability of the R&B market to major record labels (Kelley 2002). Based on the results of that study, Columbia decided to enter into a distribution deal with Stax in 1972 (Neal 1999), which served as a prototype for the distribution deal between CBS and Philadelphia International Records in 1976 (Neal 1997), and the eventual takeover of Motown by MCA/Universal in 1988 (George 2001). For the authors cited above, these deals stand as emblematic of the devolution of rhythm and blues into urban contemporary and other incarnations of crossover rhythm and blues, rendering the independent R&B tradition as "little more than a late-20th-century sharecropping system in which popular recordings were the cash crop" (Neal 1997: 126).

While I agree with the majority of George's (1988) argument, it is limited by certain changes that have occurred in the two-and-a-half decades since it was published; it requires revision. As will be demonstrated in the following pages, one of the most significant changes to have occurred is the re-emergence of the independent R&B record label as a viable force within the music industry. Daptone Records—the independent, artist-owned label on which Sharon Jones and the Dap Kings appear—must be accorded a significant share of the credit for the rebirth of rhythm and blues.[1] Before offering the main crux of this argument, however, I wish to take a detour into my first encounter with Daptone Records through the debut album of Sharon Jones and the Dap Kings.

A Fan is Born

Though I normally avoid including personal narratives in my research, I find it appropriate in this instance.[2] Over the past decade, the music produced by Daptone Records has become such an integral part of my life that it would be disingenuous to limit this essay to the purely academic. The significance of Sharon Jones and the Dap Kings' debut album is as much personal as it is cultural or economic. As an audiophile and record collector obsessed with R&B (and a sometimes radio and club DJ specializing in the genre), the successive proliferation of urban contemporary, new jack swing, ghetto pop, and new (aka neo-) soul leaves me extraordinarily unsatisfied.[3]

---

[1]   This statement is not intended to downplay the role of other labels and artists in the re-emergence of the independent tradition in R&B. Malaco continues to operate as an independent label even after decades in the industry. Stax has recently been resurrected from oblivion. Reissue labels such as the Numero Group, Light in the Attic, Soul Jazz, Now-Again, and Truth & Soul all deserve credit. In regards to artists, Bettye LaVette, Denise LaSalle, Sam Dees, Andre Williams, Lee Fields, Charles Bradley, Syl Johnson, Ronaldo Domino, The Notations, Nate Evans, and many others also deserve credit for keeping the independent tradition alive. I hope for forgiveness for leaving out all the other stalwarts. What distinguishes Daptone Records, particularly the recordings of Sharon Jones and the Dap Kings, from the rest of these will be explained during the course of this chapter.

[2]   The details included in this narrative are, to the best of my recollection, accurate. For the sake of full disclosure, however, I must admit that this instance in my life occurred nearly ten years ago. Since this narrative is the product of memory rather than recorded notes from the time, I feel it only fair to inform the reader that some misremembrance might have occurred. Nevertheless, the intent and significance of this narrative as it relates to the research included elsewhere in this chapter should not compromise either that research or the overall argument contained herein. Any factual indiscrepencies must be chalked up to the confluence of the ravages of time and the need for narrative continutiy.

[3]   Certain writers have included Sharon Jones and the Dap Kings in their discussions of neo-soul groups (Nielson 2007). I reject their inclusion into this category due to the fact that neo-soul relies heavily on digital recording and production techniques. Additionally,

I first came across *Dap-Dippin'* in early 2003, as a result of what was at that time my biweekly ritual of combing the R&B sections at Low Yo Stuff and Wuxtry Records in Athens, Georgia. I dig for old records; I have since the age of 12. Some of my earliest memories are of my mother and father playing recordings of Gladys Knight and the Pips and Booker T and the MGs on their turntable or 8-track, reel-to-reel player. Along with a little youthful hubris, this combination of an early established love for and years of research into the music had led me to believe that I was at least aware of all but the most obscure R&B recordings of the 1960s and 1970s. I was thus surprised to come across *Dap-Dippin'* in Wuxtry Records. Everything about the record suggested it had been made sometime in 1967 or 1968. [4] The graphic layout of the front cover evoked the aesthetic sensibility and printing techniques of R&B records from that time. Most striking to me was the photograph of Sharon Jones in mid-performance—bent slightly forward in a sparkling red dress, hips cocked, microphone to mouth. I flipped the record over to scan the back for production credits. Then I noticed the barcode on the shrink-wrap.

I had almost been duped into believing that a record from the late 1960s had somehow escaped my keen collector's notice. Arrogance restored, I read the liner notes, which tout Ms. Jones as "the Baddest Soul Sister on the circuit." As far as I knew, Etta James was still touring.[5] Disbelief aside, I bought the album in spite of its brazen attempts to invoke/evoke the ghost of a bygone era. I rode my bicycle back home, plugged the headphones into the stereo, and dropped the needle into the groove.

The record began with Binky Griptite, the Dap Kings' guitarist and emcee, introducing Sharon and the band at a live show. As the intro faded out, the drums of Homer Steinweiss and the bass of Bosco Mann kicked the album into high gear with a track called "Got a Thing on My Mind." By the time Sharon Jones's vocals came in, I had ripped the headphones out of their jack in the midst of doing my worst James Brown impersonation across the living room. I couldn't stop dancing as the speakers blared "What Have You Done for Me Lately?" (the only cover song on the record, first made famous by Janet Jackson), "The Dap Dip," "Give Me a Chance," and "Got to Be the Way It Is." The tempo only slowed for one track near the end of the record—"Make It Good to Me." When the pulse picked up again with "Ain't It Hard," I returned to my hip-shaking through the end of "Pick It Up, Lay It in the Cut."

---

neo-soul as a genre is characterized in part by the incorporation of hip-hop into urban contemporary.

[4]   At that time, the resurgence in popularity of the vinyl record had not yet begun. As such, very few new albums were being released on vinyl—except, of course, those records of import to DJs and turntablists.

[5]   Shortly after this chapter was written, Etta James passed away. With love and respect, RIP.

Though neither those headphones, nor my relationship at the time survived, my love of Sharon Jones and the Dap Kings has deepened and grown since that day. I own and frequently listen to not only every Dap Kings album, but also many of the other recordings either produced or distributed by Daptone Records. Besides its being significant on a personal level, however, the *Dap-Dippin'* debut stands as an important record within the independent tradition of R&B music. It is to this level of significance that the rest of this essay is dedicated.

The Rebirth of R&B

Unlike so many records produced in this current wave of R&B "revival," *Dap-Dippin'* sounds as if it were actually recorded during the mid-to-late 1960s or early 1970s. This assertion is equally true of each of the band's subsequent four albums, which could be classified alternatively as R&B or soul. One of the first reviews of *Dap-Dippin'* summed up the record's evocative power almost perfectly: "[It] recaptures the ballsy sound of vintage late-'60s club soul with mind-boggling devotion" (Morris 2002). In fact, *Big Daddy* magazine named *Dap-Dippin'* as the "best new funk record ever" (Hutton 2004).[6] Subsequent reviews of the Dap Kings' music prove equally apt to my argument. The band plays "real, dusty-groove variety" rhythm-and-blues (Ramanathan 2009), "a sensual amalgam of 60 years of rhythms and moods. At their funkiest they are Curtis Mayfield's *Superfly* band ... At their most seductive, they trace a lineage back through Motown to the 1940's R&B orchestras ... They move beyond nostalgia into a sound as natural as a spring bubbling from a mountain" (Costa 2008). The Dap Kings move effortlessly "from salty fatback and Meters-style chicken-scratch to slinky Southern soul and Motown-inflected pop," all "rife with gospel-steeped preachments and call-and-response" (Friskics-Warren 2007) expertly enabled by juke-joint guitar, "rubbery bass, hair-trigger drums [and] tricky horn counterpoint" (Harris 2006). In short, "there's no tighter, more inventive ensemble active in deep funk and soul circles today" (Friskics-Warren 2007).

Of course, not every critic is so enthusiastic. Siddhartha Mitter referred to the multiracial band's work as cultural appropriation—an exploitative act of "colonialism" (qtd. in Knafo 2008: para. 29). In this instance, Mitter is taking a reductionist view of appropriation. It can be argued that every form of art involves a level of appropriation. While it is undeniably true that the history of American popular music is also a history of white exploitation of black cultural forms, this does not automatically discount *all* cross-cultural appropriation as being essentially exploitative.

---

[6] While enthusiastic about this accolade, I must note that *Dap Dippin'* is not a funk record. It is (strictly speaking) an R&B record. The often overlooked distinction between rhythm and blues, soul, and funk is troubling, but outside the scope of the present argument.

Rhythm and blues is, of course, fundamentally a popular form of African American musical traditions.:

> To a greater extent than any other form of music, including jazz and hip-hop, soul [as well as its antecedent, R&B] reflects a broad spectrum of the African-American experience—the plantation roots and middle-class aspirations and inner-city disappointments, the sparkle and the sweat, the spirituality and sensuality, the joy and the pain, the rhythm and the blues. It was born in the black churches of the South, came of age in the Civil Rights era, embraced its African heritage during the rise of the Black Power movement and declined when nightclub owners realized it was cheaper to hire a disco DJ than a band.
> (Knafo 2008: para. 28)

But the great session bands at Stax, Muscle Shoals, and Motown were themselves multiracial. These bands were comprised of friends who were not exploiting one another, but creating a communal creative atmosphere born out of love for each other and the music (Guralnick 1986).[7] To conflate the significance of the rhythm-and-blues tradition to racial binaries is to misunderstand (or perhaps display ignorance regarding) the historical, social, and geographical contexts out of which the tradition arose. Rather than serving as a racial dividing line, R&B has always been about unity: bringing together the remnants of big band jazz with jump boogie blues and (later, in the form of soul) gospel (Shaw 1970); bringing together the troubles of personal and social life into lyrical content with a grown-up sensibility beyond the pap of most commercial pop music; bringing people together around the neighborhood, in the bedroom, and on the dance floor.[8]

Gabriel Roth (aka Bosco Mann) and Neal Sugarman (the co-founders of Daptone Records) are not exploiting the R&B tradition. Neither are the rest of the Dap Kings. Their commitment is a current-day manifestation of the pluralistic independent ethos that resides at the heart of the rhythm-and-blues tradition. Roth, Sugarman, Jones, and the rest of the Daptone family are links in a chain stretching back not to the Fordist methods of Motown, but to the musically

---

[7]   This is not to discount the exploitation of musicians by independent label owners from the 1940s through the 1970s. For instance, Berry Gordy (founder/owner of Motown) has frequently been cited as a model of exploitative label owners. Although reference could rightly be made to any number of independent label owners of the time (white or black), I use Gordy as an example here to highlight the fact that exploitation is not always dependent upon race. Oftentimes, it is about profit and control. The argument here is that studio and session bands in the rhythm-and-blues tradition were not homogenous groups. They were often racially heterogeneous, comprised of actual human beings rather than the faceless racial reductions Mitter's comment would sugest.

[8]   Those interested in more comprehensive discussions of the development of rhythm-and-blues and soul music should refer to the works of Guralnick (1986), Neal (1999), Redd (1974), Ripani (2006), Shaw (1970, 1978), and Small (1987).

passionate "anarchic impulse and [street-wise] business ethic" of Memphis and Muscle Shoals (Guralnick 1986: 18). In an age where legal status as an independent label is determined by independent means of distribution rather than production, major labels often form or subcontract to "independent" labels to avoid having to adhere to the union regulations of the American Federation of Musicians (Roberts 2002). This is not the case with Daptone, which is artist-owned and serves as a distributer for other independent labels (www.daptonerecords.com). Daptone Records maintains independent control over every facet of the label's activities, "from recording to publishing to licensing to distribution" (Sisario 2007: B7). The musicians do the work and they share the royalties (Sterdan 2010). Daptone Records embodies the best of the rhythm-and-blues tradition while seeming to avoid the economic exploitation of musicians that was characteristic of independent R&B labels from the 1940s through the 1970s, as well as the absorption of those labels into the major label system (Shaw 1970).

    No better evidence for the independent ethos of Daptone Records is found than in the person of Sharon Jones, the singer around whom both the label and the band were formed. Born in Augusta, Georgia and raised in the Bedford-Stuyvesant area of Brooklyn, Sharon Jones began singing (like so many other great R&B artists) at home, in church, and with neighborhood bands ("Me & Ms. Jones", 2008; Ryzik 2010). Her professional career started in the 1970s as a backing singer for Al Green and other R&B/soul artists. She even recorded a few disco singles under the moniker Miss Lafayette. But when the age of music videos came along, her career began to take a downturn. "They didn't mind me doing the stuff in the studio, but as far as getting on stage or getting on videos they felt I didn't have the look ... They said I was too short, I was too fat, I was too dark-skinned and I was too old" (Sharon Jones, qtd. in O'Donohue, 2006). Jones spent the next decade singing in a wedding band while working for a time as a corrections officer at Riker's Island prison (O'Donohue, 2006). In 1996, Jones went to audition as a backing singer for soul legend Lee Fields (Blackman 2008). The band for that session—the Soul Providers—was the house band for Desco, an independent label run by Roth (O'Donohue 2006). Although Desco folded soon after, Roth, Jones, and the other members of what would become the Dap Kings began playing and touring together, honing their extensive knowledge of and sincere devotion to the R&B tradition into the musical juggernaut we know today.

    The story of Sharon Jones and the Dap Kings (especially that of Jones) embodies the independent ethos that resides at the heart of the independent R&B tradition.[9] The fidelity of the sound comes not just from individual or group adherence to a certain ethos, though. Some of the Dap Kings have been touring together (in one band or another) for nearly 15 years. As Gabriel Roth put it:

---

    [9]   It must be noted that all of my information about Daptone Records comes from secondary sources. Though I attempted to establish contact with the label, my attempts were unsuccessful.

> Sharon Jones and the Dap Kings is a live act first. No matter how much studio
> experience we've had, we've had much more road experience. Most of us have
> been sitting in bands, smelling each other, rolling around the country for over ten
> years now ... There's really no substitute for that. (qtd. in Cridlin 2011)

Having seen the Dap Kings perform live on several occasions, I can attest that this
is no overstatement. Rarely have I seen a live band so proficient within a musical
idiom, so adept with their instruments, so tight as a unit, and so absolutely expert
at getting an audience to their feet in the united pleasure of dancing away the
troubles of their day. Great R&B is always road weary.

In order to translate that experience and expertise into albums, Daptone uses
recording equipment and techniques that would seem alien in a current-day studio.
The House of Soul (Daptone's recording studio) utilizes an Ampex reel-to-reel,
8-track recording machine and a Trident series 65 mixing board (Knafo 2008;
Warren 2009)—analog equipment from the 1960s and/or 1970s.[10] The Dap Kings
are recorded live with no overdubs. The horn section is recorded on a single
microphone; so are the backing vocals. "That's how you get the sound. You go in
there and you tape everything at one time. And if somebody messes up, you do it
over" (Sharon Jones, qtd. in Sterdan 2010). Shunning digital editing techniques,
Roth, who splices the session tapes with a razor blade (Cridlin 2011), asserts that:
"The technical limitations [of analog equipment] force musicians, producers and
engineers to do things right live" (qtd. in Cridlin 2011). Albums are often released
on vinyl before they are put out on CD or as MP3s (Knafo 2008).

This brings me back around to my initial point: the long-term significance
of *Dap Dippin* as a debut album is due to the fact that it enabled an independent
label to "revive" a musical and technical tradition considered by many to be dead.
Without that record, the Dap Kings would never have come to the attention of
Mark Ronson.[11] As the story appeared in the *New York Times*:

> Ronson, an acclaimed British-born music producer and DJ, had been hired
> by Island Records to produce a pop record for Amy Winehouse ... He had

---

[10]   As noted by both Garofolo (2002) and Mabry (1990), the development of R&B
in the 1940s and '50s was due in part to the inventions of analog tape and the vinyl (as
opposed to shellac) record, which allowed individuals and independent labels to operate
outside the major label system by having access to portable, more affordable recording and
pressing equipment.

[11]   This assertion is not intended to give Ronson credit for the Dap Kings' success.
Credit lies solely with Sharon Jones and the Dap Kings themselves. At best, Ronson can
be lauded for knowing a good thing when he heard it. As Sharon Jones has stated, "I'm old
enough to be Amy Winehouse's mother. How am I gonna take a back seat to that child? ...
Amy and Mark Ronson came to the Dap Kings ... They couldn't get the right sound, so
they came to us. They all came and jumped on our wagon" (qtd. in Blackman, 2008). This
statement was made before Winehouse's recent, untimely death. With love, RIP.

been striving for a classic soul sound, with little success. "We were using every computer trick in the book to make it sound old" … When he heard the Dap King's cover version of the Stevie Wonder song "Uptight (Everything's Alright)," he knew he'd found the sound he'd been looking for. He asked the band to play behind Amy Winehouse in the studio.

Roth had reservations. He didn't particularly love Winehouse's music, which, he says, was too angsty and self-involved for his taste … By this time, [the Dap Kings] had spent hundreds of hours riding around the country together in rented Econoline vans, listening to Sam Cooke and the Isley Brothers, "living and sweating the rhythm and blues," as Roth puts it. In comparison, this was an easy gig …

The album the Dap Kings played on, *Back to Black*, sold 10 million copies. Roth won a Grammy Award for engineering and received a framed platinum record. He displayed the platinum record in the studio's decrepit downstairs bathroom, propped up against the wall, a few inches from the toilet. (Knafo 2008: paras. 13-15)

This narrative is poignant because it illustrates the tension at the heart of popular discourse surrounding the current mainstream R&B "revival." While on the one hand the success of the Dap Kings might provide a level of encouragement, it should also serve a cautionary function. The A-side is that the mainstream success of *Back to Black* brought long overdue attention to a group of musicians operating within the independent R&B tradition. The B-side, however, is the fact that such success further enabled the major label system to again appropriate this tradition for its own exploitative purposes. While musicians, singers, and fans keep the real tradition alive out of love for the music, opportunists within the major label system rarely take notice unless they can market the music by packaging it with a young ingénue. The major label system takes the credit—and the money. To begin to understand the power structure at work in this instance, one need first look at what passes for "R&B" in today's market. On the flip side, however, not every act of appropriation automatically leads to exploitation.

Fortunately for the Dap Kings, the publicity they received for their work on *Back to Black* has brought some mainstream recognition to their real work with Sharon Jones. Sharon Jones and the Dap King's 2007 album *100 Days, 100 Nights* sold 105,000 copies (Concepcion 2010)—an impressive feat for an independent label. Their 2010 album *I Learned the Hard Way* debuted at #15 on the *Billboard* album chart (Sprague 2010). While the contracting of the Dap Kings to be the backing band for *Back to Black* might have served as a minor footnote in the extensive history of the consolidation-through-acquisition of independent labels by major label conglomerates (Roberts 2002), Daptone Records (under the leadership of Roth and Sugarman) did not allow mainstream success to alter its course. This success has provided Daptone Records with the ability to keep the independent R&B tradition alive without having to compromise with the major label system. Daptone Records remains as independent as it ever was, shunning not only the recording and production techniques of the major label system, but also its distribution channels and business methods.

With all the talk about the current R&B revival, it is easy to lose sight of an important fact. To even say that the tradition has been revived is inaccurate because the tradition never really died. It was kept alive by artists, labels, and fans working independently of the major label system. As Sharon Jones herself put it: "I hate that they keep saying revival. Don't put no 're' in front of me. I'm real, you know. I came up through the era. I didn't take no Soul 101. I open my mouth and it happens" (qtd. in Hana 2010). It happens, but it didn't *just* happen. It has been happening for decades due to the largely overlooked work of people who continue to make real rhythm-and-blues music out love and sweat, long drives from gig to gig, an understanding of history and tradition, an independent ethos, and the technical knowledge required to keep it playing.[12] And, thanks to the pivotal moment afforded Daptone Records by the release of *Dap Dippin' with...*, Sharon Jones and the Dap Kings will continue to make it happen.

Conclusions, Sort of ...

It is not my intention to offer any definitive summations regarding the rhythm-and-blues tradition or the role of *Dap-Dippin'* within the genre. My aim, instead, has been to offer an argument that would open up a more generative discussion regarding the evolution of rhythm-and-blues and its continued significance—personal, historical, cultural, technological, critical, and economic. The independent tradition that characterizes the best of what R&B can be must not be bookended. Rhythmand blues is not dead. Though marginalized within the music industry and popular music discourse for the better part of the past three decades, real R&B remains as vital to those of us who love it as it was before the intrusion of the corporations that operate major labels. Fortunately, Daptone Records—enabled by the success of Sharon Jones and the Dap Kings—are doing more than their fair share to ensure that rhythm and blues not only survives and thrives, but does so by remaining true to the fiercely independent tradition that led to its initial rise. The music speaks for itself, without further interpretation or interference.

---

[12]　I am aware of the difficulties associated with distinguishing urban contemporary, etc., from "real" R&B. It is admittedly a matter of personal preference—one consistent, however, with the argument contained herein.

Chapter 21
Pilfering the Past or Postmodern Punks?: The Libertines' *Up the Bracket*

Micah Rueber

In early 2003, EMI released the Libertines' first album in the United States. Recorded "live" in the studio and featuring minimal overdubs, *Up the Bracket* placed the band in the same basic oeuvre of other then-current hipsters the Strokes, the White Stripes, and the Hives. Like those groups, the Libertines' guitar-driven tunes were at once modern and retro, a blend that for all its musical touchstones represented something rather unique. Wildly popular among both critics and the modish in their native England, the Libertines reached similar groups in the States, appearing on numerous "best albums" lists albeit never quite finding mainstream success.[1]

The Libertines never really fulfilled the promise of *Up the Bracket*. Tensions between the band's front men and songwriters Karl Barat and Pete Doherty—fueled primarily by Doherty's increasing drug use and general unreliability—led to canceled shows, a sloppy, if occasionally stunning, second record, and Doherty's expulsion from the group. Doherty quickly became tabloid fodder on both sides of the Atlantic, both for his growing rap sheet—he has been arrested at least a dozen times for various drug and drink infractions—his engagement to supermodel (and onetime Johnny Depp muse) Kate Moss, and his friendship with the tragically troubled Amy Winehouse. In the meantime, Barat continued touring under the Libertines moniker while Doherty found an outlet—and modest success—with his new band Babyshambles. However, neither achieved the success they had while working together, and in 2010 the pair finally resolved their issues to the point where they could reunite for a series of well-received—and sold out—concerts in the UK. Critics, though happy to hear the band in good form, noted that the Libertines of 2010 amounted to an oldies band, playing the same old tunes for an increasingly nostalgic if more well-heeled audience.[2]

---

[1] The Libertines, *Up the Bracket*, Rough Trade #83213, Audio CD, 2003. *Rolling Stone* named the album #94 on its online "Best of the 00's" list and British music magazine *NME* named it #2—and the top British album—on its "Top 50 Records of the Noughties [*sic*]."

[2] Neil McCormick, in an online review for the *Daily Telegraph* of one of the reunion concerts, called the show "a sentimental evening," while Alex Petridis, writing for *NME* in 2010, referred to the Libertines' set as "trailing an undertow of wistfulness."

But that was in the future. Back to 2002: the Libertines entered the studio and recorded their first album. Produced and mixed by former Clash member Mick Jones, the debut features few—if any—overdubs and is notable primarily for the frenzied guitar stylings and vocals of the group's leaders, Barat and Doherty. In the background—in the studio, on stage, and, from all reports, contractually— drummer Gary Powell and bassist John Hassell keep the group together.

Indeed, what makes the record—and, according to critics, the Libertines' live show—work is the rhythm section: for all the craziness layered on top, the bass and drums miss nary a cue. Hassell's bass work is crisp, walking a fine line between laying down a solid harmonic foundation and offering little melodic asides and leads. Powell's drumming is even better: taut and powerful, knowing when to spur the band on and when to hold them back. The pair act as a sort of musical glue, holding together the songs when they threaten to fracture apart, and, in doing so, set the Libertines apart from much of their competition.

But nobody—or very few, at most—buys these records because of the rhythm work. The simplest assessment of the frontmen's instrumental skill is that the guitar playing of Barat and Doherty is sloppy—almost extravagantly so. But it is a different sort of nonchalance than that purveyed by the various lo-fi bands of the 1990s probably best exemplified by the likes of Pavement. Pavement's sloppy play and out-of-tune guitars suggest that they are either too lazy or too cool to care. The Libertines, on the other hand, sound like they cannot sit still long enough— though whether that stems from mere restlessness or knowing that they are late to make a drug connection remains unclear.[3]

And that is not to say they are *bad* guitar players, exactly. Though it is usually impossible to tell who is playing what, it does not really matter: no traditional distinction between rhythm- and lead-playing here—no Lennon/Harrison, Richards/whoever, Joe Perry/the "other" guy from Aerosmith. Instead, they are both playing lead and rhythm, sometimes at the same time. The duality usually works out better than it should. And that, in a nutshell, *is* the Libertines: it *all* somehow works out better than it should.

The album's opening track, "Vertigo," sets the tone for the album. Over a sinister, hip shuffle Doherty and Barat work their magic as their sloppy, interlocking guitar parts and slurred, indistinct vocals weave their way around the solid groove laid down by the bass and drums. Charming in a sinewy way, the lyrics provide a clue about what is to come: though the song's "drunken prophet" might well "see everything," his view, and by implication that of the singers, of the surroundings is clearly a perspective from the gutter. Unlike the Beatles' "Penny Lane," which offers a bird's-eye view of its characters' thoughts and actions—to say nothing of the Kinks' snapshots of contemporary (and changing) England in the 1960s

---

[3]   Kalefa Sanneh (2003), reviewing a concert performed soon after the American debut of *Up the Bracket*, wrote "the flubbed guitar notes helped create the illusion of great effort," while Betty Clarke (2003), describing a Libertines' gig for the *Guardian*, refers to the guitar work as both "messy" and "frenzied."

and 1970s—the Libertines look "up" rather than "down," and it remains unclear whether they really wish to crawl out of the mess.[4]

Maybe even more telling is the song's advice to make a fortune with a "lead pipe." Deliciously ambiguous about theft, to the American ear the line sounds like a scenario from the board game Clue ("Libertines used the lead pipe in the music room," perhaps), it also hints at the traditional fallback of English thieves, who would strip the roofing and pipes off buildings. Either way, the line rings as a confession: the first instance suggests the Libertines have appropriated—violently—their style; in the second, that they have "borrowed" it from others, melted it down, and created a new amalgam. And in either case the admission confirms what the listener already suspects, that they have heard this all before. Or have they?

If the lyrics of "Vertigo" imply (mis)appropriation, the album's second song, "Death on the Stairs," is, among other things, a meditation on the past. Appropriately for post-modern rockers, Barat and Doherty seem unsure whether to reject or embrace what came before. One verse scolds the listener who will not (or cannot) "leave the past behind." The singer, on the other hand, professes unfamiliarity with "yesterday" though it remains unclear whether this amounts to ignorance or enlightenment. Sly nod to the Beatles' "Yesterday" aside, the third verse probably best sums up their stance: singing about "meeting the past" in order to "keep it sweet," the vocalist concludes "It's just like nothing at all." In a disavowal of the past and a denial of its importance, the singer implores the listener not to "bring that ghost round to my door."[5]

The album's next two songs, "Horror Show" and "Time for Heroes," continue the Libertines' musings on temporality and, in fact, act as flip sides of the coin. In "Horror," the listener learns of a future in there is "nothing changing," and that "it's all sorrow." Again the lyrics dance around the ebb and flow of time—in this case a static future reminiscent of the Talking Heads' "Heaven"—a "place where nothing ever happens." "Time for Heroes," on the other hand, suggests that this possibility it not wholly undesirable. Commenting on the squalor of the contemporary "scene," the singer promises that "Time will strip it away." Putting together the rebus, we find that the "Time for Heroes" "obscene scene" will give way to a "tomorrow" where "there's nothing changing."

Of course, "Time for Heroes" asks more questions than it answers: is *now* the time for heroes? Or will they be needed (or appear) sometime in the future? And, more obviously, who are the "heroes"? The Libertines themselves? The lyrics suggest that possibility: "It's all in my hands," the singer admits. Another clue

---

[4]   Barat/Doherty, "Vertigo," EMI Music Publishing Ltd., 2002. Critic John Robinson, writing for *The Guardian* (London) in 2008, referred to the album as "a new and suitably murky installment from … London's 'seamy underbelly'… a self-created demi-monde that smells faintly of cheese."

[5]   Throughout the remainder of this text, all lyric citations of the songs from *Up the Bracket* are credited to Barat/Doherty, EMI Music Publishing Ltd., 2002.

can be gleaned in the song's reference to Bill Bones, a mysterious and sometimes contradictory character in Robert Louis Stevenson's *Treasure Island*. Again, we have the Libertines wrapping themselves in mystery.

The Libertines' songs teem with sordid street scenes: illicit sex, voyeurism, drug use, insobriety, fights, riots, seemingly taking place in the wee hours when the more respectable members of society are safely at home. Quite frankly, it seems like a Kerouac-ish put-on, the antics of spoiled brats slumming in the streets. Which does not imply the band has not had its problems: Doherty's multiple (at last count somewhere north of a dozen) arrests for drink, drugs, and burglary— of band mate Barat's flat, no less—imply a certain awareness of the life's darker corners, but even this seems like a charade if not a chimera—another costume put on by Doherty who, despite his obvious intelligence and musical talent, seems either by inclination or design (or both) to care as much about sustaining the sordid fantasy he has weaved around himself as about actually realizing the vision he espouses.[6]

In terms of both musicality and sensibility, the Libertines' persona seems to consist of an accumulation of tropes gathered from the dustbin of British rock. More mythos than history, their background, whether fiction, fact, or a combination of the two, amount to an olio, an amalgamation of the past: teenaged Barat and Doherty meet and find they share some sort of musical vision (Lennon/McCartney, Jagger/Richards, Townsend/Daltrey, etc.); the band is "discovered" by a promoter who insists that Barat and Doherty become the focal point of the band (the Brian Epstein role? Sex Pistols' mastermind Malcolm McLaren, perhaps?); rumors of a physical relationship between Barat and Doherty which they coyly—or savvily— refused to confirm or deny.[7]

In this sense the real counterpart for the Libertines are not fellow rockers the Strokes, the Hives, et al., with whom they are usually compared but rather American band the White Stripes, who very consciously created their own mythology in large part by keeping their mouths shut. By adopting the last name White, Jack and Meg implied a relationship. Rumors spread that they were brother and sister, or married, or both. In truth, the pair had been married—and divorced—

---

[6] Carl Wilson, writing for the *Globe and Mail* (Canada), eloquently captured something of this when he said: "The Libertines are worldly and seductive, their approach highly calculated. But in their case, not cynically so. Most potentially good rock bands have (or fake) a secret agenda" (2003).

[7] The rumors were fueled by the fact that Barat and Doherty were photographed kissing, though whether this was a stolen tender scene or simply a staged shot has never been entirely clear. Of course, English rock stars have longed played with gender identities and bisexuality: David Bowie's Ziggy Stardust character reveled in some combination of androgyny and pan-sexuality; openly gay Elton John was once closeted and married, apparently not entirely unhappily; Freddy Mercury enjoyed scores of lovers of both genders though he was careful to maintain a "macho"—if not always entirely "masculine"—image on stage.

before they found fame outside their native Detroit. Still, by doing nothing more than remain mum and allow the rumor mill to take over they fostered, if they did not exactly create, their own mythology. The British press did much the same with the Libertines.

Should the Libertines' past matter? That is a more difficult question. Other postmodern acts have produced good music. Tenacious D, for one, works precisely because—their send-up of rock and the whole experience of membership in a band beside—they make great music. Their "A Tribute to the Best Song in the World" would not pack such a punch, nor provoke such mirth, if it were not a pretty good song in its own right. While Tenacious D relies on parody, the homage offered to heavy metal by the Queens of the Stone Age—best exemplified on *Songs for the Deaf*, the group's third release—also works because it is, in the end, good music.

And that's not to imply the Libertines don't—or at least didn't—make good music. *Up the Bracket* remains fresh, powerful, and moving, even after a decade and countless listenings. Like the best debut albums it offers hints of everything the band will become. Granted, in the case of the Beatles this amounted to roughly a dozen more albums—ending, with 1970's *Let it Be*, almost exactly where they started, while the Libertines first record amounted to precisely half their (as of 2011) recorded output. But the point is valid. A good friend of some half-century musical experience once remarked that "virtually everything a band is going to be is evident at their first gig"—the implication being that after a band starts gigging the time and drive to create is tempered by the pressures and commitments of the gigs themselves. Doherty said at the time: "I knew I had a better album than *Up the Bracket* in me and I wanted to record it. But I was told we've got to keep touring, keep promoting. That was the first time I realized we were on a conveyor belt" (Clarke 2004).

This tension between appearances and reality is nowhere more apparent than in "Boys in the Band"—the obvious answer song to "Time for Heroes"—which begins with the singer calling out all pretenders, who run away rather than "sing," "dance," or "fight." In short, the song questions those whose walk does not match their talk. While not especially profound, the question at least seems "punk." Meanwhile, the listener is left asking the same things about the Libertines themselves. Posture and pretense aside, what had (at least at the time this album appeared) the Libertines actually accomplished? A single? A handful of (by all accounts sloppy) gigs? Perhaps the question is not fair: the same could be said of most bands that had just released their debut album. On the other hand, not all bands try so hard to wish or imagine themselves into the musical tradition. Instead, the Libertines seem to assume that if you *act* like you belong than you *do*, in fact, belong.

Consider the ways by which the Libertines attempt to align themselves with their British musical forbears. As the bridge of "Boys" reminds the listener, the Libertines' audience "twist and scream and shout" for The Boys in the Band — a nice trick linking their debut album to the Beatles' first recording session. But it goes deeper than that. Because the Libertines came of age at a time when

MTV remained musically, rather than culturally, relevant, it seems appropriate to briefly consider the video for their debut album's title song. The video begins with a scene of the four band members walking down the street. Approximately one minute into the video the shot cuts to a pile of vinyl records—themselves largely rendered obsolescent by cassettes and (slightly later) compact discs by the time MTV appeared—on the top of which rests, quite visibly, and certainly not coincidentally, a copy of the Beatles' second LP, *With the Beatles.* This quick camera shot is the essence of postmodernism: it suggests either that time does not exist, or that all times are equally valid. In either case, the video, like the band's lyrics, seem engaged in an intricate dance with temporality.[8]

Immediately after the quick shot of this heap of records—whether it comprises a treasure trove to be raided or a pile of refuse is unclear—the camera finds the Boys "playing" their song: dressed in Sgt. Pepper jackets, no less, and shaking their carefully disheveled hair in obvious parody or homage to the Fab Four. Another post-modern moment, the quick juxtaposition of the Beatles' second record with *Sgt. Pepper*'s is significant. First, it reminds the viewer of how far the Beatles progressed in a scant five years. Second, that for the Libertines—and whether this is true for a whole generation is a subject for another debate—the Beatles' entire history is not a sequence but a whole to be mined at will: that for the Libertines the Beatles, early or late, are simply a discrete piece of the past to be mined, mimicked, cut-and-pasted. Moreover, a quick cut—blink and you'll miss it—shows the boys back in their street clothes while a quartet of young birds have donned the Sgt. Pepper garb. Again, this merely emphasizes that point that, at least for this band, the past is merely a costume or aesthetic that can be as easily assumed as shed.[9]

And the Libertines seem to confirm this postmodern temporal sensibility in some of their interviews. Critics made much of the fact that the Libertines seem wistful for some sort of forever-lost—or perhaps never-was—England, one reviewer likening them to "the cherubic-faced link between Noel Coward and the Clash" (Clarke 2003). Another spoke of the Libertines "referencing their arch nostalgia for a certain indefinable quality of Englishness" (McCormick 2003). The Libertines' response is telling. Said Barat, "People accuse us of being in love with

---

[8]   For what it is worth, the other vinyl record that is recognizable to the viewer is a copy of Marc Bolan and T. Rex's *Best of the 20th Century Boy* compilation—a band that again, probably not coincidentally, many critics compared to the Libertines.

[9]   Of course, this skewed sense of the past is not new with the Libertines, as critic/crank Richard Meltzer noted in his 1970 screed *The Aesthetics of Rock*: "Just as the realm of rock repetition easily copes with the experience of sameness, the several varieties of tongues can easily deal with the experience of apparently unbreachable disparity. To rock the distance between *Pride and Prejudice* and *Last Exit to Brooklyn* is no more than that between, for example, Magritte's 'The Human Condition II,' 1935, and his later 'Les promenades d'Euclide,' 1955. Thus can 'I Want to Hold Your Hand' and 'Being for the Benefit of Mr. Kite!' be viewed simultaneously ..." (1970: 137).

the colours of an old world and dusty tins." Doherty expanded on this sentiment: "But it's an age that exists now. You can own the tin now. It's not like time-travelling or pretending you live in another era. *You can appreciate the beauty of something whenever it was made*" (McCormick 2003, emphasis added).

In a sense, the Libertines echo, almost certainly unintentionally, critic Greil Marcus's essay "History Lesson." Taking as a starting point the line "Don't know much about history" from Sam Cooke's song "Wonderful World," Marcus argues that the myriad histories presented in common culture actually act to free moderns from the "burden" of the past: that all these competing mythologies, in effect, cancel each other out. As a result, the "parts of history" that "don't fit the story a people wants to tell itself, can survive only as haunts and fairy tales, accessible only as specters and spooks" (Marcus 1995: 21-24). Taken from this perspective, the Libertines' entire mythology becomes rather more interesting: post-modern punks living in a past of their own creation, they are no longer tethered to any fixed notion of the past, and are free to draw meaning where/when they find it. Whether this temporal timelessness is a good thing is up for debate, but at least from an artistic standpoint the Libertines seems to have found success.

Depending on one's thoughts about the nature of time and the role of history, *Up the Bracket* as a whole can be read as homage to the Beatles. Alternatively, if the Libertines and the Beatles exist in the same moment, the Libertines can be seen as writing themselves into the Beatles myth—and, vice versa. That might or might not have been the Libertines' intention, but the similarities of the recording process as well as the various "clues" scattered throughout both album and video suggest such a reading is as valid as any other: after all, if the band refuses to play straight they cannot very well expect their audience to act differently.

Already this article has noted in passing some of the possible Beatles references, but things come to a head in the song "The Boy Looked at Johnny." Ostensibly (and quite likely actually) written about Razorlight front man and one-time Libertine Johnny Borrell, the song can be interpreted instead as an ode to John Lennon. The opening couplet alone—"Like in a saddle with his gun / We're in slow motion eating breakfast"—makes reference to three Beatles tunes: "Happiness is a Warm Gun," "Good Morning Good Morning," and "A Day in the Life"—all of them (save the bridge of "A Day...") written by Lennon. Also telling is the chorus's reference to New York City, a nice connection to the iconic photograph of Lennon sporting the popular I (Heart) NY t-shirt.

The Lennon connection continues with "The Boy...": "But oh don't you miss Soho." That little "oh," though probably superfluous, has all sorts of resonance for the Lennon-phile. Lennon himself was fond of playing with the "oh," from songs (*Imagine*'s "Oh My Love" as well as "Oh Yoko") to Lennon's self-styled sometimes moniker and recording pseudonym, Dr. Winston O'Boogie. Now, it must be acknowledged that Paul McCartney also had a bit of an "oh" fascination himself, from "Oh Darling" to "Ob-La-Di, Ob-La-Da." In fact, the babble of nonsense syllables—"La de di la de di da diddy"—in the chorus of "The Boy..." can certainly be read as a comment/satire/response to "Ob-La-Di," a Macca tune that Lennon famously panned on at least one occasion as "Paul's granny shit." Put together, that Libertines chorus— "don't you miss Soho / Where everybody goes / La de di la de di da diddy"—can be taken as a question not to Johnny Borrell but to John Lennon himself, asking Lennon if, as an expatriate living in New York, he does not sometimes miss both London and McCartney.[10]

Interestingly—and appropriately—for all their genre-jumping, the Libertines rarely sound nostalgic. True, they purloin pieces of the past. Critics describing the album have compared the Libertines' sound to a gamut of (mostly British) bands: the Clash, the Sex Pistols, the Jam, the Kinks, Marc Bolan, and, probably most often, the Buzzcocks. No doubt the likely lads owe more than a nod to these and to others; depending on the listener's familiarity with the British rock oeuvre, he or she will find bits and pieces they will swear they have heard before. But what makes *Up the Bracket* a really good—and quite perhaps great—album is that, for all their borrowing, the Libertines make it sound uniquely their own. These songs are not, in any real sense, homage to their musical heroes. Instead, it is a debut that could only have appeared when it did, how it did.

Lyrically, Doherty and Barat fit, not altogether surprisingly given their quite earnest Britishness, somewhere in the land claimed earlier by the Kinks and, to a certain extent, the Jam, both bands who, in their own way, found their sensibilities not in the American past but in a bygone or disappearing England. All British rock bands owe a certain debt to America, but most of them—the Rolling Stones, Cream, Led Zeppelin—clearly hope to best the Americans at their own game. Only the Beatles really straddled the oceanic divide comfortably: every quintessentially British tune such as "Penny Lane" has a companion in a fundamentally American number like "Oh Darling"; part of the Beatles' genius was this ability to combine the two aesthetics so seamlessly.

The closest American touchstones for the Libertines music are the Velvet Underground and, especially musically, the Ramones. The Ramones' hard-driving, relentless guitar attack underpins much of their work. The influence of the Velvet Underground comes through primarily lyrically, in the fascination with the darker corners of the London night: tales of fights, random sex, and drug use. And though Sonic Youth rarely gets the credit they deserve, the Libertines—and, whether they know it or not, most "alternative" bands formed since the mid-1980s—owe them a certain debt: the first 40 seconds of "Begging"—and, for that matter, the full last minute—could have come straight off a 1980s era Sonic Youth record: driving drums, atmospheric guitars, cryptic vocals, and all the rest.

The one moment nostalgia does creep in is, appropriately enough, "The Good Old Days." Granted, the nostalgia is tempered. Reminding the listener that the spirit of Queen Boadicea (the first-century AD British princess who led a revolt against the Romans and was mentioned by Tacitus) "lives on" in her "children's children's children," and that it "would be wrong" to lose the spirit, the narrator

---

[10]   This writer would posit that Lennon's response would most likely consist of a resounding "NO."

curtly asserts that "there were no good old days / These are the good old days." The album closes with the title song, "Up the Bracket," the lyrics of which neatly sum up the band's whole approach. The lyric's two main themes involve "two shadowed men" and "these two crooked fingers." The first term, "shadowed men," is British slang for either underground cops, spies, or, in some cases, the criminals they're after. Either meaning works: ostensibly the shadowy figures are pursuing the singer after offering to pay for "your"—the song's intended audience's— address. The singer (Doherty) shows the men "these two cold fingers"—the British equivalent of the American "one-fingered salute"—a salute to both the shadowy men and the Libertines' audience that somehow works perfectly.

For what the Libertines—whether they realize it or not—demonstrate is that it is nearly impossible in the post-millennial era to come up with something entirely novel. The Libertines cannot be the Beatles, or Elvis, or the Sex Pistols, or any other of the truly original artists whose debuts made the listener sit up and pay attention. Instead, much like Lady Gaga almost a decade later, the Libertines mined that past, choosing bits and pieces to combine in new ways, relying less on originality than on new interpretations or juxtapositions of the past. Though at least one reviewer chastised the Libertines for their "derivative music," the truth is that virtually all music is derivative to some degree. The Libertines' allure lies in part in the brazenness with which they confront the listener with the familiar; but their genius is in their ability to do so in such a compelling manner (Smith 2002).

Chapter 22

Cinematic Fantastic Sampledic Funky Found-Sound Sifting:
The Go! Team's *Thunder, Lightning, Strike*

George Plasketes and Rivers Plasketes

Perhaps the most exuberantly intriguing and irresistible sounds (intentionally plural) to emerge from our son's ever expanding music collection at age 14 were those generated by The Go! Team's *Thunder, Lightning, Strike* (Memphis Industries 2004/Columbia 2005).[1] When I initially overheard the record, I assumed it was a soundtrack. The songs were predominantly instrumental. They were upbeat, offbeat, occasionally cheesy, but in a familiar and funky sort of way. Keenly aware of the clearly defined, hip posturing parameters and parent-child bonding boundaries of advancing adolescence, I approached our son about the record with delicate curiosity. Without too much suspicion of a parent trap or set-up, he responded like a newly enlisted Fan Clubber who had completed his music homework beyond his headsets, but at the same time remained true to tweendom with an interrogation succinct four-fragment response: "new group; lot of Internet buzz; from the UK; The Go! Team."

Before becoming a Team, the Brighton-based band's beginnings were as a homemade hobby rooted in the solo sound-tinkerings of Ian Parton, a Discovery Channel film documentarian. Parton culled through and combined some of his "favorite things"—detuned no-wave guitars, Motown brass, old school hip hop beats, cheerleader chants, action-movie soundtrack music—and, with the engineering assistance of his brother Gareth, mixed a batch of samples with live instruments on a four-track recorder in their parents' kitchen. Ian Parton, whose "plan was always to be a gang," posted a London classified seeking vocalists, musicians and players. Within weeks, he assembled an energetic, eclectic, multinational sextet, some with exotic action-figure names—Sam Dook, Kaori Tsuchida, MC Ninja and Silke Steidinger—almost too good to be true to the band's *Scooby Doo* sensibility and *Speed Racer* cartoon-worthy name. The "Go! Team" title, which derives from the units that are dispatched to clean up the wreckage

---

[1]   There are two versions of *Thunder, Lightning, Strike*. The first was a UK release in 2004 on Memphis Industries, followed by a US/UK version, with two new songs, on Columbia in 2005. The stateside distribution was delayed due to sample clearance issues. Keep reading, a more detailed discussion lies ahead in this chapter.

after a plane crash, is an appropriate, if not ideal designation for the gang of sound sifters.[2]

Three singles soon circulated into Internet sensations—"Get It Together," released on Pickled Egg in 2002, followed by "Junior Kickstart" in 2003. "The Power is On" preceded the *Thunder, Lightning, Strike* debut in 2004. Mainstream appeal and airplay were not the group's primary goals. Parton set out to make "dirty" pop songs that were chaotic and catchy. "It wasn't ever going to be a polished, radio-friendly outfit," said Parton. "That's why I went with Memphis [Industries]. I would bring in a mix and they would tell me to go back and make it dirtier. That was a good sign" (Visakowitz 2007).

The resulting *Thunder, Lightning, Strike* is a sampledelic, cinematic fantastic soundtrack in search of a screenplay. Or a fitting score for an aerial-view high-speed chase "breaking news" on cable television. Perhaps an ad jingle pumping the volume for nostalgia and hipster fashion at urban clothing outfitters. The three words in the album title—"Thunder, Lightning, Strike"— might as well be code for "Holland, Dozier, Holland," though that might be too musically restrictive. The record's image-rich sound spectrum spans 1960s soul, from Curtis Mayfield to Motown moments, to kids educational *Schoolhouse Rock*, 1970s television and film cops *Starsky and Hutch* and *Shaft!*, to Toni Basil's Big 80s hit "Mickey," to contemporary club and convertible hip hop "Hollaback Girl" Gwen Stefani, to Sonic Youthfulness. The album's expansive sonic palette is chaotic, but controlled, its convergence conjuring feelings of summer and school spirit; Kung Fu and cowboys; jump ropes, junk yards, and gymnasiums; double Dutch and *Drumline*.

The Go! Team brings da' funk and da' noise, jump starting the record's race pace with "Panther Dash," making it instantly obvious why there is an exclamation point placed in the band's name. The velocity is predominantly high energy; "1970s Red Bull," "sunshine funk," and "Day-Glo bubble-dance-pop" are among the colorful critical characterizations of the sound style. The tempo sprints; it is steady on straightaways with sudden shifts in syncopation, and variations that include middledistance diversions and a cool cool-down. It's anything but a marathon. Even with its two added tracks, the US version's running time clocks in at around 41 minutes. However, the mix masters pack a fun fusion into the abbreviated time frame, demonstrating an "everything but the kitsch(en) sink" resourcefulness. The outfit utilizes cheers and chants, marching band bursts, an occasional siren and whistle, handclaps, Northern soul horns, and plangent harmonica, 1-2-3-4 countdowns to launch songs, flutes and fuzzy guitars, flourishes of electronica and old skool hip hop, trashcans and turntables, surf chords and strings, Bacharach and banjo, scratching and sampling.

The lyrics are lo-fi to the loud; they are sparse and supplementary, straining through the megaphone mix. Decipherable phrase fragments such as "fantastic," "romantic," "power," and "let's go" seem to surface subliminally, while "shake it

---

[2]   The origins of the band name may in part explain the noisy 39-second "Air Raid GTR" eight cuts into the album.

down to the bone" and "come on everybody let's rock this" are decipherable in the rapid-fire rap and rant of "Bottle Rocket" and "Huddle Formation's" shouts. The exception is the jungle gym playground soliloquy, "Hold Yr Terror Close," which soothes over a toy piano composition.

Parton miraculously manages to avoid a messy mish-mashup. The production is comprehensive and cluttered, but orchestrally cohesive. The inventive layering and extractions are not so much a Spectorian Wall of Sound as a Wall of Graffiti tagged with vibrant sheets of sound and soundalikes. The excavations relocated in Team Territory are bountiful: feature films, the Holland/Dozier/Holland songbook, blues/jazz compositions of Billy Davis, Carl William Smith and Raynard Miner, 1960s soul of Shirley Ellis, Fred Neil's "Everybody's Talkin'," Laura Nyro, and the Clash documentary *Westway to the World.* The word choice of "contains elements" rather than "samples" in the credits suggests a scientific and archeological approach in field recording fashion, with Parton and company digging, collecting, experimenting, excavating, and arranging musical molecules in the sound lab.

Whether swiped or simply subtle, there are some "swear-that-sounds-like" moments on the record that are surprisingly not credited or cited. [3] One of the most conspicuous ricochets is Archie Bell and the Drells' soul classic "Tighten Up" bedded in the hook-happy "Ladyflash," one of the record's richest, multifarious arrangements. Most of the borrowed bits on *Thunder, Lightning, Strike* are not as blatant as those that had routinely resurfaced in radio's rotations. Among the ex(s) amples are: America's "Ventura Highway" hook intro in Janet Jackson's "Someone to Call My Love"; Sean "Puffy" Combs (aka "Puff Daddy"/"P. Diddy"/"Diddy") copping the Police's "Every Breath You Take" on "I'll Be Missing You"; or Jessica Simpson ripping John Mellencamp's "Jack and Diane" riffs on "I Think I'm In Love With You." To their credit, the Go! Team's abstractions are more nuanced, teasing the listener's memory bank with the traces ranging from Van McCoy's "Hustle" to the Jackson Five to the Japanese jive of Shonen Knife. There is a hint of the Cure's "In Between Days" running through "Huddle Formation," while "Hold Yr Terror Close" is reminiscent of the Thrills, and "Everyone's a V.I.P. to Someone" evokes Burt Bacharach.

The entire record is not at car chase pace. There are breath-catching, mid-tempo moments that balance the block party. "Feel Good by Numbers" features an innocent Vince Guraldian piano melody. The homage would be an ideal comic strip soundtrack for one of cartoonist Charles Schulz's lost *Peanuts* panels, with Snoopy transformed into Snoop Dogg, twisting on top of the dog house while Charlie Brown diligently labors over the sequencing and selections for a Ramsey Lewis mix tape for Lucy. The campfire harmonica that tails out the tune may be the best of the brilliantly sweet sound-sprinkles throughout the record.

---

[3] The music, film, and sound samples are more clearly cited in the liner notes of the US version of the album (Columbia 2005).

There are also what might be described as "East meets West(ern)" interludes on "Get It Together" and "Friendship Update." The instrumentation—flute, pennywhistle, hollow drums, harmonica flutters, bold horns, piano and keyboards—combine to create a riding-the-range crescendo that connects Kung Fu with classic Western, David Carradine meets Gary Cooper. Both compositions are pure Go! Team; there are no borrowed rudiments that accent their other songs. Though "Everyone's a V.I.P. to Someone" is more derivative, the sound results are similar. Banjo blends with harmonica, horns and flute, merge into a medley that re-grooves the Rascals' "Groovin'" with the Fifth Dimension's version of Laura Nyro's "Stone Soul Picnic" melody. The 1960s reprise evokes clouds and credits rolling, and provides calming closure that rides *Thunder, Lightning, Strike* off into the sunset. The band is particularly adept at this solitary, sentimental, Shanghai Noon style, which eventually emerged as one of its signature sounds. There is further evidence of the Go! Team's fondness for this musical mode on "Phantom Broadcast," their contribution to *Help! A Day in the Life* (2005), a charity record for children of war. The song could have fit seamlessly into the sound and sequence of the debut.

The extensive sampling of elements that defines *Thunder, Lightning, Strike*'s pastiche aesthetic also resulted in legal and distribution complications that became a part of the Team's debut narrative. *Thunder, Lightning, Strike*'s initial release in 2004 on the UK label Memphis Industries—even though nominated for Britain's prestigious Mercury Music Prize in 2005—was unavailable in the US due to the album's sprawling sample list. Seattle-based Sub Pop was among the labels interested in providing a stateside home for the album, but clearance costs were prohibitive. "At that point in time we just didn't have the muscle to pull it together and get all the samples cleared. It was just way too much money," said Sue Busch, Sub Pop head of radio promotion (Visakowitz 2007). Memphis Industries' Ollie Jacob and the independent-minded Parton negotiated a deal with Sony BMG. "We decided on a joint venture for the one album, knowing it would help get Ian to a stage where he could later do a lot of smaller deals around the world with indie labels," said Jacob (Visakowitz 2007). Eighteen months after its initial release, The Go! Team's debut was slightly tweaked and remixed to suit sampling clearance issues, and re-released by Sony subsidiary Columbia in 2005 in the US and UK. The reconfigured version included two additional songs totaling five minutes— "We Just Won't Be Defeated" and "Hold Yr Terror Close." Predictably, a sticker on the album's cover provides herald and highlight to maximize marketability: "*Mercury Prize Nominee. U.S. release includes two new tracks.*" The new songs were not included as typical "bonus material" footnotes fastened to the end of the original recording, but were integrated seamlessly into the sequence as tracks 6 and 11. Despite selling only 48,000 copies in the US, *Thunder, Lightning, Strike*'s international sales reached a quarter-million.

The Go! Team is an impressive, imaginative group of audio archival rearrangers and abstract expressionists. The Pep squad hipsters orchestrated an incredibly colorful, catchy collage of convergent commotion without reducing the record to novelty or gimmick. *Thunder, Lightning, Strike* is a striking debut, as playful and picturesque as it is sweet and smart. Perhaps its most admirable, noteworthy qualities lie in the familiar fragments of musical heritage that the Team has mined from various soundscapes, styles, and eras. Ironically, the sense of homage, whether intentional or not, may be overlooked, as the majority of the sample sources are likely unknown to many younger listeners who are the band's primary audience.[4] While bits and pieces may be lost in translation, The Go! Team is about found sound and exotic resonance within the familiar. Their resourceful, rambunctious retro reverberations of musical flotsam and jetsam provided a fleet alternative and fresh spin to the strands of hip hop, girl pop, rap, gangsta, dance tracks, and mashups that were prevalent in music and its ancillary outlets in broadcast, cable, film, advertising, and the Internet.

In the six years following their hyper-kinetic entrance on The Scene, The Go! Team still goes gleefully, their pom pom presence, the exclamation point in their name, and the shout in their sound all still in motion in fast forward mode. With its subsequent recordings, the team has remained true to its cool, their thunder and lightning striking twice in the same place on *Proof of Youth* (2007) and *Rolling Blackouts* (2011). Beyond the solid succession of albums, the Go! Team debut fragments intermittently surface outside and inside the mainstream. In a small club scene in the film, *Nick and Norah's Infinite Playlist* (2008), there is a glimpse of a Go! Team gig poster in the background of a shot. Sound clips from their songs "Get it Together" and "Ladyflash" are part of the US's National Public Radio's rotation segueing segments and bedded under promos for popular programs such as Terri Gross's cultural interview forum *Fresh Air.* Other songs have been adroitly adapted into advertising. The car chase pace of "Huddle Formation" is a perfect fit for the jump-cut visuals of a drive-around-the-world scene featuring a character who awakens and divides into seven versions of himself in a Honda Civic. "We Just Won't Be Defeated" underscores the red-and-white series of animated adventures of a flat figure's acrobatics while pushing a shopping cart in a rush to Target for the two-day sale commencing the consumer holiday holy day "Black Friday."

Their widest sound exposure surfaces in a somewhat unlikely source. In 2010, the National Football League began its sponsorship of a youth fitness program designed to promote health and counter obesity. "Play 60" encourages children to be physically active 60 minutes a day rather than playing stationary or Play Station(ing) indoors. In a public service announcement promoting the initiative, a group of professional football players are aboard a school bus, ride sharing with the school-age passengers. The Go! Team's "The Power is On" is hazily distinct on the soundtrack, as if audio eavesdrop leaking from headsets at a damaging decibel level. The sound steadily rises. Seated, the athletes are gently rocking back and forth, heads bobbing, slight smiles to the spirited song. The youngsters

---

[4]   Recognizing that presumption, I seized the opportunity for parental musicological reciprocation and played as many of the original sources of the samples used in *Thunder, Lightning, Strike* as I could for Rivers.

are energized as well. The gladiator-like figures exit the bus with the children, a swarm spilling enthusiasm, onto a park field. The slogan—"Join the Movement"— superimposes on the screen. The energy-encouraging expression punctuates and propels, a fitting phrase not only for the "Play 60" program, but an appropriate logo for the inventive found-sound synthesis and fringe force of The Go! Team.

Appendix A
Debut Album Discography

This discography features the 23 debut albums that are presented in the chapters of this volume. The albums are listed chronologically (as they appear in the book), with each entry identifying the artist, album title, record label, catalog number, and release date. Please note that many of the albums have multiple versions/editions such as US, UK, stereo, mono, and reissue, often on different record labels.

The Crickets. *The "Chirping" Crickets* (Brunswick BL 54038), 1957.
Little Richard. *Here's Little Richard* (Specialty SP-100), 1957.
Huey "Piano" Smith and His Clowns. *Having A Good Time* (Ace LP-1004), 1959.
Joan Baez. *Joan Baez* (Vanguard VRS-9078), 1960.
Roger Miller. *Dang Me/Chug A Lug* (Smash MGS27049), 1964.
Wilson Pickett. *Midnight in Memphis* (Atlantic 8114), 1965.
Jackson C. Frank. *Jackson C. Frank* (EMI Columbia 33SX 1788), 1965.
Nick Drake. *Five Leaves Left* (Island ILPS 9105), 1969.
George Harrison. *All Things Must Pass* (Apple STCH 639), 1970.
Willis Alan Ramsey. *Willis Alan Ramsey* (Shelter SR-2124), 1972.
New York Dolls. *New York Dolls* (Mercury SRM1-675), 1973.
Warren Zevon. *Warren Zevon* (Asylum 7E-1060), 1976.
Elvis Costello. *My Aim Is True* (Stiff Records SEEZ3), 1977.
Steve Forbert. *Alive on Arrival* (Nemperor/Epic JZ 35538), 1978.
Jandek. *Ready for the House* (Corwood Industries 0739), 1978.
Rickie Lee Jones. *Rickie Lee Jones* (Warner Bros. BSK3296), 1979.
Metallica. *Kill 'Em All* (Megaforce Records MRI 069), 1983.
Pearl Jam. *Ten* (Epic 468884-2), 1991.
LeAnn Rimes. *Blue* (Curb D2-77821), 1996.
Third Eye Blind. *Third Eye Blind* (Elektra 62012-2), 1997.
Sharon Jones and the Dap-Kings. *Dap-Dippin' with Sharon Jones and the Dap-Kings* (Daptone Records Dap 001), 2002.
The Libertines. *Up the Bracket* (Rough Trade 06076-83213-2), 2002.
The Go! Team. *Thunder, Lightning, Strike* (Memphis Industries Ltd. M104LP), 2004.

Appendix B
Grammy Award Winners and Nominees "Best New Artist" (1959-2013)

The Grammy winner is listed first and with an asterisk. The album listed for each artist is their record released closest to their Grammy nomination, and not necessarily their debut.

2013
fun,*, *Some Nights* (Fueled by Ramen, 2012)
Alabama Shakes, *Boys & Girls* (Ato, 2012)
Hunter Hayes, *Hunter Hayes* (Atlantic, 2011)
Frank Ocean, *Channel Orange* (Def Jam, 2012)
The Lumineers, *The Lumineers* (Dualtone Music Group, 2012)

2012
Bon Iver*, *Bon Iver* (Jagjaguwar, 2011); *For Emma, Forever Ago* (Jagjaguwar, 2008)
The Band Perry, *The Band Perry* (Republic Nashville, 2010)
J. Cole, *Cole World; The Sideline Story* (Roc Nation/Columbia, 2011)
Nicki Minaj, *Pink Friday* (Young Money Cash Money, 2010)
Skrillex, *More Monsters and Sprites; Bangarang* (his fourth and fifth EPs) (Big Beat, 2011)

2011
Esperanza Spalding*, *Chamber Music Society* (Heads Up International, 2010)
Justin Bieber, *My World 2.0* (Island/RBMG, 2010)
Drake, *Thank Me Later* (Young Money Entertainment/Cash Money Records/ Universal Motown Records, 2010)
Florence and the Machine, *Lungs* (Island, 2009)
Mumford and Sons, *Sigh No More* (Island/Glassnote, 2009)

2010
Zac Brown Band*, *The Foundation* (Atlantic/Home Grown/Bigger Picture, 2008)
Keri Hilson, *In a Perfect World* (Mosley/Zone 4, 2009)
MGMT, *Oracular Spectacular* (Columbia/Red Ink, 2007)
Silversun Pickups, *Swoon* (Dangerbird, 2009)
The Ting Tings, *We Started Nothing* (Columbia, Red Ink, 2008)

2009
Adele*, *19* (XL/Allido/Columbia, 2008)
Duffy, *Rockferry* (A&M/Mercury, 2008)
The Jonas Brothers, *A Little Bit Longer* (Hollywood, 2008)
Lady Antebellum, *Lady Antebellum* (Capitol Nashville, 2008)
Jazmine Sullivan, *Fearless* (J/Arista, 2008)

2008
Amy Winehouse*, *Back to Black* (Island, 2006)
Feist, *The Reminder* (Cherrytree/Polydor/Arts and Crafts, 2007)
Ledisi, *Lost and Found* (Verve Forecast, 2007)
Paramore, *Riot!* (Fueled by Ramen, 2007)
Taylor Swift, *Taylor Swift* (Big Machine, 2006)

2007
Carrie Underwood*, *Some Hearts* (Arista, 2005)
James Blunt, *Back to Bedlam* (Atlantic, 2004)
Chris Brown, *Chris Brown* (Jive, 2005)
Imogen Heap, *Speak For Yourself* (Megaphonic/RCA/White Rabbit, 2005)
Corrine Bailey Rae, *Corrine Bailey Rae* (EMI, 2006)

2006
John Legend*, *Get Lifted* (GOOD Music/Columbia Records, 2004)
Ciara, *Goodies* (LaFace, 2004)
Fall Out Boy, *From Under the Cork Tree* (Island, 2005)
Keane, *Hopes and Fears* (Island, 2004)
Sugarland, *Twice the Speed of Life* (Mercury Nashville, 2004)

2005
Maroon 5*, *Songs About Jane* (J, 2002)
Los Lonely Boys, *Los Lonely Boys* (Epic Records, 2004)
Joss Stone, *Mind Body and Soul* (Relentless, 2004)
Kanye West, *The College Dropout* (Roc-A-Fella/Def Jam, 2004)
Gretchen Wilson, *Here for the Party* (Epic Nashville, 2004)

2004
Evanescence*, *Fallen* (Wind-up, 2003)
50 Cent, *Get Rich or Die Tryin'* (Aftermath/Shady/Interscope, 2003)
Fountains of Wayne, *Welcome Interstate Managers* (S-Curve/Virgin Records, 2003)
Heather Headley, *This Is Who I Am* (RCA, 2002)
Sean Paul, *Dutty Rock* (VP/Atlantic Records, 2002)

2003
Norah Jones*, *Come Away with Me* (Blue Note, 2002)
Ashanti, *Ashanti* (Murder Inc./Island Def Jam, 2002)
Michelle Branch, *The Spirit Room* (Maverick Records, 2001)
Avril Lavigne, *Let Go* (Arista, 2002)
John Mayer, *Room for Squares* (Sony, 2001)

2002
Alicia Keys*, *Songs in A Minor* (J, 2001)
India.Arie, *Acoustic Soul* (Motown Records, 2001)
Nelly Furtado, *Whoa, Nelly!* (DreamWorks, 2000)
David Gray, *Lost Songs 95-98* (RCA/ATO, 2001)
Linkin Park, *Hybrid Theory* (Warner Bros., 2000)

2001
Shelby Lynne*, *I Am Shelby Lynne* (Mercury/Island Records, 1999)
Brad Paisley, *Who Needs Pictures* (Arista Nashville, 1999)
Papa Roach, *Infest* (DreamWorks, 2000)
Jill Scott, *Who is Jill Scott? Words and Sounds Vol. 1* (Hidden Beach/Epic, 2000)
Sisqó, *Unleash the Dragon* (Def Soul Recordings, 1999)

2000
Christina Aguilera*, *Christina Aguilera* (RCA, 1999)
Macy Gray, *On How Life Is* (Epic Records, 1999)
Kid Rock, *Devil Without a Cause* (Lava/Atlantic/Top Dog, 1998)
Britney Spears, *...Baby One More Time* (Jive, 1999)
Susan Tedeschi, *Just Won't Burn* (Tone Cool, 1998)

1999
Lauryn Hill*, *The Miseducation of Lauryn Hill* (Columbia/Ruffhouse Records, 1998)
Backstreet Boys, *Backstreet's Back* (Jive, 1997)
Andrea Bocelli, *Bocelli* (Polygram International, 1995)
Dixie Chicks, *Wide Open Spaces* (Monument, 1998)
Natalie Imbruglia, *Left of the Middle* (RCA, 1997)

1998
Paula Cole*, *This Fire* (Imago/Warner Bros. Records, 1996)
Fiona Apple, *Tidal* (Clean Slate/Epic Records, 1996)
Erykah Badu, *Baduizm* (Kedar Records, 1997)
Seam Combs, *No Way Out* (Bad Boy, 1997)
Hanson, *Middle of Nowhere* (Independent, 1997)

1997
LeAnn Rimes*, *Blue* (Curb, 1996)
Garbage, *Garbage* (Almo Sounds, 1995)
Jewel, *Pieces of You* (Atlantic Records, 1995)
No Doubt, *Tragic Kingdom* (Trauma/Interscope, 1995)
Tony Rich, *Words* (LaFace/Arista, 1996)

1996
Hootie and the Blowfish*, *Cracked Rear View* (Atlantic Records, 1994)
Brandy Norwood, *Brandy* (Atlantic Records, 1994)
Alanis Morissette, *Jagged Little Pill* (Maverick, 1995)
Joan Osborne, *Relish* (Blue Gorilla Records, 1995)
Shania Twain, *The Woman in Me* (Mercury Nashville, 1995)

1995
Sheryl Crow, *Tuesday Night Music Club* (A&M Records, 1993)
Ace of Base, *Happy Nation/The Sign* (Warner, 1993)
Counting Crows, *August and Everything After* (Geffen Records, 1993)
Crash Test Dummies, *God Shuffled His Feet* (BMG/Arista, 1993)
Green Day, *Dookie* (Reprise, 1994)

1994
Toni Braxton*, *Toni Braxton* (LaFace, 1993)
Belly, *Star* (Sire/Reprise, 1993)
Blind Melon, *Blind Melon* (Capitol Records, 1992)
Digable Planets, *Reachin' (A New Refutation of Time and Space)* (Pendulum/
Elektra Records, 1993)
SWV, *It's About Time* (RCA, 1992)

1993
Arrested Development*, *3 Years, 5 Months and 2 Days in the Life of...* (Chrysalis,
1992)
Billy Ray Cyrus, *Some Gave All* (PolyGram/Mercury Records, 1992)
Sophie B. Hawkins, *Tongues and Tails* (Columbia Records, 1992)
Kris Kross, *Totally Krossed Out* (Ruffhouse/Columbia Records, 1992)
Jon Secada, *Jon Secada* (SBK, 1992)

1992
Marc Cohn*, Marc Cohn (Atlantic Records, 1991)
Boyz II Men, *Cooleyhighharmony* (Motown, 1991)
C+C Music Factory, *Gonna Make You Sweat* (Columbia Records, 1990)
Color Me Badd, *C.M.B.* (Giant, 1991)
Seal, *Seal* (ZTT, 1991)

1991
Mariah Carey*, *Mariah Carey* (Columbia, 1990)
Black Crowes, *Shake Your Money Maker* (American Recordings, 1990)
The Kentucky Headhunters, *Pickin' on Nashville* (Mercury Records, 1989)
Wilson Phillips, *Wilson Phillips* (SBK, 1990)
Lisa Stansfield, *Affection* (Arista, 1989)

1990
Milli Vanilli*, *Girl You Know It's True* (Arista, 1989)
Neneh Cherry, *Raw Like Sushi* (Virgin, 1989)
Indigo Girls, *Indigo Girls* (Epic, 1989)
Soul II Soul, *Keep on Movin'* (Virgin, 1989)
Tone Lōc, *Lōc-ed After Dark* (Delicious Vinyl, 1989)

1989
Tracy Chapman*, *Tracy Chapman* (Elektra, 1988)
Rick Astley, *Whenever You Need Somebody* (RCA Records, 1987)
Toni Childs, *Union* (A&M, 1988)
Take 6, *Take 6* (Warner Bros., 1988)
Vanessa L. Williams, *The Right Stuff* (Wing/Mercury, 1988)

1988
Jody Watley*, *Jody Watley* (MCA Records, 1987)
Breakfast Club, *The Breakfast Club* (MCA Records, 1987)
Cutting Crew, *Broadcast* (Virgin, 1986)
Terence Trent D'Arby, *Introducing the Hardline According to Terence Trent D'Arby* (Columbia, 1987)
Swing Out Sister, *It's Better to Travel* (Mercury, 1987)

1987
Bruce Hornsby and the Range*, *The Way It Is* (RCA, 1986)
Glass Tiger, *The Thin Red Line* (Capitol, 1986)
Nu Shooz, *Tha's Right* (Poolside Records, 1985)
Simply Red, *Picture Book* (WEA Records, 1985)
Timbuk 3, *Greetings from Timbuk 3* (I.R.S., 1986)

1986
Sade*, *Promise* (Epic, 1985)
A-ha, *Hunting High and Low* (Warner Bros., 1985)
Freddie Jackson, *Rock Me Tonight* (Capitol Records, 1985)
Katrina and the Waves, *Katrina and the Waves* (Capitol, 1985)
Julian Lennon, *Valotte* (Atlantic/Charisma/Virgin, 1984)

1985
Cyndi Lauper*, *She's So Unusual* (Portrait/Epic, 1983)
Sheila E., *The Glamorous Life* (Warner Bros. Records, 1984)
Frankie Goes to Hollywood, *Welcome to the Pleasuredome* (ZTT/Island Records, 1984)
Corey Hart, *First Offense* (EMI/Aquarius, 1983)
The Judds, *Why Not Me* (RCA/Curb Records, 1984)

1984
Culture Club*, *Colour by Numbers* (Virgin, 1983)
Big Country, *The Crossing* (Mercury Records, 1983)
Eurythmics, *Sweet Dreams (Are Made of This)* (RCA, 1983)
Men Without Hats, *Rhythm of Youth* (Statik Records/MCA/Virgin, 1982)
Musical Youth, *The Youth of Today* (MCA, 1982)

1983
Men at Work*, *Business as Usual* (Columbia Records, 1981)
Asia, *Asia* (Geffen Records, 1982)
Jennifer Holliday, *Feel My Soul* (Geffen Records, 1983)
The Human League, *Dare* (Virgin/A&M, 1981)
Stray Cats, *Built for Speed* (EMI America, 1982)

1982
Sheena Easton*, *Take My Time* (EMI/EMI America, 1981)
Adam Ant, *Kings of the Wild Frontier* (Epic Records, 1980)
The Go-Go's, *Beauty and the Beat* (IRS, 1981)
James Ingram, *The Dude* (A&M, 1981)
Luther Vandross, *Never Too Much* (Epic/Legacy Recordings, 1981)

1981
Christopher Cross*, *Christopher Cross* (Warner Bros., 1979)
Irene Cara, *Fame* (RSO, 1980)
Robbie Dupree, *Robbie Dupree* (Elektra Records,1980)
Amy Holland, *Amy Holland* (Capitol Records, 1980)
Pretenders, *Pretenders* (Real/Sire, 1980)

1980
Rickie Lee Jones*, *Rickie Lee Jones* (Warner Bros., 1979)
Blues Brothers, *Briefcase Full of Blues* (Atlantic, 1978)
Dire Straits, *Communiqué* (Vertigo/Warner Bros., 1979)
The Knack, *Get The Knack* (Capitol, 1979)
Robin Williams, *Reality...What a Concept* (Casablanca Records, 1979)

1979

A Taste Of Honey*, *A Taste of Honey* (Capitol Records, 1978)
The Cars, *The Cars* (Elektra Records, 1978)
Elvis Costello, *This Year's Model* (Radar/Columbia, 1978)
Chris Rea, *Whatever Happened to Benny Santini?* (Magnet, 1978)
Toto, *Toto* (Columbia Records, 1978)

1978

Debby Boone*, *You Light Up My Life* (Warner Brothers, 1977)
Stephen Bishop, *Careless* (Warner Brothers, 1976)
Shaun Cassidy, *Shaun Cassidy* (Warner, 1977)
Foreigner, *Foreigner* (Atlantic Records, 1977)
Andy Gibb, *Flowing Rivers* (RSO Records, 1977)

1977

Starland Vocal Band*, *Starland Vocal Band* (RCA, 1976)
Boston, *Boston* (Epic Records, 1976)
Dr. Buzzard's Original Savannah Band, *Dr. Buzzard's Original Savannah Band* (RCA, 1976)
The Brothers Johnson, *Look Out for #1* (A&M, 1976)
Wild Cherry, *Wild Cherry* (Epic, 1976)

1976

Natalie Cole*, *Inseparable* (Capitol, 1975)
Morris Albert, *Feelings* (RCA, 1975)
Amazing Rhythm Aces, *Stacked Deck* (ABC, 1975)
The Brecker Brothers, *The Brecker Brothers* (Arista, 1975)
KC and the Sunshine Band, *KC and the Sunshine Band* (TK, 1975)

1975

Marvin Hamlisch*, *The Entertainer* (MCA Records, 1974)
Bad Company, *Bad Company* (Swan Song Records, 1974)
Johnny Bristol, *Hang On In There Baby* (Motown, 1974)
David Essex, *Rock On* (Columbia, 1973)
Phoebe Snow, *Phoebe Snow* (Shelter Records, 1974)
Graham Central Station, *Release Yourself* (Warner Bros., 1974)

1974

Bette Midler*, *The Divine Miss M* (Atlantic, 1972)
Eumir Deodato, *Percepção* (Creed Taylor Inc., 1972)
Maureen McGovern, *The Morning After* (20th Century, 1973)
Marie Osmond, *Paper Roses* (MGM, 1973)
Barry White, *I've Got So Much to Give* (20th Century, 1973)

1973
America*, *America* (Warner Brothers, 1971)
Harry Chapin, *Heads and Tales* (Elektra Records, 1972)
Eagles, *Eagles* (Asylum Records, 1972)
Loggins and Messina, *Sittin' In* (Columbia, 1971)
John Prine, *John Prine* (Atlantic, 1971)

1972
Carly Simon*, *Carly Simon* (Elektra, 1971)
Chase, *Chase* (Epic, 1971)
Emerson, Lake and Palmer, *Tarkus* (Island/Manticore, 1971)
Hamilton, Joe Frank and Reynolds, *Hamilton, Joe Frank and Reynoldsm* (Dunhill, 1971)
Bill Withers, *Just as I Am* (Sussex, 1971)

1971
The Carpenters*, *Close to You* (A&M Records, 1970)
Elton John, *Elton John* (DJM, 1970)
Melba Moore, *I Got Love* (Mercury Records, 1970)
Anne Murray, *This Way Is My Way* (Capitol, 1969)
The Partridge Family, *The Partridge Family Album* (Bell Records, 1970)

1970
Crosby, Stills and Nash*, *Crosby, Stills and Nash* (Atlantic Records, 1969)
Chicago, *The Chicago Transit Authority* (Columbia, 1969)
Led Zeppelin, *Led Zeppelin* (Atlantic, 1969)
The Neon Philharmonic, *The Neon Philharmonic* (Warner Brothers, 1969)
Oliver, *Good Morning Starshine* (Crewe Records, 1969)

1969
José Feliciano*, *Feliciano!* (RCA, 1968)
Cream, *Wheels of Fire* (Polydor, 1968)
Gary Puckett and the Union Gap, *Woman, Woman* (Richmond, 1968)
Jeannie C. Riley, *Harper Valley PTA* (Plantation, 1968)
O.C. Smith, *Hickory Holler Revisited* (Collectables, 1968)

1968
Bobbie Gentry, *Ode to Billie Joe* (Capitol, 1967)
Lana Cantrell, *Stay/I Love Him* (RCA Victor, 1966)
The 5th Dimension, *Up, Up and Away* (Soul City, 1967)
Harpers Bizarre, *Feelin' Groovy* (Warner Bros., 1967)
Jefferson Airplane, *Surrealistic Pillow* (RCA Victor, 1967)

1967
The Grammys did not present an award for Best New Artist in this year.

1966
Tom Jones*, *It's Not Unusual* (Parrot, 1965)
The Byrds, *Mr. Tambourine Man* (Columbia, 1965)
Herman's Hermits, *Herman's Hermits* (EMI/Columbia, 1965)
Horst Jankowski, *The Genius of Jankowski* (Mercury Records, 1965)
Marilyn Maye, *Meet Marvelous Marilyn Maye* (RCA, 1965)
Sonny and Cher, *Look at Us* (Atco, 1965)
Glenn Yarbrough, *It's Gonna Be Fine* (RCA, 1965)

1965
The Beatles*, *A Hard Day's Night* (United Artists, 1964)
Morgana King, *With a Taste of Honey* (Mainstream Records, 1964)
Petula Clark, *Downtown* (US Warner Bros., 1965)
Astrud Gilberto, *The Astrud Gilberto Album* (Verve Records, 1964)
Antonio Carlos Jobim, *The Composer of Desafinado Plays* (Verve Records, 1963)

1964
The Swingle Sisters*, *Jazz Sébastien Bach* (Philips, 1963)
Vikki Carr, *Color Her Great* (Collectables, 1963)
John Gary, *Catch a Rising Star* (RCA Victor, 1963)
The J's With Jamie, *The Remarkable J's with Jamie* (Columbia, 1962)
Trini Lopez, *Live at PJ's* (Reprise Records, 1963)

1963
Robert Goulet*, *Always You* (Columbia Records, 1962)
The Four Seasons, *Sherry and 11 Others* (Vee-Jay, 1962)
Vaughn Meader, *The First Family* (Cadence Records, 1962)
The New Christy Minstrels, *Presenting the New Christy Minstrels* (Columbia, 1962)
Peter, Paul and Mary, *Peter, Paul and Mary* (Warner Bros., 1962)
Allan Sherman, *My Son, the Folk Singer* (Warner Bros., 1962)

1962
Peter Nero*, *Piano Forte* (RCA, 1961)
Ann-Margret, *And Here She Is... Ann-Margret* (RCA, 1961)
Dick Gregory, *In Living Black and White* (Colpix Records, 1961)
The Lettermen, *A Song For Young Love* (Capitol Records, 1962)
Timi Yuro, *Hurt!* (Liberty Records, 1961)

1961

Bob Newhart*, *The Button-Down Mind of Bob Newhart* (Warner Bros., 1960)
The Brothers Four, *The Brothers Four* (Columbia, 1960)
Miriam Makeba, *The Many Voices of Miriam Makeba* (Kapp, 1960)
Leontyne Price, *Arias* (RCA, 1961)
Joanie Summers, *Positively the Most!* (Warner Bros., 1960)

1960

The Grammy Awards were not held this year.

1959

Bobby Darin*, *Bobby Darin* (Atco, 1958)
Edd Byrnes, *Kookie, Kookie—Lend Me Your Comb* (Warner Bros., 1959)
Mark Murphy, *Meet Mark Murphy* (Decca, 1956)
Johnny Restivo, *Oh Johnny!* (RCA Italiana, 1959)
Mavis Rivers, *Take a Number* (Capitol Records, 1959)

Appendix C
"The 100 Greatest Debut Albums"
Uncut Magazine (August 2006)

1. The Velvet Underground and Nico, *The Velvet Underground and Nico* (Verve, 1967)
2. Television, *Marquee Moon* (Elektra, 1977)
3. The Jimi Hendrix Experience, *Are You Experienced* (Track, 1967)
4. The Stone Roses, *The Stone Roses* (Silvertone, 1989)
5. The Band, *Music From Big Pink* (Capitol, 1968)
6. The Clash, *The Clash* (CBS, 1977)
7. Led Zeppelin, *Led Zeppelin* (Atlantic, 1969)
8. Joy Division, *Unknown Pleasures* (Factory, 1979)
9. Roxy Music, *Roxy Music* (Island/Reprise, 1972)
10. The Stooges, *The Stooges* (Elektra, 1969)
11. The Who, *My Generation* (Brunswick, 1965)
12. Ramones, *Ramones* (Sire, 1976)
13. The Byrds, *Mr. Tambourine Man* (Columbia, 1965)
14. Pink Floyd, *The Piper At The Gates Of Dawn* (Capitol/EMI Records, 1967)
15. The Rolling Stones, *The Rolling Stones* (Decca, 1964)
16. New York Dolls, *New York Dolls* (Mercury, 1973)
17. The Beatles, *Please Please Me* (Parlophone, 1963)
18. Patti Smith, *Horses* (Arista, 1975)
19. The Sex Pistols, *Never Mind The Bollocks, Here's The Sex Pistols* (Virgin/Warner Bros., 1977)
20. The Specials, *The Specials* (2 Tone Records, 1979)
21. The Smiths, *The Smiths* (Rough Trade, 1984)
22. R.E.M., *Murmur* (I.R.S., 1983)
23. The Flying Burrito Brothers, *The Gilded Palace of Sin* (A&M, 1969)
24. Big Star, *#1 Record* (Ardent, 1972)
25. The Mothers of Invention, *Freak Out!* (Verve, 1966)
26. Buffalo Springfield, *Buffalo Springfield* (Atco, 1967)
27. My Bloody Valentine, *Isn't Anything* (Creation, 1988)
28. The Doors, *The Doors* (Elektra, 1967)
29. Nick Drake, *Five Leaves Left* (Island, 1969)
30. Oasis, *Definitely Maybe* (Creation, 1992)
31. Elvis Costello, *My Aim Is True* (Stiff/Columbia, 1977)
32. MC5, *Kick Out The Jams* (Elektra, 1969)

33.   Gang of Four, *Entertainment!* (EMI/Warner Bros., 1979)
34.   Steely Dan, *Can't Buy A Thrill* (ABC, 1972)
35.   Black Sabbath, *Black Sabbath* (Vertigo, 1970)
36.   Arctic Monkeys, *Whatever People Say I Am, That's What I'm Not* (Domino, 2006)
37.   Magazine, *Real Life* (Virgin, 1978)
38.   Captain Beefheart and His Magic Band, *Safe as Milk* (Buddah, 1967)
39.   Bruce Springsteen, *Greetings From Asbury Park, NJ* (Columbia, 1973)
40.   Wire, *Pink Flag* (Harvest, 1978)
41.   Public Enemy, *Yo! Bum Rush The Show* (Def Jam/Columbia, 1987)
42.   The Modern Lovers, *The Modern Lovers* (Beserkley, 1976)
43.   Siouxsie and the Banshees, *The Scream* (Polydor/Geffen, 1978)
44.   Orange Juice, *You Can't Hide Your Love Forever* (Polydor, 1982)
45.   Jeff Buckley, *Grace* (Columbia, 1994)
46.   The Slits, *Cut* (Island, 1979)
47.   NWA, *Straight Outta Compton* (Ruthless, 1989)
48.   The Pretenders, *Pretenders* (Real/Sire, 1980)
49.   Talking Heads, *77* (Sire, 1977)
50.   The Jesus and Mary Chain, *Psychocandy* (Blanco y Negro, 1985)
51.   Moby Grape, *Moby Grape* (Columbia, 1967)
52.   ABC, *The Lexicon of Love* (Neutron/Mercury, 1982)
53.   De La Soul, *3 Feet High and Rising* (Tommy Boy/Warner Bros., 1989)
54.   Randy Newman, *Randy Newman* (Reprise, 1968)
55.   Ian Dury, *New Boots and Panties!!* (Stiff, 1977)
56.   Bob Dylan, *Bob Dylan* (Columbia, 1962)
57.   Pixies, *Come On Pilgrim* (4AD, 1987)
58.   Tim Hardin, *Tim Hardin 1* (Verve Forecast, 1966)
59.   U2, *Boy* (Island, 1980)
60.   Richard Hell and The Voidoids, *Blank Generation* (Sire, 1977)
61.   Leonard Cohen, *The Songs Of Leonard Cohen* (Columbia, 1968)
62.   The Associates, *The Affectionate Punch* (Fiction, 1980)
63.   Pere Ubu, *The Modern Dance* (Blank, 1978)
64.   Neu!, *Neu!* (Brain, 1972)
65.   Dexys Midnight Runners, *Searching For The Young Soul Rebels* (EMI, 1980)
66.   Beastie Boys, *Licensed To Ill* (Def Jam/Columbia, 1986)
67.   Suicide, *Suicide* (Red Star, 1977)
68.   Buzzcocks, *Another Music In A Different Kitchen* (United Artists, 1978)
69.   Echo and The Bunnymen, *Crocodiles* (Korova, 1980)
70.   Judee Sill, *Judee Sill* (Asylum, 1971)
71.   Scritti Politti, *Songs To Remember* (Rough Trade, 1982)
72.   The Strokes, *Is This It* (RCA, 2001)
73.   Pavement, *Slanted And Enchanted* (Matador, 1992)
74.   Kate Bush, *The Kick Inside* (EMI, 1978)

75.   The La's, *The La's* (Go!/London, 1990)
76.   Guns N' Roses, *Appetite For Destruction* (Geffen, 1987)
77.   Eminem, *The Slim Shady LP* (Aftermath/Web, 1999)
78.   The Libertines, *Up The Bracket* (Rough Trade, 2002)
79.   Jackson Browne, *Jackson Browne* (Asylum, 1972)
80.   Cheap Trick, *Cheap Trick* (Epic, 1977)
81.   Pearl Jam, *Ten* (Epic, 1991)
82.   The Pop Group, *Y* (Radar/Rhino, 1979)
83.   Little Feat, *Little Feat* (Warner Bros., 1971)
84.   Tricky, *Maxinquaye* (Island, 1995)
85.   Elvis Presley, *Elvis Presley* (RCA, 1956)
86.   The Undertones, *The Undertones* (Sire/Rykodisc, 1979)
87.   Dr Feelgood, *Down By The Jetty* (United Artists, 1974)
88.   Tom Petty and The Heartbreakers, *Tom Petty and The Heartbreakers* (Shelter, 1976)
89.   Elastica, *Elastica* (Deceptive, 1994)
90.   Franz Ferdinand, *Franz Ferdinand* (Domino, 2004)
91.   Throwing Muses, *Throwing Muses* (4AD, 1986)
92.   Spiritualized, *Lazer Guided Melodies* (Dedicated, 1992)
93.   The Birthday Party, *Prayers On Fire* (4AD, 1981)
94.   Mercury Rev, *Yerself Is Steam* (Columbia, 1991)
95.   The White Stripes, *The White Stripes* (Sympathy, 1999)
96.   PJ Harvey, *Dry* (Too Pure, 1992)
97.   Vashti Bunyan, *Just Another Diamond Day* (Philips, 1970)
98.   Foo Fighters, *Foo Fighters* (Capitol/Roswell, 1995)
99.   Suede, *Suede* (Nude, 1993)
100. The Arcade Fire, *Funeral* (Merge, 2005)

Appendix D
"The 50 Greatest Debut Albums Ever"
New Musical Express (*NME*)
(November 6, 2010)

The editors of the British indie music magazine employed a chronological approach for their list of 50, selecting one debut album for each year, beginning in 1960 and continuing through 2009.

1960   Joan Baez, *Joan Baez* (Vanguard)
1961   The Shadows, *The Shadows* (Amiga)
1962   Bob Dylan, *Bob Dylan* (Columbia)
1963   The Beatles, *Please Please Me* (Capitol)
1964   Dusty Springfield, *A Girl Called Dusty* (Phillips)
1965   The Who, *My Generation* (Brunswick/MCA)
1966   The Mothers of Invention, *Freak Out!* (Verve)
1967   The Velvet Underground and Nico, *The Velvet Underground and Nico* (MGM/Verve)
1968   The Band, *Music From Big Pink* (Capitol)
1969   The Stooges, *The Stooges* (Elektra)
1970   Black Sabbath, *Black Sabbath* (Warner Brothers)
1971   Thin Lizzy, *Thin Lizzy* (Dream)
1972   Neu!, *Neu!* (Brain Records)
1973   New York Dolls, *New York Dolls* (Mercury)
1974   Brian Eno, *Here Comes The Warm* (EG)
1975   Patti Smith, *Horses* (Arista)
1976   The Ramones, *The Ramones* (Sire)
1977   The Sex Pistols, *Never Mind the Bollocks* (Warner Brothers)
1978   Devo, *Are We Not Men? We Are Devo!* (Warner Brothers)
1979   Joy Division, *Unknown Pleasures* (Qwest)
1980   Killing Joke, *Killing Joke* (EG)
1981   Depeche Mode, *Speak and Spell* (Sire)
1982   ABC, *The Lexicon of Love* (Neutron/Mercury)
1983   R.E.M., *Murmur* (I.R.S.)
1984   The Smiths, *The Smiths* (Sire)
1985   The Jesus and Mary Chain, *Psychocandy* (Def American)
1986   Beastie Boys, *License to Ill*, (Def Jam)
1987   Guns N' Roses, *Appetite For Destruction* (Geffen)

1988   My Bloody Valentine, *Isn't Anything* (Creation/Sire)
1989   The Stone Roses, *The Stone Roses* (Silvertone)
1990   The La's, *The La's* (London)
1991   Massive Attack, *Blue Lines* (Virgin)
1992   Manic Street Preachers, *Generation Terrorists* (Columbia)
1993   Suede, *Suede* (Nude/Columbia)
1994   Oasis, *Definitely Maybe* (Epic)
1995   Elastica, *Elastica* (Geffen)
1996   Super Furry Animals, *Fuzzy Logic* (Creation)
1997   Roni Size, *New Forms* (Talkin' Loud)
1998   Lauryn Hill, *The Miseducation of Lauryn Hill* (Ruffhouse)
1999   Eminem, *The Slim Shady LP* (Interscope)
2000   Coldplay, *Parachutes* (Parlophone)
2001   The Strokes, *Is This It* (RCA)
2002   The Libertines, *Up the Bracket* (Rough Trade)
2003   Dizzee Rascal, *Boy In Da Corner* (XL)
2004   Kanye West, *The College Dropout* (Rock-A-Fella/Def Jam)
2005   Arcade Fire, *Funeral* (Merge)
2006   The Arctic Monkeys, *Whatever People Say I Am, That's What I'm Not* (Domino)
2007   The Klaxons, *Myths of the Near Future* (Polydor)
2008   Crystal Castles, *Crystal Castles* (Different/Last Gang/Lies)
2009   The XX, *XX* (Young Turks)

Appendix E
"The 100 Best Debut Albums of All Time"
Rolling Stone (March 2013)

The editorial panel that compiled this list focused on debuts that provided "the thrill of an act arriving fully-formed, ready to reinvent the world in its own image." The criteria placed less emphasis on artists who achieved significant success following their debuts, while allowing "extra recognition" to great debuts that the artist never matched. In addition, solo debuts by artists from well-known bands were not considered (http://www.rollingstone.com/music/lists/the-100-greatest-debut-albums-of-all-time-20130322).

1. Beastie Boys, *License to Ill* (Def Jam, 1986)
2. Ramones, *Ramones* (Sire, 1996)
3. Jimi Hendrix Experience, *Are You Experienced* (Reprise, 1967)
4. Guns N' Roses, *Appetite for Destruction* (Geffen, 1987)
5. Velvet Underground and Nico, *The Velvet Underground and Nico* (MGM/ Verve, 1967)
6. N.W.A., *Straight Outta Compton* (Priority, 1988)
7. The Sex Pistols, *Never Mind the Bollocks* (Warner Brothers, 1977)
8. The Strokes, *Is This It* (RCA, 2001)
9. The Band, *Music From Big Pink* (Capitol, 1968)
10. Patti Smith, *Horses* (Arista, 1975)
11. Nas, *Illmatic* (Columbia, 1994)
12. The Clash, *The Clash* (Epic, 1979)
13. The Pretenders, *Pretenders* (Sire, 1980)
14. Jay-Z , *Reasonable Doubt* (Rock-A-Fella, 1996)
15. Arcade Fire, *Funeral* (Merge, 2004)
16. The Cars, *The Cars* (Elektra, 1978)
17. The Beatles, *Please Please Me* (Parlophone, 1963)
18. R.E.M., *Murmur* (I.R.S., 1983)
19. Kanye West, *The College Dropout* (Rock-A-Fella/Def Jam, 2004)
20. Joy Division, *Unknown Pleasures* (Factory, 1979)
21. Elvis Costello, *My Aim Is True* (Columbia, 1977)
22. Violent Femmes, *Violent Femmes* (Slash, 1983)
23. The Notorious B.I.G., *Ready to Die* (Bad Boy, 1994)
24. Vampire Weekend, *Vampire Weekend* (XL, 2008)
25. Pavement, *Slanted and Enchanted* (Matador, 1992)
26. Run-D.M.C., *Run-DMC* (Profile/Arista, 1984)

27.   Van Halen, *Van Halen* (Warner Bros., 1978)
28.   The B-52's, *B-52's* (Warner Bros., 1979)
29.   Wu-Tang Clan, *Enter the Wu Tang Clan (36 Chambers)* (Loud/RCA, 1993)
30.   The Arctic Monkeys, *Whatever People Say I Am, That's What I'm Not* (Domino, 2006)
31.   Portishead, *Dummy* (Go! Discs, 1994)
32.   De La Soul, *Three Feet High and Rising* (Tommy Boy, 1989)
33.   The Killers, *Hot Fuss* (Island, 2004)
34.   The Doors, *The Doors* (Elektra, 1967)
35.   Weezer, *Weezer* (DGC, 1994)
36.   The Postal Service, *Give Up* (Sub Pop, 2003)
37.   Bruce Springsteen, *Greetings From Asbury Park, N.J.* (Columbia, 1973)
38.   The Police, *Outlandos d'Amour* (A&M, 1978)
39.   Lynyrd Skynyrd, *Pronounced 'leh-'nérd 'Skin-'nérd* (MCA,1973)
40.   Television, *Marquee Moon* (Elektra, 1977)
41.   Boston, *Boston* (Epic, 1976)
42.   Oasis, *Definitely Maybe* (Creation, 1994)
43.   Jeff Buckley, *Grace* (Columbia, 1994)
44.   Black Sabbath, *Black Sabbath* (Warner Bros., 1970)
45.   The Jesus and Mary Chain, *Psychocandy* (Reprise, 1985)
46.   Pearl Jam, *Ten* (Epic, 1991)
47.   Pink Floyd, *Piper At the Gates of Dawn* (Tower, 1967)
48.   The Modern Lovers, *The Modern Lovers* (Berserkley, 1976)
49.   Franz Ferdinand, *Franz Ferdinand* (Domino, 2004)
50.   X, *Los Angeles* (Slash, 1980)
51.   The Smiths, *The Smiths* (Sire, 1984)
52.   U2, *Boy* (Island, 1980)
53.   New York Dolls, *New York Dolls* (Mercury, 1973)
54.   Metallica, *Kill 'Em All* (Megaforce/Elektra, 1983)
55.   Missy "Misdemeanor" Elliott, *Supa Dupa Fly* (The Goldmine/Elektra, 1997)
56.   Bon Iver, For Emma, *Forever Ago* (Jagjaguar, 2008)
57.   MGMT, *Oracular Spectacular* (Columbia, 2008)
58.   Nine Inch Nails, *Pretty Hate Machine* (TVT, 1989)
59.   Yeah Yeah Yeahs, *Fever To Tell* (Interscope, 2003)
60.   Fiona Apple, *Tidal* (Columbia, 1996)
61.   The Libertines, *Up the Bracket* (Rough Trade, 2002)
62.   Roxy Music, *Roxy Music* (Reprise, 1972)
63.   Cyndi Lauper, *She's So Unusual* (Epic/Legacy, 1983)
64.   The English Beat, *I Just Can't Stop It* (I.R.S., 1980)
65.   Liz Phair, *Exit From Guyville* (Matador, 1993)
66.   The Stooges, *The Stooges* (Elektra, 1969)
67.   50 Cent, *Get Rich or Die Tryin'*, (Interscope, 2003)

68. Talking Heads, *Talking Head: 77* (Sire, 1977)
69. Wire, *Pink Flag* (Harvest, 1977)
70. P.J. Harvey, *Dry* (Too Pure, 1992)
71. Mary J. Blige, *What's the 411* (Uptown/MCA, 1992)
72. Led Zeppelin, *Led Zeppelin* (Atlantic, 1969)
73. Norah Jones, *Come Away With Me* (Blue Note, 2002)
74. The XX, *XX* (XL/Young Turks, 2009)
75. The Go Go's, *Beauty and the Beat* (I.R.S., 1981)
76. Devo, *Q: Are We Not Men? A: We Are Devo!* (Warner Bros., 1978)
77. Drake, *Thank Me Later* (Young Money/Cash Money/Universal/Motown, 2010)
78. The Stone Roses, *The Stone Roses* (Silvertone, 1989)
79. Elvis Presley, *Elvis Presley* (RCA, 1956)
80. The Byrds, *Mr. Tambourine Man* (Columbia, 1965)
81. Gang of Four, *Entertainment!* (Warner Bros., 1979)
82. The Congos, *Heart of the Congo* (Black Ark, 1977)
83. Erik B. and Rakim, *Paid in Full* (4th and Broadway/Island, 1987)
84. Whitney Houston, *Whitney Houston* (Arista, 1985)
85. Rage Against the Machine, *Rage Against the Machine* (Epic, 1992)
86. Kendrick Lamar, *good kid, m.A.A.d. city* (Top Dog/Aftermath/Interscope, 2012)
87. The New Pornographers, *Mass Romantic* (Mint, 2000)
88. Daft Punk, *Homework* (Virgin, 1997)
89. Yaz, *Upstair's at Eric's* (Mute, 1982)
90. Big Star, *#1 Record* (Ardent/Stax, 1972)
91. M.I.A., *Arular* (XL, 2005)
92. Moby Grape, *Moby Grape* (Columbia, 1967)
93. The Hold Steady, *Almost Killed Me* (Frenchkiss, 2004)
94. The Who, *The Who Sings My Generation* (MCA, 1965)
95. Little Richard, *Here's Little Richard* (Specialty, 1957)
96. Madonna, *Madonna* (Sire, 1983)
97. DJ Shadow, *Entroducing...*(London/Mo Wax, 1996)
98. Joe Jackson, *Look Sharp!* (A&M, 1979)
99. The Flying Burrito Brothers, *The Gilded Palace of Sin* (A&M, 1969)
100. Lady Gaga, *The Fame* (Interscope, 2009)

Appendix F
"The 20 Greatest Debut Albums of All-Time"
"And 40 more outstanding debuts …"
dkpresents.wordpress.com (2008)

Albums are listed chronologically.

The 20 Greatest Debut Albums of All-Time

The Doors. *The Doors* (Elektra 1967)
The Jimi Hendrix Experience. *Are You Experienced?* (Reprise 1967)
Moby Grape. *Moby Grape* (San Francisco Sound 1967)
Captain Beefheart. *Safe as Milk* (Buddah 1967)
The Band. *Music From Big Pink* (Capitol 1968)
Led Zeppelin. *Led Zeppelin* (Atlantic 1969)
Nick Drake. *Five Leaves Left* (Hannibal 1969)
Black Sabbath. *Black Sabbath* (Warner Brothers 1970)
John Prine. *John Prine* (Atlantic 1971)
Steely Dan. *Can't Buy A Thrill* (MCA 1972)
Patti Smith. *Horses* (Arista 1975)
Ramones. *Ramones* (Sire 1976)
Sex Pistols. *Never Mind the Bollocks* (Warner Brothers 1977)
Van Halen. *Van Halen* (Warner Brothers 1978)
Joy Division. *Unknown Pleasures* (Qwest 1979)
Dead Kennedys. *Fresh Fruit for Rotting Vegetables* (Cherry Red/Alternative Tentacles 1980)
Guns N' Roses. *Appetite for Destruction* (Geffen 1987)
Eric B and Rakim. *Paid in Full* (1987)
Massive Attack. *Blue Lines* (Virgin 1991)
Jeff Buckley. *Grace* (Columbia 1994)

And 40 more outstanding debuts …

Elvis Presley. *Elvis Presley* (RCA 1956)
Rolling Stones. *England's Newest Hitmakers* (Decca 1964)
The Byrds. *Mr. Tambourine Man* (Columbia 1965)

Fred Neil. *Bleecker and MacDougal* (Elektra 1965)

Neil Diamond. *Just For You* (Bang 1967)

Dr. John. *Gris Gris* (Repertoire 1968)

Funkadelic. *Funkadelic* (Westbound 1970)

Lynyrd Skynrd. *Prounounced Leh-Nerd Skin-Nerd* (MCA 1973)

Bob Marley and the Wailers. *Catch a Fire* (Island 1973)

New York Dolls. *New York Dolls* (Mercury 1973)

Tom Waits. *Closing Time* (Asylum 1973)

Dr. Feelgood. *Down by the Jetty* (United Artists 1975)

Jonathan Richman and the The Modern Lovers. *The Modern Lovers* (Berserkley 1976)

Tom Petty and the Heartbreakers. *Tom Petty and the Heartbreakers* (Shelter 1976)

The Clash. *The Clash* (CBS 1977)

Talking Heads. *Talking Heads: 77* (Sire 1977)

The Cars. *The Cars (Elektra 1977)*

Dire Straits. *Dire Straits* (Warner Brothers 1978)

The Undertones. *The Undertones* (Rykodisc 1979)

Black Flag. *Damages* (SSI 1981)

Metallica. *Kill 'Em All* (Elektra 1983)

Stevie Ray Vaughn. *Texas Flood* (Epic 1983)

Beastie Boys. *Licensed to Ill* (Def Jam 1986)

Public Enemy. *Yo! Bum Rush the Show* (Def Jam 1987)

Nirvana. *Bleach* (Sub Pop 1989)

Stone Roses. *Stone Roses* (Silvertone 1989)

The Black Crowes. *Shake Your Moneymaker* (Def American 1990)

Pearl Jam. *Ten* (Epic 1991)

PJ Harvey. *Dry* (Indigo 1992)

Wu Tang Clan. *Enter the Wu Tang Clan (36 Chambers)* (Loud 1993)

Nas. *Illmatic* (Columbia 1994)

DJ Shadow. *Endtroducing* (Mo' Wax 1996)

Queens of the Stone Age. *Queens of the Stone Age* (Loosegroove 1998)

The Strokes. *Is This It* (RCA 2001)

Kings of Leon. *Youth and Young Manhood* (RCA 2003)

Arcade Fire. *Funeral* (Merge 2004)

Clap Your Hands Say Yeah. *Clap Your Hands Say Yeah* (Wichita 005)

LCD Soundsystem. *LCD Soundsystem* (DFA 2005)

Bon Iver. *For Emma, Forever Ago* (Jagjaguwar 2008)[1]

Fleet Foxes. *Fleet Foxes* (2008)

---

[1]   I have corrected this entry from the dk listing of Bon Iver's second record, *Bon Iver, Bon Iver* (2011) as the debut. *For Emma, Forever Ago* is the band's debut released three years earlier.

Appendix G

"The 20 Best and 10 Most Disappointing Debut Albums" Dave Marsh and James Bernard, *The New Book of Rock Lists* (1994): 120-122

The 20 Best Debut Albums

1.   Jimi Hendrix. *Are You Experienced* (Reprise, 1967)
2.   The Beatles. *With the Beatles* (Capitol, 1963)[1]
3.   Elvis Presley. *Elvis Presley* (RCA, 1956)
4.   Little Richard. *Here's Little Richard* (Specialty, 1956)
5.   Guns N' Roses. *Appetite for Destruction* (Geffen, 1987)
6.   John Lennon/Plastic Ono Band. *John Lennon/Plastic Ono Band* (Capitol, 1970)
7.   The Clash. *The Clash* (Epic, 1977)
8.   Ice Cube. *AmeriKKKa's Most Wanted* (Priority, 1990)
9.   Dr. Dre. *The Chronic* (Death Row, 1992)
10.   The Band. *Music from Big Pink* (Capitol, 1968)
11.   Terence Trent D'Arby. *Introducing the Hard Line According to Terence Trent D'Arby* (Columbia, 1987)
12.   Bob Dylan. *Bob Dylan* (Columbia, 1962)
13.   The Rolling Stones. *The Rolling Stones* (London, 1964)
14.   PM Dawn. *Of the Heart, Of the Soul, Of the Cross: The Utopian Experience* (Gee Street, 1991)
15.   Lynyrd Skynrd. *Pronounced Leh-Nerd Skin-Nerd* (MCA, 1973)
16.   Seal. *Seal* (Sire, 1991)
17.   Elvis Costello. *My Aim Is True* (Rykodisc, 1977)
18.   Jerry Lee Lewis. *Jerry Lee Lewis* (Sun, 1958)
19.   The Pretenders. *Pretenders* (Sire, 1980)
20.   R.E.M. *Murmur* (I.R.S., 1983)

---

[1]   *Please Please Me* is the Beatles' debut, its March 1963 release preceding *With the Beatles* November release later the same year.

The 10 Most Disappointing Debut Albums

1.   Blind Faith. *Blind Faith* (RSO, 1969)
2.   The Grateful Dead. *The Grateful Dead* (Warner Brothers, 1967)
3.   Crosby, Stills and Nash. *Crosby Stills and Nash* (Atlantic, 1969)
4.   Paul McCartney. *McCartney* (Capitol, 1970)
5.   Wilson Phillips. *Wilson Phillips* (1990, SBK)
6.   Janis Joplin. *I Got Dem Ol' Kozmic Blues Again, Mama* (Columbia, 1969)
7.   Whitney Houston. *Whitney Houston* (Arista, 1985)
8.   Van Dyke Parks. *Song Cycle* (Warner Brothers, 1968)
9.   Simon and Garfunkel. *Wednesday Morning, 3 AM* (Columbia, 1965)
10.   Sex Pistols. *Never Mind the Bollocks, Here's the Sex Pistols* (Warner Brothers, 1977)

Bibliography

"10 Pupils Burned to Death in School Near Buffalo." *New York Times* (April 1, 1954): A1.

Alden, Grant, and Gilbert, Jeff. "Seattle: Everything You Always Wanted..." *Guitar World*, I (1993): 6-42.

Allen, Jim. "Jackson C. Frank: An American Tragedy." *Mojo*, 186 (May 2009): 68-74.

Androutsopoulos, Jannis K. "What Names Reveal About the Music Style: A Study of Naming Patterns in Popular Music." Paper presented to the 7th International Pragmatics Conference, Budapest, July 2000. At: http://bandnames.archetype. de/bandnames.PDF.

Anderson, Kyle. *Grunge: The End of Rock and Roll* (London: Aurum, 2007).

Antonia, Nina. *The New York Dolls: Too Much Too Soon* (London: Omnibus, 1998).

Azerrad, Michael, "Grunge city." *Rolling Stone*, 628 (1992): xx.

————."Introduction." In Charles Peterson, Michael Azerrad, and Bruce Pavitt, eds., *Screaming Life: A Chronicle of the Seattle Music Scene* (New York: HarperCollinsWest, 1995): 1-15.

Baez, Joan. *And a Voice to Sing With* (New York: Summit Books, 1987).

————. *Daybreak* (New York: Dial Press, 1968).

Bakhtin, Mihail. *Rabelais and His World*, trans. Helène Iswolsky (Bloomington: Indiana UP, 1984).

————. "Unitary Language." In Lucy Burke, Tony Crowley, and Alan Girvin, eds., *The Routledge Language and Cultural Theory Reader* (London: Routledge, 2000): 269-279.

Bell, Thomas, "Why Seattle? An Examination of an Alternative Rock Culture Hearth." *Journal of Cultural Geography*, 18.1 (1998): 35-47.

Berry, Jason, Jonathan Foose, and Tad Jones. *Up from the Cradle of Jazz* (Athens, GA: University of Georgia Press, 1986).

Blackman, G. "Her Time Starts Now." *Sunday Age* (Melbourne, Australia) (February 17, 2008): 22.

Blackwell, Bumps. "Up Against the Wall with Little Richard." In William McKeen, ed., *Rock and Roll is Here to Stay: An Anthology* (New York: W.W. Norton and Company, 2000): 100-101.

Bloom, Harold. *A Map of Misreading* (Oxford: Oxford UP, 1975).

Boucher, Geoff. "Facing Mortality with Mischief Rather than Tears." *L.A. Times* (September 13, 2002): F1.

Bowen, Pete. "Little Richard—The Specialty Years." *Now Dig This*, 80 (November 1989): 4-8.

Bowman, Rob. *Soulsville, USA: The Story of Stax Records* (New York: Schirmer Books, 1997).

Boyd, Joe. *White Bicycles: Making Music in the 1960s* (London: Serpent's Tail, 2006).

Broven, John. *Rhythm and Blues in New Orleans* (Gretna, LA: Pelican Publishing, 1978.)

California State University, Northridge (2006). *Mike Curb Biography*. Retrieved from http://www.csun.edu/pubrels/MikeCurb/bio.html.

Callahan, Mike. "New Orleans Rock and Roll." *Goldmine*, 57 (February 1981): 155-159.

Carr, Joe and Alan Munde. *Windy Days and Dusty Skies* (Flying Fish, 1995).

"Chart Beat: Rimes Puts the Blues Behind Her" (March 1, 1997). Retrieved from www.billboard.biz/bbiz/others/chart-beat-rimes-puts-the-blues-behind-her-752538.story.

Christanen, M. "Cycles in Symbol Production? A New Model to Explain Concentration, Diversity and Innovation in Music Industry." *Popular Music*, 14 (1995): 55-93.

"Chuck E. Weiss and Rickie Lee Jones." At: http://www.tomwaitslibrary.com/extras/rickieandchuck.html (retrieved on 10 August 2011).

Chusid, Irwin. *Songs in the Key of Z: The Curious Universe of Outsider Music* (Chicago: A Capella Books, 2000).

Clarke, Betty. "Pop: The Libertines Play Guttersnipe Pop." *The Guardian* (London) (February 14, 2003).

———. "Us Against the World." *The Guardian* (London) (July 30, 2004).

The Clash: Westway to the World. Dir. Don Letts. 3DD Entertainment, 2000. DVD.

Cocks, Jay. "Huey 'Piano" Smith's Rock & Roll Revival!" In Greil Marcus, ed., *Stranded: Rock and Roll for A Desert Island* (New York: Alfred A. Knopf, 1979): 148-160.

———. "The Duchess of Coolsville." *Time* (May 21, 1979). At: http://www.time.com/time/printout/0,8816,920372,00.html (retrieved August 26, 2011).

Colapinto, John. "Famous Names: Does It Matter What a Product Is Called?" *The New Yorker* (October 3, 2011): 38-43.

Coleman, Rick. Liner Notes. *Little Richard: "The Specialty Sessions"* (Specialty SPCD 8508) (London: Specialty/Ace Records, 1989): 18-27.

Colvin, Shawn. Liner notes, *Cover Girl* (Sony, 1994).

Concepcion, M. "Sharon Jones: Still Learning, Still Growing." *Billboard* (April 3, 2010).

Considine, J.D. "Steve Forbert" (Record review). In Dave Marsh and John Swenson, eds., *The New Rolling Stone Record Guide* (New York; Random House/Rolling Stone Press, 1983): 182.

Cooper, B. Lee. "Track-By-Track Commentary," in *Funky Midnight Mover: The Atlantc Studio Recordings, 1962-1978* (Burbank, CA: Rhino Hand Made, 2009): 15-70.

———. "Architects of the New Orleans Sound, 1946-2006: A Bio-Bibliography." *Popular Music and Society*, 31 (May 2008): 221-261.

———. "In Memoriam: Wilson Pickett, 1941-2006." *Popular Music and Society*, 29 (July 2006): 387-388.

Costa, M. Review of the Dap Kings. *The Guardian* (London) (April 18, 2008): 40.

Costello, Elvis. Liner Notes to *My Aim Is True* (Reissue) (Rhino Entertainment Company, 2001).

"Country Corner" (August 31. 1996). At http://billboard.biz/bbiz/others/country-corner/759670.story (retrieved on December 21, 2011).

"Country Corner: Can you say greatest gainer" (December 21, 1996). At: http://billboard.biz.bbiz/others/country-corner/77056.story (retrieved on December 2, 2011).

"Country Music Spotlights." "Dang Me" in Singles Reviews, *Billboard* (May 16, 1964).

"Country Music: The state of the country after the gold rush." (October 5, 1996). At: http://billboard.biz/bbbiz/others/country- music-the-state-of-the-country-after-759682.story (retrieved December 21, 2011).

Crang, Mike, *Cultural Geography* (London: Routledge, 1998).

Cridlin, J. "King of the Dap Kings." *St. Petersburg Times* (Florida) (March 2, 2011): 29.

Dahl, Bill. "The South: Tennessee, Alabama, Georgia, Virginia, Carolinas," in *The Blackwell Guide to Soul Recordings*, ed. by Robert Pruter (Cambridge, MA: Blackwell, 1993): 230-263.

Dasein, Deena. "Megadeth: Countdown to Conventional?" *C.A.M.M.*, 3.6 (September 15-October 15, 1992): 14-16.

"Dateline Music City." "Sessions in Progress for Skeeter Davis, Roger Miller and the Avons." *Music Reporter* (November 16, 1963).

Davies, Hunter, *The Beatles* (London: William Heinemann, 1968).

Dellio, P. "I Want Something Else: Semi-charmed Second Life." *The Village Voice*, 44.49 (December 14, 1999): 92.

Denny, Sandy. "Next Time Around." *The North Star Grassman and the Ravens* (Island ILPS 9165, Warlock Music Ltd., 1971).

Doerschuk, Bob, ed. *Rock Keyboard* (New York: Quill/Keyboard Books, 1985).

———. "The Rock Piano Story: From Boogie to B. Bumble." *Keyboard*, 8 (February 1982): 44-45, 49-61.

Doggett, Peter. "Little Richard: The Specialty Sessions." *Record Collector*, 125 (January 1990): 62-65.

———. "Wilson Pickett." *Record Collector*, 48 (August, 1983): 18-21.

———. "Little Richard." *Record Collector*, 25 (September 1981): 20-25.

Doughton, K.J. "The History of Metallica." In Jeff Kitts, Brad Tolinski, and Harold Steinblatt, eds., *Guitar World Presents Metallica* (Milwaukee: Hal Leonard, 1997): 1-9. (Reprinted from *Guitar World*, October 1991.)

Edmonds, Ben. "New York Dolls Greatest Hits Volume 1." *Creem* (October 1973). Reprinted in Robert Matheu and Brian J. Bowe, eds., *Creem: America's Only Rock 'n' Roll Magazine* (New York Collins, 2007): 99-101.

Eliot, Marc. *To the Limit: The Untold Story of the Eagles* (Cambridge, MA: DeCapo, 2005).

Epstein, Brian. *A Cellarful of Noise* (London: Souvenir Press, 1964).

Epstein, Dan. "The History of American Thrash." *Revolver Magazine* (February 2009) at: http://www.revolvermag.com/content/history-american-trash 02/17/2009.

Ericson, S. "Rimes is Blue for the first time this day in country music—September 13" (September 13, 2011). Retrieved from http://kicks105.com/keith-urban-puts-you-in-a-song-and-leanne-rimes-is-blue-for-the-first-time-this-day-in-country-music-september-13th/.

Evans, D.E. "Curb's Rimes a Country Music Conqueror: Chart-topping Teen's Star Continues to Rise." *Billboard*, 109.49 (December 6, 1997): 43.

Farina, Richard. "Baez and Dylan: A Generation Singing Out" In David A. De Turk and A. Poulin, Jr., eds., *The American Folk Scene* (New York, 1967): 253. (Originally printed in *Mademoiselle* (March 1964).)

Flanagan, Bill. Liner notes. *The Best of Steve Forbert, What Kinda Guy* (Nemperor/ Epic Legacy, 1993).

———. "Steve Forbert Escapes from Hell: The frighteningly true story of a rock 'n' roll singer/songwriter who endured the musician's worst nightmare." *Musician* (October 1988).

———. *Written in My Soul: Conversations with Rock's Great Songwriters* (Chicago: Contemporary, 1987).

Forbert, Steve. Personal interviews with George Plasketes (September 30, 2011; October 4, 2011; January 24, 2012).

———. Liner notes. *Young, Guitar Days* (Rolling Tide, 2001).

Friskics-Warren, B. "Recordings: Quick Spins." *Washington Post* (October 7, 2007): C05.

Frith, Simon, *Sound Effects: Youth, Leisure, and the Politics of Rock 'n' Roll* (New York: Pantheon, 1981).

Frushour Kelly, Amy. Interview on *Jandek on Corwood* DVD. Directed by Paul Fehler and Chad Friedericks (United States of America: Unicorn Stencil, 2004).

Fuss, Charles. *Joan Baez: A Bio-Bibliography* (Westport, CT: Greenwood Press, 1996).

Gaar, Gillian G. *She's A Rebel: The History of Women in Rock ans Roll* (Seattle: Seal Press, 1992).

Gardiner, Michael E. *Critique of Everyday Life* (London: Routledge, 2000).

Gardner, Elysa. "The Singer and the Song." In Barbara O'Dair, ed., *Trouble Girls: The Rolling Stone Book of Women in Rock* (New York: Random House 1997): 359-363.

Garofolo, R. "Crossing Over: From Black Rhythm and Blues to White Rock 'n' Roll." In N. Kelley, ed., *Rhythm and Business: The Political Economy of Black Music* (New York: Akashic Books, 2002): 112-137..

George, N. *The Death of Rhythm and Blues* (New York: Pantheon Books. 1988).

————. *Buppies, B-boys, Baps, and Bohos: Notes on Post-soul Black Culture* (Cambridge, MA: De Capo Press, 2001).

Gerron, P.S. and G. Cameron. *Whatever Happened to Peggy Sue?* (Oklahoma City: Togi Entertainment, 2008).

Gilbert, Jeff. "Alive and kicking: Pearl Jam's Stone Gossard and Mike McCready." In Jeff Kitts, Brad Tolinski, and Harold Steinblatt, eds., *Nirvana and the Grunge Revolution* (Milwaukee, WI: Hal Leonard Corporation, 1998).

Goldrosen, J. *Buddy Holly: His Life and Music* (Bowling Green, OH: Popular Press, 1975).

———— and J. Beecher. *Remembering Buddy* (London: Omnibus Press, 1996).

Greene, Joshua M., *Here Comes The Sun* (New York: Wiley, 2006).

Griffiths, Dai. "Allusion and Influence in Elvis Costello." *Popular Music History*, 2.2 (2007): 201-221.

Gunderson, Edna. "Sad Fate for an Excitable Boy." *USA Today* (September 13, 2002): 12D.

Guralnick, Peter. *Sweet Soul Music: Rhythm and Blues and the Southern Dream of Freedom* (New York: Harper and Row, 1986).

Guthrie, J. "He can see clearly now: Third Eye Blind's Stephan Jenkins looks at success, love, creativity." *SFGate* (2003, April 20). Retrieved from http://www. sfgate.com/cgi-bin/article.cgi?f=/chronicle/archive/2003/04/20/PK64418. DTL&type=entertainment.

Hamil, Pete. "Sinatra: The Legend Lives." *New York Magazine* (April 28, 1980): 30-35.

Hana, J. "Rapid Fire: Sharon Jones." *The Sunday Mail* (Queensland, Australia) (May 2, 2010): 3.

Hannusch, Jeff. "Huey 'Piano' Smith: Don't You Just Know It," in *I Hear You Knockin': The Sound of New Orleans Rhythm and Blues* (Ville Platte, LA: Swallow Press, 1985): 35-44.

Harper, Colin. Liner Notes. *Jackson C. Frank: Blues Run the Game* (Castle Music CMEDD762, 2003).

Harris, K. "Sharon Jones Gives Dap Kings a Groove." *The Philadelphia Enquirer* (February 20, 2006): E08.

Harrison, George. WABC-TV radio interview, New York (April 25, 1970).

————. Sleeve notes. *All Things Must Pass* (EMI 7243 53047429, January 2001).

Harrison, Olivia. *George Harrison: Living in the Material World* (New York: Abrams, 2011).

Hermes, Will. *Love Goes to Buildings on Fire: Five Years in New York that Changed Music Forever* (New York: Faber and Faber, 2011).

Hetfield, James. *Kerrang! Legends: Metallica*. Cited at: http://www.last.fm/user/suzallica/journal (posted July 20, 2009)..

Hirshey, Gerri. "High-Octane Dreams", in *Nowhere to Run: The Story of Soul Music* (New York: Penguin Books, 1984): 42-53.

Holden, Stephen. "Rickie Lee Jones in the Cool World." *Rolling Stone* (May 31, 1979): 9, 12-13.

"Hoots and Hollers on Campus." *Newsweek* (November 27, 1961): 84

Hoskyns, Barney. *Hotel California: The True-Life Adventures of Crosby, Stills, Nash, Young, Mitchell, Taylor, Browne, Ronstadt, Geffen, the Eagles, and their Many Friends* (Hoboken, NJ: Wiley and Sons, 2006).

———. *Waiting for the Sun: A Rock and Roll History of Los Angeles* (New York: Backbeat: 2003).

Humphries, Patrick. *Nick Drake* (New York: Bloomsbury, 1998).

Hutton, J. "The guide." *The Guardian* (London) (January 3, 2004): 27.

Jandek 1985. Interview by John Trubee (Originally tape recording). "Special features," *Jandek on Corwood*. DVD. Directed by Paul Fehler and Chad Friedericks (Columbia, MO:, Unicorn Stencil, 2004).

Jenkins, Stephan. "Third Eye Blind's Stephan Jenkins talks 'Ursa Major,' fierce fans." *Rolling Stone* (2009, August 11). Retrieved from http://www.rollingstone.com.

Jensen, J. *The Nashville Sound: Authenticity, Commercialization and Country Music* (Nashville: Vanderbilt UP, 1998).

Kelley, N. "Notes on the Political Economy of Black Music." In N. Kelley, ed., *Rhythm and Business: The Political Economy of Black Music* (New York: AkashicBooks, 2002): 6-23.

Kirby, David. *Little Richard: The Birth of Rock 'n' Roll* (New York: Continuum International Publishing, 2009).

Knafo, S. "Soul Reviver." *New York Times* (December 7, 2008): 38.

Knopper, S. "Third Eye Blind sees promise in Elektra: Heavily courted act's debut eases into market." *Billboard*, 109.11 (March 15, 1997): 22, 24.

Laing, D. *Buddy Holly* (Bloomington, IN: Indiana UP, 2010).

Lally, J. "Ultragrrrl doesn't understand Stephan Jenkins." *AbsolutePunk* (July 29, 2009). Retrieved from http://www.absolutepunk.net.

Leavell, Chuck. "Radiatin' the 88s: Rock Piano's Ancestry." *Musician*, 141 (July 1990): 82-84, 113.

Leckie, John. "How to Make the Perfect Debut." *Uncut* (August 2006): 56.

Lee, Cosmo. "Metallica—The First Four Albums." *Invisible Oranges* (July 29, 2011). At: htp://www.invisibleoranges.com/2011/06/metallica-the-first-four-albums-kill-em-all.

Leigh, S. *Everyday: Getting Closer To Buddy Holly* (London: SAF, 2009).

Lévi-Strauss, Claude. *The Savage Mind* (Chicago: University of Chicago Press, 1962).

Lewitinn, S. "Third Eye Blind explained." *Ultragrrrl* (July 29, 2009). Retrieved from http://ultragrrrl.blogspot.com/2009/07/third-eye-blind-explained.html.

Lichtenstein, Grace and Laura Dankner. *Musical Gumbo: The Music of New Orleans* (New York: W.W. Norton and Company, 1993).

Lieberman, Josh. "The members of 'The Next Bob Dylan Club'" (March 2, 2012). Retrieved from www.theawl.com/2012/03/the-members-of-the-bob-dylan-club.

Love, Robert, ed. *Harrison: By the Editors of Rolling Stone* (New York: Simon & Schuster, 2002).

Lubow, Arthur. "Remember Nick Drake." *New Times*, 10.10 (May 1, 1978): 57-58, 60, 62.

Mabry, D.J. "The Rise and Fall of Ace Records: A case study in the independent record business." *Business History Review*, 64.3 (1990): 411-450.

Maiscott, Mary Lyn. "Q. & A. Rickie Lee Jones Is Not In Love." Retrieved August 10, 2011 http://www.vanityfair:com/online/daily/2011/07/qa-rickie-lee-jones-is-not-in-love.

Male, Andrew. "The Strange Tale of Jackson C. Frank." *Mojo Online* (24 July 2009), at: http://www.mojo4music.com/blog/2009/04/the_strange_tale_of_jackson_c.html (retrieved October 19, 2011).

Marcus, Greil. "Warren Zevon's Red Harvest." *Village Voice* (March 6, 1978).

———, ed. *Stranded: Rock and Roll for a Desert Island* (New York: Knopf, 1979).

———. "Elvis Costello Repents," in *In the Fascist Bathroom: Punk in Pop Music 1977-1992* (Cambridge: Harvard UP, 1993): 221-234.

———. *The Dustbin of History* (Cambridge: Harvard University Press, 1995).

Marek, Ed, ed. "Memoirs of Those Who Lived Through the Cleveland Hill Elementary School Fire of 1954." *Talking Proud Archives* at: http://www.talkingproud.us/Culture/CleveHillFire/CleveHillFireIntro.html (retrieved on November 24, 2011).

Marsh, Dave. "Soul On Ice," in *Fortunate Son; The Best of Dave Marsh* (New York: Random House, 1985): 286-290.

——— and James Bernard. *The New Book of Rock Lists* (New York: Fireside, 1994).

——— and John Swenson, eds. *The New Rolling Stone Record Guide* (New York: Random House/Rolling Stone Press, 1983).

Martin, George, *Summer Of Love: The Making Of Sgt Pepper* (London: Macmillan, 1994).

Maslin, Janet. "Salty Margaritas." *Newsweek* (2 August 1976): 72-73.

Mazullo, Mark. "The Man Whom the World Sold: Kurt Cobain, Rock's Progressive Aesthetic, and the Challenges of Authenticity." *Musical Quarterly*, 84.4 (2000): 713-749.

McCartney, Paul. Sleeve notes. *McCartney* (Apple PCS 7102, April 1970).

McCombe, John. "'A Complete Loser': Masculinity and Its Discontents in Elvis Costello's *My Aim Is True* and *This Year's Model*." *Journal of Popular Music Studies*, 21.2 (2009): 192-212.

McCormick, Neil. "On the Road with the Best New Band in Britain." *The Daily Telegraph* (London) (March 8, 2003).

———. Online review of the Libertines. *The Telegraph* at: http://www.telegraph.co.uk/culture/music/live-music-reviews/7965666/The-Libertines-HMV-Forum-review.html (accessed January 25, 2012).

McGrath, T.J. "Lost Singer Found." *Dirty Linen*, 57 (April/May 1995). Reprinted on *The Unofficial Jackson C. Frank Homepage* at: http://www.hut-six.co.uk/jcfrank/froots.html (retrieved on October 19, 2011).

McNutt, Randy. "New Orleans: Sea Cruise," in *Guitar Towns: A Journey to the Crossroads of Rock 'N' Roll* (Bloomington: Indiana University Press, 2002): 6-29

"Me & Ms. Jones." *The Irish Times* (March 28, 2008): 6.

Means, Andrew. "Game, Set, Blues: Whatever Happened to Jackson C. Frank." *Folk Roots*, 146/147 (August-September 1995). Reprinted on *The Unofficial Jackson C. Frank Homepage* at http://www.hut-six.co.uk/jcfrank/froots.html (retrieved on October 19, 2011).

Mehr, Bob. "In the Beginning Was the Word..." *Mojo*, 163 (June 2007): 90-95.

———. Liner Notes. *Warren Zevon* (reissue) (Rhino 2008).

Mellers, Wilfrid. *Twilight of the Gods: The Beatles in Retrospect* (London: Faber, 1973).

Meltzer, Richard. *The Aesthetics of Rock* (New York: Da Capo Press, 1970).

Mendelsohn, J. "Country's Teen of Hearts." *USA Weekend* (September 27-29, 1996): 4-5.

Milstein, Phil. "The Units: Ready for the House." *Op*, issue "L" (1983).

Monthland, J. "Music's Teen Queen: The little girl with the big voice is in it for the long haul." *Texas Monthly*, 25 (1997): 107-110.

Morris, C. "Declarations of Independents." *Billboard* (May 18, 2002): 68.

NA. "Dave Mustaine: The Story Behind Metallica's 'The Four Horsemen.'" *Blabbermouth* (August 15, 2011) at: http://www.roadrunnerrecords.com/blabbermouth.net.

Neal, M.A. "Sold Out on Soul: The corporate annexation of black popular music." *Popular Music & Society*, 21.3 (1997): 117-135.

———. *What the Music Said: Black Popular Music and Public Culture* (London: Routledge, 1999).

Needs, Kris, and Dick Porter. *Trash! The Complete New York Dolls* (London: Plexus, 2006).

Neely, Kim. *Five Against One: The Pearl Jam Story* (Harmondsworth: Penguin, 1998).

Nelson, Paul. "Warren Zevon: How He Saved Himself from a Coward's Death." *Rolling Stone* (March 19, 1981): 28-34, 70.

———. "A Pair of Aces: Ian Hunter, Steve Forbert: Autumn Fire, Spring Fever" (Record review). *Rolling Stone* (July 26, 1979): 57, 59.

——— and Jan Panake, "Record Reviews." *Little Sandy Review*, 18 (September 1961): 3-6.

New York Dolls. Dir. Greg Whiteley. Vivendi Entertainment, 2005. DVD.

Nielson, A.L. "Foreword: Preliminary Postings from a Neo-Soul." *African American Review*, 41.4 (2007): 601-608.

NME (New Musical Express). "Top 50 Records of the Noughties." At: http://www.guardian.co.uk/music/2009/nov/17/nme-top-albums-decade-noughties (accessed January 25, 2012).

Nooger, Dan. "Wilson Pickett: The Golden Years." *Goldmine*, 179 (June 5, 1987): 79-80, 92.

O'Connor, Pat. "Shockwaves Interview with Ron McGovney" (1997). At: http://www.metallicaworld.co.uk/Interviews/1997_ronmcgovney.htm (accessed November 16, 2010).

O'Dair, Barbara, ed. *Trouble Girls: The Rolling Stone Book of Women in Rock* (New York: Random House, 1997).

O'Donohue, S. "How video almost killed the soul star." *Herald Sun* (Australia) (April 20, 2006): 110.

Palmer, Robert. "Hit and Myth: Searching for Steve Forbert." *Rolling Stone* (March 20, 1980): 8-10.

Pato, Greg. *Grunge Is Dead: The Oral History of Seattle Rock Music* (Ontario: ECW Press, 2009).

Petridis, Alex. *NME* website, http://www.guardian.co.uk/music/2010/aug/26/the-libertines-live-review-forum (accessed January 25, 2012).

Petrusich, Amanda. *Pink Moon* (New York: Continuum, 2007).

Pierce, J.E. *Off the Record: Country Music's Top Label Executives Tell Their Stories* (Lanham, MD: Madison Books, 2000).

Plasketes, George. "Warren Zevon (1947-2003). The Grim and Grin Reaper in the Songwriter's Neighborhood, From A to Zevon." *Popular Music and Society*, 28.1 (February 2005: 95-109.

———. *B-Sides, Undercurrents and Overtones; Peripheries to Popular Music, 1960 to the Present* (Aldershot, UK: Ashgate, 2009).

"Playboy Interview: Joan Baez." *Playboy* (July 1970): 54-62.

Quintana, Ron. "San Francisco Heavy Metal. The Birth of a Scene." Cited at: http://www.ilikethat.com/metallica.

Ramanathan, L. "Washington Does a Little Soul-searching. *Washington Post* (December 4, 2009): E08.

Raper, Jim. "Classic Cuts: *Here's Little Richard* (1957)." *Now Dig This*, 59 (February 1988): 18-19.

Redd, L.N. *Rock Is Rhythm and Blues: The Impact of Mass Media* (Spartanburg, MI: Michigan State University Press, 1974).

Reece, D. "Third Eye Blind Shines: Elektra act shows keen vision." *Billboard*, 109.22 (May 31, 1997): 11, 17, 20.

Reeves, M. (Writer). "LeAnn Rimes" [Television series episode]. In M. Reeves and K. Palmer's (Producers), *Backstory*. Knoxville, TN: Scripps Network (2011).

Reid, Jan. *The Improbable Rise of Redneck Rock* (Austin, TX: University of Texas Press, 2004).

RIAA (n.d.). *RIAA—Recording Industry Association of America.* Retrieved from http://www.riaa.com/goldandplatinumdata.php?table=SEARCH_RESULTS &artist=Third%Eye%Blind&album=Third%Eye%Blind&go=Search&perPage=50

Rickie Lee Jones Interview. *1001 Songs* (June 5, 2011), at http://1001-songs. blogspot.com/2011/06/in-more-than-30-years-since-chuck-e.html (retrieved on August 10, 2011).

Ripani, R.J. *The New Blue Music: Changes in Rhythm and Blues 1950-1999* (Jackson, MS: UP of Mississippi, 2006).

Roberts, Chris. "Unknown Pleasures *M2OH:* Great Lost Albums." *Uncut* (26 August 2006): 122.

Roberts, M. "Papa's Got a Brand-new Bag: Big music's post-Fordist regime and the role of independent music labels." In N. Kelley, ed., *Rhythm and Business: The Political Economy of Black Music* (New York: Akashic Books, 2002): 24-43.

Robinson, John. "This Week's New Singles." *The Guardian* (London) (September 28, 2002).

Rockwell, John. "Disbanding of the Dolls Tells a Tale of One City." *New York Times* (April 25, 1975): 23.

———. "Steve Forbert, New Folk Singer." *The New York Times* (December 3, 1977).

———. "The Pop Life: One critic's top 10 for 1978." *The New York Times* (December 22, 1978): C21.

———. "Pop Music: Steve Forbert." *The New York Times* (December 22, 1978): C33.

———. "Living in the USA." In Greil Marcus, ed., *Stranded: Rock and Roll for a Desert Island* (New York: Knopf, 1979): 188-218.

Rodnitzky, Jerome. "Joan Baez: A Pacifist St. Joan," in *Minstrels of the Dawn: The Folk-Protest Singer as a Cultural Hero* (Chicago: Nelson-Hall, 1976): 83-99.

Rolling Stone, online. "Best of the 00's" list, at: http://www.rollingstone.com/ music/lists/100-best-albumsof-the-2000s-20110718/the-libertines-up-the- bracket-196912131 (accessed January 25, 2012).

Rushdie, Salman. Side bar. *Vanity Fair* (January 2012): 67.

Ryzik, M. "From Jameson to Fela Kuti, preshow rites of a soul band." *New York Times* (April 25, 2010): AR15.

Sacks, Leo. Liner notes. "The Best of Wilson Pickett," in *A Man and A Half: The Best of Wilson Pickett* (New York: Rhino/Atlantic Records, 1992): 1-11.

Sanneh, Kalefa. "In Performance: Rock," *New York Times* (May 6, 2003).

Schaffner, Nicholas, *The Beatles Forever* (New York: McGraw-Hill, 1977).

Schulian, John. "One Album to His Name, but It Is the Stuff of Legend." *The New York Times* (August 27, 2000). Retrieved 19 July 2011 at http://www.nytimes. com/2000/08/27/arts/music-one-album-to-his-name-but-it-s-the-stuff-...

Scoppa, Bud. "Album by Album: Jackson Browne." *Uncut* (August 2010): 64-66.

Seabrook, J. "The Money Note: Can the Record Business Survive?" *New Yorker* (July 2003): 42-55.

Shankar, Ravi. *Raga Mala: An Autobiography* (London: Genesis, 1992).

Shannon, Bob and John Javna. "In The Midnight Hour—Wilson Pickett," in *Behind the Hits: Inside Stories of Classic Pop and Rock and Roll* (New York: Warner Books, 1986): 122.

Shapiro, Peter. "Wilson Pickett," in *The Rough Guide to Soul and R&B* (New York: Rough Guides, 2006).

Shaw, A. *The World of Soul: Black America's contribution to the popular music scene* (New York: Cowles Book Co., 1970).

Shaw, Greg. "The Story of New Orleans Rock 'n' Roll". *Phonograph Record*, 3 (July 1973): 16-21.

Shevory, Thomas, 'Bleached Resistance: The Politics of Grunge." *Popular Music and Society*, 19.2 (1995): 23-28.

Silvester, Peter. *A Left Hand Like God: The Story of Boogie Woogie* (New York: Omnibus Books, 1988).

Simels, Steve. *Gender Chameleons: Androgeny in Rock 'n' Roll* (New York: Arbor House, 1985).

Sisario, B. "She's Not Anybody's Backup Act." *New York Times* (September 29, 2007): B7.

Small, C. *Music of the Common Tongue: Survival and Celebration in Afro-American Music* (London: John Calder Publications, 1987).

Smith, Alan, "Meanwhile Ringo Keeps in the World's Eye." *New Musical Express* (February 21, 1970): 2.

Smith, David. "Hyperactive Likely Lads on Best Behaviour." *The Evening Standard* (London) (October 29, 2002).

Sprague, D. "Sharon Jones and the Dap Kings." *Daily Variety* (May 3, 2010): 9.

Sprech, J. "I Forget to Remember to Forget: Elvis Presley in Texas—1955." *Journal of Texas Music History*, 3.1 (2003): 1-7.

Stark, P. "Rimes' 'Blue' is Radio Magic: Curb Teen Country Artist Taking Off." *Billboard.biz* (June 1, 1996). Retrieved from http://www.billboard.biz/bbiz/others/rimes-blue-is-radio-magic-756345.

Stegall, Tim. "Doll Parts." *Guitar World* (July 2005): 72+.

Steinke, Darcey. "Smashing Their Heads on the Punk Rock." *Spin* (October 1993): 71.

Sterdan, D. "Jones breaks out." *Toronto Sun* (April 9, 2010): 57.

Strong, Catherine, "Grunge, riot grrrl and the forgetting of women in popular culture." *Journal of Popular Culture*, 44.2 (2011): 398-416.

Tannenbaum, R. "In defense of Third Eye Blind." *New York Magazine* (August 20, 2009). Retrieved from http://nymag.com/daily/entertainment/2009/08/in_defense_of_third_eye_blind.html

Taylor, C. "Third Eye Blind finds another audience connection with latest crossover cut." *Billboard*, 110.5 (January 31, 1998): 86.

"The 20 Greatest Debut Albums of All-Time" (August 17, 2008). At: http://dkpresents.wordpress.com/2008/08/17/the-20-grestest-debut-albums-of-all-time/ (retrieved April 23, 2010).

"The 50 Best Debut Albums Ever," *New Musical Express* (November 6, 2010): 24-27.

"The 100 Greatest Debut Albums of All Time" (March 2013). Retrieved from http://www.rollingstone.com/music/lists/the-100-greatest-debut-albums-of-all-time-20130322.

"The 100 Greatest Debuts." *Uncut* (August 2006): 48-71.

"The 100 Records that Changed the World." *Mojo*, 163 (June, 2007): 60-95.

"The 500 Greatest Albums of All Time." *Rolling Stone* (December 11, 2003): 83+.

Thomson, Graeme. *Complicated Shadows: The Life and Music of Elvis Costello* (New York: Canongate, 2004).

Tow, Stephen, *The Strangest Tribe: How a Group of Seattle Rock Bands Invented Grunge* (Seattle, WA: Sasquatch Books, 2011).

Tramontana, Giancula. "Country and Southwestern." *Mojo* (November 2000): 126.

Uhelzski, J. "Third Eye Blind's second coming." *SFGate* (2007, March 11). Retrieved from http://www.sfgate.com/cgi-bin/article.cgi?f=/c/a/2007/03/11/PKGLEOFQM21.DTL&type=music.

Ulrich, Lars and Malcolm Dome. "Encyclopedia Metallica." *RAW*, 3 (September 28-October 11, 1988): 27-34.

VH1.com. "Interviews: Warren Zevon: Dirty Life and Times" (August 11, 2003). At: http://www.vh1.com/shows/dyn/inside_out/68383/episode_interviews_int.jhtml?start=1 (retrieved August 11, 2003).

Vine, Katy. "Jandek and Me." *Texas Monthly* (August, 1999).

Visakowitz, Susan. "Doing It Their Way: The Go! Team Returns to Indie-Land." *Billboard*, 119.34 (2007): 46.

Von Appen, Ralph and Doehring, Andre. "Never Mind The Beatles, Here's Exile 61 and Nico: 'the top 100 records of all time'—a canon of pop and rock albums from a sociological and an aesthetic perspective." *Popular Music*, 25.1 (2006): 21-39.

Wakefield, Dan. "Interview with Joan Baez: I'm Really a Square." *Redbook* (January, 1967): 115-117.

Walker, Michael. *Laurel Canyon: The Inside Story of Rock and Roll's Legendary Neighborhood* (New York: Fraser and Fraser, 2006).

Warner Music Group. Press release. "Warner Music Group and Mike Curb expand relationship" (July 23, 2002). Retrieved from www.prnewswire.com.

Warren, M.R. "Burglary stuns a studio, but can't stop the music." *New York Times* (February 23, 2009): 20.

Watson, Tony. "Little Richard's Specialty Sessions." *Blues and Rhythm*, 50 (March 1990): 24-26.

Wenner, Jann, *Lennon Remembers* (San Francisco: Straight Arrow, 1971).

Wexler, Jerry, with David Ritz. *Rhythm and the Blues: A Life in American Music* (New York: Knopf, 1993).

Whitburn, Joel. *Top R&B /Hip Hop Singles, 1942-2004* (Menomonee Falls, WI: Record Research, 2004).

———. *Top Pop Singles, 1955-2008* (Menomonee Falls, WI: Record Research, 2009).

White, Adam and Fred Bronson. "In The Midnight Hour by Wilson Pickett," in *The Billboard Book of Number One Rhythm and Blues Hits* (New York: Billboard Books, 1993): 8-9.

White, Charles. *The Life and Times of Little Richard: The Quasar of Rock* (1984; New York: Da Capo Press, 1994).

White, Timothy. "Rickie Lee Jones: A Walk on the Jazz Side of Life." *Rolling Stone* (August 9, 1979): 40-45.

———. "Rickie Lee Jones; The Great Disconnected's Leading Lady Flirts with Happiness." *Rolling Stone* (August 6, 1981): 36-41.

Whiting, S. "Third Eye Blind spots a big gig: Unsigned S.F. band to open for Oasis." *SFGate* (April 13, 1996). Retrieved from http://www.sfgate.com/cgi-bin/article.cgi?f=/c/a/1996/04/13/DD24339.DTL.

Whitman, Andy. "Jackson Browne: Moving Farther In." *Paste Magazine* (July 2008):28.

Wiederhorn, Jon. "Seattle Reign: The Rise and Fall of Seattle Grunge." In Jeff Kitts, Brad Tolinski, and Harold Steinblatt, eds., *Nirvana and the Grunge Revolution* (Milwaukee, WI: Hal Leonard Corporation, 1998): 1-12.

Williams, Richard. "The Beatles: Produced by George Martin." *Melody Maker* (August 21, 1971. Reprinted in W. Fraser Sandercombe, *The Beatles: Press Reports* (Burlington, Ont.: 2007): 313.

Wilson, Carl. "A Punk-like Stab at the British Heart." *Globe and Mail* (Canada) (August 7, 2003).

Winner, Langdon. "Little Richard." In Anthony DeCurtis and James Henke, eds., with Holly George-Warren, *The Rolling Stone Illustrated History of Rock and Roll* (rev. edition) (New York: RandomHouse, 1992): 52-59.

———. "The Sound of New Orleans." In Jim Miller, ed., *The Rolling Stone Illustrated History of Rock and Roll* (rev. edition) (New York: Random House/Rolling Stone Press Book, 1980): 35-44.

Wood, Jennifer. "Pained expression: metaphors of sickness and signs of 'authenticity' in Kurt Cobain's *Journals*." *Popular Music*, 30.3 (2011): 331-349.

Yarm, Mark. *Everybody Loves Our Town: A History of Grunge* (London: Faber and Faber, 2011).

Young, Neil. *Waging Heavy Peace: A Hippie Dream* (New York: Blue Rider Press, 2012).

Zevon, Crystal. *I'll Sleep When I'm Dead: The Dirty Life and Times of Warren Zevon* (New York: Ecco/Harper Collins, 2007).

Zollo, Paul. "Riding on the Horses: Rickie Lee Jones," in *Songwriters on Songwriting* (Cincinnati, OH: Writers Digest Books, 1991): 133-139.

———. "Faith, Hope and Love: Steve Forbert," in *Songwriters on Songwriting* (Cincinnati, OH: Writers Digest Books, 1991): 153-157.

Index